UNDERSTANDING
THE
DALAI
LAMA

Hay House Titles of Related Interest

YOU CAN HEAL YOUR LIFE,
the movie, starring Louise L. Hay & Friends
(available as a 1-DVD program and an expanded 2-DVD set)
Watch the trailer at: **www.LouiseHayMovie.com**

THE SHIFT,
the movie, starring Dr. Wayne W. Dyer
(available as a 1-DVD program and an expanded 2-DVD set)
Watch the trailer at: **www.DyerMovie.com**

ALL YOU EVER WANTED TO KNOW FROM HIS HOLINESS THE
DALAI LAMA ON HAPPINESS, LIFE, LIVING, AND MUCH MORE:
Conversations with Rajiv Mehrotra

THE GURU OF JOY: Sri Sri Ravi Shankar & the Art of Living,
by François Gautier

CHANTS OF A LIFETIME,
by Krishna Das (book-with-CD; available March 2010)

IN MY OWN WORDS:
An Introduction to My Teachings and Philosophy, by His Holiness
The Dalai Lama; edited by Rajiv Mehrotra

A NEW WAY OF THINKING, A NEW WAY OF BEING:
Experiencing the Tao Te Ching, by Dr. Wayne W. Dyer
(available November 2009)

YOUR SOUL'S COMPASS: What Is Spiritual Guidance?
by Joan Borysenko, Ph.D., and Gordon Dveirin, Ed.D.

All of the above are available at your local bookstore, or may be ordered
by visiting: Hay House USA: **www.hayhouse.com**®
Hay House Australia: **www.hayhouse.com.au**
Hay House UK: **www.hayhouse.co.uk**
Hay House South Africa: **www.hayhouse.co.za**

UNDERSTANDING
THE
DALAI
LAMA

Edited by Rajiv Mehrotra

HAY HOUSE, INC.
Carlsbad, California • New York City
London • Sydney • Johannesburg
Vancouver • Hong Kong • New Delhi

Published and distributed in the United States by: Hay House, Inc.: www.hay house.com • *Published and distributed in Australia by:* Hay House Australia Pty. Ltd.: www.hayhouse.com.au • *Published and distributed in the United Kingdom by:* Hay House UK, Ltd.: www.hayhouse.co.uk • *Published and distributed in the Republic of South Africa by:* Hay House SA (Pty), Ltd.: www .hayhouse.co.za • *Distributed in Canada by:* Raincoast: www.raincoast.com

Editorial supervision: Jill Kramer • *Design:* Riann Bender

Library of Congress Cataloging-in-Publication Data

Understanding the Dalai Lama / edited by Rajiv Mehrotra.
   p. cm.
Previously published: New Delhi ; New York : Viking, 2004.
   ISBN 978-1-4019-2327-3 (hardcover : alk. paper) 1. Bstan-'dzin-rgya-mtsho, Dalai Lama XIV, 1935- I. Mehrotra, Rajiv, 1953-
   BQ7935.B777U63 2009
   294.3'923092--dc22

                          2008018587

ISBN: 978-1-4019-2327-3

12 11 10 09   4 3 2 1
1st edition, May 2009

Printed in the United States of America

To:

The long life of my Guru, Gyalwa Rinpoche

His Holiness the Dalai Lama

The memory of my mother, Shanti Mehrotra

And for:

My father, H. N. Mehrotra

Sarada Gopinath

And my best friend, fellow traveler, and wife, Meenakshi Gopinath

CONTENTS

PREFACE

"Don't be nervous," I said. "He's the most
human person you could ever hope to meet."
She gave me a shocked glance. "He is a living Buddha!" she protested.
"Well, isn't it the same thing?" I asked her.

The Foundation for Universal Responsibility is honored and delighted to present this collection of essays: *Understanding the Dalai Lama*. To Tibetans, the Dalai Lama is known as *Yeshi Norbu*, the precious Wish-Fulfilling Gem—the reincarnation of the Buddha aspect of compassion, *Avalokiteshvara*. To others, he is known by his Mongol title—the Dalai Lama, or Ocean of Wisdom. To the more initiated, he is quite simply . . . His Holiness. He describes himself as Tenzin Gyatso, a simple Buddhist monk.

The book attempts the impossible. It is incomplete and inadequate. Yet, perhaps born of the vanity and blessings of being led by a great master, the Foundation felt we owed it to history and to the millions around the world whose lives he has touched—more often through his ideas than his physical person, although he remains one of the most accessible, self-effacing public figures of our times—to offer these contemporary insights into his personality and work by those who have met him and, in most cases, are well acquainted with him. We can never completely know and understand the many layers and facets of a human being, less so when that human form is a manifestation of a Buddha—the epitome of human striving.

As with all truly great, inspiring men and women, his life by itself is his message and philosophy. The Dalai Lama represents a progressive and logical continuum of a mind that has evolved through lifetimes and the institution of the Dalai Lamas, of whom he is the 14th reincarnation. He has come to represent a singular, if idealistic, response to the individual and collective crises, imperatives, and needs of our times.

The contributors to this book explore some facets of this extraordinary man. Tibetologist Jeffrey Hopkins served as His Holiness's official interpreter for more than a decade. He gives a syllable-by-syllable translation in English of the Dalai Lama's full name: "leader, holiness, gentleness, renown, speech, dominion, mind, goodness, primordial, wisdom, teaching, hold, vastness, ocean, being, triad, controlling, unparalleled, glory, integrity."

Robert Thurman was one of the Dalai Lama's first Western students. "His Holiness is a giant of spiritual development, a living exemplar of the best qualities of a Buddhist monk: an inspired practitioner and teacher of the ethical, religious, and philosophical paths of the bodhisattva; and an elegant and energetic wielder of the vajra scepter of the Tantric adept."

Matthieu Ricard, a monk himself, notes:

> He always describes himself as a simple Buddhist monk, but to various writers he has been the god-king of Tibet; to the Chinese, a splittist; to most politicians, the true head of Tibet; to Dharma students everywhere, a great teacher and a perfect living example of what he teaches; and to the world at large, a Nobel laureate, a great statesman, the leading advocate of nonviolence and peace, the voice of Buddhism, and, in general, our best hope for the future. To the Tibetan people, His Holiness has always been the living manifestation of Chenrezig Avalokiteshvara, the Buddha of Compassion.

Tenzin Gyatso evokes a range of views, analyses, and descriptions so similar and yet diverse as he impacts us in varied ways and dimensions. Each contribution in this collection represents a personal response to the charisma of a supremely integrated yet manifold-faceted personality. What holds it all together? . . . It is that he is intensely human.

What is it that best describes him? It is not just what he says that gives meaning to all that makes him unique, but also because, as writer Pico Iyer suggests, "the heart of the man . . . exists in silence." It is not a severe silence, but one that ever brims with joy and the infectious laughter that frequently spills over, disarming us and moving us all a step closer to our real selves.

Psychologist and author Daniel Goleman observes that the roots of empathy are latent in compassion. He suggests that empathy and ethics are closely linked and empathy underlies many facets of moral judgment and actions. The Dalai Lama's secular philosophy of universal responsibility, bred of a profound insight of our interdependence, has had an enormous impact. Goleman explains:

> Science and technology have brought immense control over nature, but power without wisdom is dangerous. We need to balance our modern capabilities with an ancient wisdom. . . . [The Dalai Lama] has said, also, that just because these times are so dire, it is a great honor to be alive now, at this moment, on this planet. It is we who bear the responsibility, who face the challenge, who must take care of the planet—not just for ourselves, but for the future of our children.

How would the Dalai Lama have the world remember him? "Just as a human being; perhaps as a human being who often smiles." While discussing Tibet, Ela Gandhi, granddaughter of the Mahatma, describes the Dalai Lama as a "simple smiling monk." She writes: "His power comes from a life of ethics, the force of truth. In Tibetan, he speaks with a range, depth, inspiration, humor, and sincerity that inspire insight and motivate dedication to others' welfare."

Describing him as "a very human . . . human being," writer Mary Craig emphasizes that he is a "uniquely luminous person who could make you want to laugh aloud for the sheer job of being alive." In an unexpectedly extended afternoon she got to spend with His Holiness, she saw several sides of the Dalai Lama . . . one of them pedaling a brand-new exercise bike with the enthusiasm of a small child. She cites a 19th-century yogi who says: *Look at my delighted laughter! The delight of a vast, free mind.* What the writer has learned to value most in His Holiness is his genuine humility and refusal, in spite of everything, to hate the Chinese.

This compilation of personal narratives as well as scholarly interactions brings out facets of an extraordinary life. It is altogether too early to make any judgments about what his intellectual legacy will be, but as Thubten Jinpa, the translator and interpreter for His Holiness, observes, "his life mirrors the wider picture of classical Tibetan culture's encounter with modernity."

In our increasingly fragmented and fractured world, the Dalai Lama has sought dialogues with other faiths. Brother Wayne Teasdale writes: "His Holiness's commitment to interreligious dialogue, which is really a dialogue of life itself, is not a stiff, formal activity as it often is in academic forums." He adds, "Basically, what I discern in his example is a highly developed humanism rooted in spiritual practice and extended to all sentient beings."

The Dalai Lama's exile has meant that he has reached out to a much larger world extraordinarily receptive to his personality and message—beyond the remote Shangri-la of the isolated Tibet rudely awakened from the slumber of history by the Chinese invasion in the 1950s. Identified as the incarnation of the Great 13th Dalai Lama by representatives of the Tibetan theocracy and groomed from early childhood in the ancient traditions and practices of Tibetan Buddhism, the Dalai Lama has, remarkably, bridged the ancient with the modern. Journalist Swati Chopra writes:

> Science grows from a spirit of discovery; and I know that Buddhism, and certainly the Dalai Lama, have always been interested in leading explorations into the area beyond the circumference of doctrinal beliefs. I am particularly reminded of a public meeting some years ago, where I had been struck by the open attitude, and humbleness, of His Holiness. When asked about reincarnation, he had said: "In Buddhism, we believe in being open. For example, I now have flown in an airplane and have seen that

there is no Mount Meru and that the earth is not flat. So I have proof that these are not true, even though they are believed in our scriptures. So far I believe in reincarnation because I have not seen proof that it isn't so."

For more than four decades, the Dalai Lama has lived in exile, while Chinese oppression in Tibet has continued, as has the systematic decimation of its culture and heritage. He has remained a transient on a refugee's passport, dependent on the generosity of foreigners.

For the Tibetans whose cause he represents, he wears both a political and spiritual hat. He has led the struggle for a free Tibet and the survival of its ancient heritage. Researcher Senthil Ram observes: "From exile, the Dalai Lama pursued various landmark reforms, on the one hand to democratize the Tibetan polity, and on the other to nonviolently handle the conflict with China." Dalip Mehta, a former Indian diplomat, notes how . . .

> . . . he has succeeded in keeping alive the aspirations and hopes of the Tibetan people and in preserving Tibet's unique culture. He has achieved the delicate task of adhering to his principles and at the same time not jeopardizing the interests of his adopted homeland. And he has ensured that the Tibetan diaspora—not just in India, but elsewhere in the world—has developed and progressed in the modern world, even while remaining rooted in their traditions. In his quest for "freedom in exile" in India, the Dalai Lama has perhaps achieved far more than he would have if destiny had not forced him to flee Tibet.

His Holiness has been widely received and applauded at many capitals around the world by politicians, who, anxious not to offend the Chinese, greet him as a great spiritual leader, paying at best discreet lip service to his political cause.

Although he embodies the aspirations of a free Tibet and the survival of its unique heritage, his message of universal responsibility, of compassion, altruism, and peace, have made him a global anchor for our troubled times.

As one of His Holiness's personal, if most unworthy, *chelas,* I feel twice blessed and privileged—to have helped put together this collection of essays by minds more incisive and erudite than mine, and to be able to write these words and in a small way help make available this collection of contemporary insights of a living Buddha. I dedicate any merit gained to the benefit of all sentient beings and acknowledge total responsibility for any errors in this book.

— **Rajiv Mehrotra**
Secretary/Trustee
Foundation for Universal Responsibility

(**Editor's Note:** In the essays that follow, please note that when the Dalai Lama is quoted, his words have occasionally been edited slightly for clarity.)

THE DALAI LAMA: AN INTRODUCTION

by Rajiv Mehrotra

Tenzin Gyatso is a Buddhist monk. His message of compassion, altruism, and peace have made him a statesman for our troubled times. For six million of his followers, he is Holy Lord, Gentle Glory, Eloquent, Compassionate, Learned, Defender of the Faith, Ocean of Wisdom—His Holiness, the 14th Dalai Lama of Tibet. The Nobel Peace Prize awarded to him in December 1989 became a formal global acknowledgment of his personal spiritual striving and the goal of liberating Tibet from the Chinese oppression that he personifies.

In awarding the Nobel Prize to a religious leader, the Nobel Committee identified three specific elements of his philosophy: nonviolence, the interrelatedness of social and individual human rights, and the critical need in our generation to confront the threat of a global environmental disaster. It is significant that the ecological issue has been put on the agenda of the Nobel Peace Prize by a spiritual leader. He combines rationality, humanism, and religious tradition as foundations for moral responses to the great challenges of our times. Nor did the Nobel Committee shrink from identifying the Dalai Lama as the "political and spiritual leader" of the

Tibetan people and his struggle for the "liberation" of Tibet, despite strong Chinese protests.

Tibet today is at once a tragedy and a triumph, a stark example of modern totalitarianism fighting to a draw against an unwilling traditional society. A number of delegations from the Dalai Lama first visited Tibet in the 1980s, evoking powerful emotions among Tibetans there. Following the death of Mao, delicate and potentially substantive contacts were first established between the Dalai Lama and Beijing. This was followed by a virtually decade-long impasse after the student protests at Tiananmen Square in the spring of 1989 created by, in the words of the Chinese government, counter-revolutionaries, capitalist agents, and enemies of the people. Protests and demonstrations continued in Tibet. Martial law was in force for more than a year, and only supervised tourist groups were allowed into the capital, Lhasa. The Chinese government repeatedly, rhetorically, accused the Dalai Lama of instigating anti-Chinese and antinational sentiments. There has been increasing Chinese nervousness over growing popular global support for the Dalai Lama and international pressure to resolve the Tibetan question, even if usually under the guise of drawing attention to human-rights issues in Tibet.

Recently, a promising dialogue has resumed through direct contacts and visits to Beijing by representatives of the Dalai Lama. While these have been described as a confidence-building step, it seems that the Tibetan position draws on more than the decade-old proposal of a five-point peace plan set out by the Dalai Lama.

His Holiness has proposed the transformation of Tibet into a zone of peace, a respect for fundamental human rights, an abandonment of China's population transfer, the protection of Tibet's environment, and the commencement of earnest negotiations. This was followed by an offer renouncing Tibetan independence and any political role for himself in the Tibet of the future, made before the European Parliament. The Dalai Lama had warned that if there is no concrete response from the Chinese in the near future, he will be obliged to reconsider his position.

The Dalai Lama has been exiled in India since 1959 by the Chinese occupation of Tibet. But to the Tibetans both inside and outside Tibet, he has remained their spiritual and temporal leader, embodying the ideal of the religion he heads and the people he represents but no longer directly rules. He represents the past, as well as future, history of Tibet.

Tenzin Gyatso is heir to a religious tradition that began in India more than 2,500 years ago when, seated under a tree, a young Indian prince from deep meditation attained decisive knowledge of the human condition and the unshakable certainty that he was released from its suffering. He had become the Buddha, the Enlightened One. The core of the Buddhist path is the recognition that life is an endless round of suffering, disease, death, and rebirth: a cycle caused by a desire bred of ignorance and of an innate misconception of reality.

Liberation of enlightenment occurs when through a training of the mind, the mind itself is transcended. There is then an experience of the innate nature of reality, the recognition that all matter exists only in the manner of an illusion and in an ultimate void. Some beings who have attained enlightenment and thus liberation from rebirth opt for reincarnation voluntarily out of compassion for others in order to teach and serve humanity. They are called *bodhisattvas*. The Dalai Lama is a reincarnation of the patron saint of Tibet, the Buddha aspect of compassion—*Avalokiteshvara*, a bodhisattva.

Buddhism, from its earliest forms, included the finest moral philosophy with a vast range of mind development and pioneer psychology. As it traveled the globe, it evolved into religion, advanced philosophy, mysticism, metaphysics, and the triple yogas of India: the paths of reason, devotion, and action. It was not enough to be told to be moral and ethical. Buddhism became an adventure in "how."

A constant theme of the Dalai Lama's teaching is that the essence of a Buddhist's life lies in a person's own efforts to purify his mind. By replacing its coarse, deluded states such as anger, attachment, and ignorance with patience, wisdom, and equanimity, a lasting internal happiness can be achieved independent of external conditions.

Spreading 2,000 miles from China in the east to Afghanistan in the west, with India the home of much of its culture in the south, Tibet is a severe Himalayan plateau 15,000 feet above sea level. Tibetans were confronted by natural grandeurs so cruel that it brought an intense awareness of the contrasting splendors and terrors in the universe, relieved by a few pleasant plains and a spiritual quest. It was a remote, secret Shangri-la so deeply inspired by the Buddhist cosmic view that it pursued its religion in splendid isolation with an unusual fervor. Hunting and killing ceased because it meant an arbitrary interruption in that being's own evolution. Armies disbanded and became monks. The traditional kings were replaced by religious rule. The essential peace-loving nature of their religion encouraged a simplicity and quiet pragmatism in the people. Famine was unknown; disease rare.

The Dalai Lama has acknowledged, "Unfortunately, some monasteries and institutions became like landlords, not practicing well. The general public's practice of Buddha Dharma declined; although there was a great deal of devotion, there was little actual education."

The social structure was feudal. Most Tibetans were peasants paying taxes to the great monastic and noble estates. One in four Tibetans was a monk or nun and constituted its de facto ruling class. Naturally warmhearted, with an innate sense of order and humor, the various classes had been immutably defined for centuries. Inside the cloisters flourished a rich culture and tradition.

In 1933, the Great 13th Dalai Lama passed on to the Honorable Fields. Two years later, Tibet's regent journeyed to its sacred lake seeking a vision of the one who would be the new leader, returned in a new body. In the waters, he was shown a monastery, a nearby house, and a baby.

Other omens directed the search party to the northeast, to the monastery and the house of the vision. A two-and-a-half-year-old boy approached and recognized the disguised lamas and called them by name. He spoke in the dialect of the capital, Lhasa, more than 1,000 miles away. He identified as his own the rosaries, walking stick, and hand drum of the 13th Dalai Lama. On the child's body were the marks distinguishing the Dalai Lamas, including the large ears, tiger-skin-like streaks on the legs, and the conch-shell print on the palm.

On a bright October morning in 1939, the now-four-year-old boy entered the great city of Lhasa in a brilliant procession, where thousands lined the yellow and white route cheering and waving. There was no doubt that this was indeed the holy one himself, the 14th Dalai Lama of Tibet.

Talking of his reincarnation, he says, "The original Dalai Lamas, the first, second, third—these were no doubt the reincarnations of Avalokiteshvara, so that means Buddha. I believe I am a blessed one. My own spiritual level is not high. I am still practicing. . . ."

The philosopher-king born of peasant parents began his long, arduous training while a regent held temporary power. Surrounded by tutors and attendants, he lived in splendid but disciplined isolation. He was soon recognized as an exceptional student. As most of Lhasa watched, His Holiness the Dalai Lama won his doctorate of Buddhist philosophy with honors, in public debates, at the age of 24.

Meanwhile, China had begun to assert a claim on Tibet, contending that the nation was part of the Chinese motherland because the Tibetans, descended from the Mongolians, were a part of the five races comprising the Chinese. On New Year's Day in 1950, the Dalai Lama, at only 16 years old, began his education in real politics. The new People's Republic of China announced its intentions to "liberate" Tibet. As its armies marched into a nation physically and temperamentally unprepared for war, at the urging of the state oracle and his people, Tenzin Gyatso assumed formal temporal power of Tibet as the 14th Dalai Lama to steer the country through its darkest hours.

On March 17, 1959, after nine years of fruitless attempts at compromise with the Chinese, as atrocities against the Tibetans grew, on a night of firing, shelling, and popular revolt in Lhasa, the Dalai Lama, guarded by Tibetan guerillas, slowly began his long, dangerous escape into India. Over the next few weeks, an estimated

87,000 Tibetans were killed, 25,000 were imprisoned, and 100,000 followed him into exile.

Speaking on this topic, the Dalai Lama comments, "As a Buddhist, all these tragedies, the basic factor or cause, is because of one's own previous karma. The external factors are the Chinese forces, but the basic cause is one's own previous bad karma. Although personally that enemy is harming you, forget that so-called enemy. Look at him as a human being just like you or me who also wants happiness. With that reason you can develop genuine sympathy or compassion."

The 1960 report of the International Commission of Jurists recognized Tibet's status as that of a fully sovereign state. China was found guilty of "the gravest crime of which any nation can be accused: the intent to destroy, in whole or in part, a national ethnic, racial or religious group" as such—genocide.

At the end of the "cultural" revolution, the new Chinese order revealed that 45 of Tibet's 6,000 monasteries remained. The number is soon to be increased to 53. Of the more than 500,000 monks and nuns, 1,300 survived in Tibet. These numbers may increase. However, a Socialist education is today a prerequisite for permission to enter the monkhood.

Ever looking for insights and understanding, the Dalai Lama began to study Marxism, searching for a common ground: "I think in Buddhism there is much emphasis on love and compassion. In Marxism, somehow the basis of the class struggle is hatred. Also, of course, Buddhism is not only thinking of *this* life, but the next. But both believe that the individual is capable of taking control of his own destiny; there is no belief in a creator in either. I believe that the two can coexist."

On the afternoon of March 31, 1959, the Dalai Lama entered India and exile. The Dalai Lama's seeking political asylum in India initially embarrassed its government. Although India and Tibet shared a long religious and cultural history, Prime Minister Nehru was obliged to take into account the then-recent delicate rapprochement between India and China. However, humanity triumphed over politics and asylum was granted. The Dalai Lama became an honored guest in the land of Buddha's birth. Although there was profound sympathy and substantial material support for the refugees, there was little political backing. Tibet's isolation had given it no experience of international diplomacy and few friends.

In India, the Dalai Lama plunged into frenetic activity, serving as leader and shock absorber to a traumatized people uprooted from their natural habitat and relocated into the heat and dust of India. They not only survived change but flourished, drawing upon a philosophy that provided important insights into the permanent nature of change and flux, of how "becoming" is a vital aspect of "being."

The Dalai Lama found residence in Dharamsala, a day away from Delhi. Out of the graciousness of a foreign government, a residential area of less than two acres was now the Dalai Lama's physical domain. He was stripped of the external symbols that attested to his power and authority in Tibet. It was a call to Tenzin Gyatso to build a much vaster empire sourced on an inner kingdom. For the Dalai Lama, the cultivation of inner peace and a refined integrity are the ultimate weapons that an individual can use to make a difference in this seemingly mad world.

While the world soon prepared to put Tibet back on the shelves of myth and legend, the Dalai Lama and his people were driven by a different perception of reality. Religion was their wellspring, and it had top priority.

Preserving, and as it evolved, perpetuating, Tibetan religion and culture became an essential strategy in exile and countered Chinese attempts to decimate it. The Tibetan identity would not be allowed to die. For every major monastery destroyed in Tibet, a new, if smaller, one was built in India, continuing the same lineage and practices as in Tibet. Children, the hope of any exiled people, continued to be ordained as monks, and senior lamas now began to reincarnate in exile.

His Holiness explains, "Because I am outside Tibet, still the pure form of Tibetan culture has survived. Now today, strangely, the true Tibetan culture or community is found outside Tibet—not inside."

The major challenge was rehabilitation. By the 1990s, 44 Tibetan settlements linked by commercial, political, and religious ties, housing almost all of the 100,000 exiles, looked to Dharamsala as their headquarters. The refugees arrived with few assets and little immunity to the many diseases unknown in Tibet's dry atmosphere but prevalent in subtropical India. Slowly the survivors began to weave a small economic miracle. Their former feudal lives were quickly relinquished. The barren land was equitably distributed, and a marketing and purchasing collective established. Tibetan medicine, arts and crafts, and education were encouraged. The Tibetans in exile have carved out one of the most successful stories of the rehabilitation of a people—of vigorously maintaining their own identities yet harmonizing with their new environments to remain welcome by their hosts.

One of the first tasks the Dalai Lama undertook in India was the establishment of an education system that would inculcate traditional Tibetan values and culture while imparting instruction in modern ways. The first Tibetan schools were for orphans, but soon a network of schools accommodated all children. Many of them went through Indian universities and now serve in the administration in exile.

The Dalai Lama's keen personal interest in the modernization of a medieval social system has been rewarded with the emergence of a new generation of Tibetans fiercely loyal to their cause, the first children to see maps of the world and hear about people other than their own.

While still in Tibet, the Dalai Lama had recognized the disadvantages and the injustices of the old ways. Always drawn toward the lowest strata in society, he now included them in a power-sharing scheme with their former rulers: "Here we have a draft constitution made in 1963 that has subsequently evolved. It is based on the basic principles of the democratic system. In Buddhist practice, especially monk-system, it's really a democratic system, so in a draft constitution we are making, I mentioned 'according to principles of Buddhist teaching we are making [a] democratic constitution.' So we are trying to make as much as we can while we are exiled in a different country. Now in the future, as I often mention, I regard myself as a free spokesman of Tibetan people, so in future the final decision will be taken by people inside Tibet."

The text of the constitution draws heavily on the Universal Declaration of Human Rights, but it is uniquely Tibetan; the preamble refers to the principle of justice, equality, and democracy laid down by the Lord Buddha. Today the Dalai Lama stands as the head of the government, assisted by a directly elected *Kalon Tripa* or de facto prime minister and his cabinet. A parliament consists of deputies chosen in popular elections among the exiled community. An annual general meeting enables the public questioning of individual departments.

Article 36, Section (e) of the draft constitution provides for the suspension of the Dalai Lama's executive functions by a two-thirds majority of the Assembly.

The Dalai Lama has personally laid the foundation for his administration in exile: a cabinet, a liaison bureau with the Indian government, and a civil service that was established early in 1959. Although no country has recognized his government in exile, the Dalai Lama has representatives overseas in several countries, including the U.S., Britain, Switzerland, France, South Africa, Taiwan, and Japan, often working as centers of Tibetan culture rather than as his political nominees. Together they have managed to keep the Tibetan issue on the international agenda. His emphasis on the interconnectedness of all things has helped generate a new sensitivity to the significance of our environment and the real potential for a truly secular interreligious dialogue.

Tibet's cause is never far from the pilgrim's thoughts. Today there is renewed hope, a Nobel Peace Prize that reflects a measure of consensus in international public opinion in support of both his cause and the strategy he embodies. Forty-odd years later, the U.S. Congress, the European Parliament, and numerous groups across the political spectrum have articulated their concern over human-rights violations, the threat to the environment in Tibet, and the future of its people.

The Dalai Lama believes that only by building up a collective merit of good karma through overcoming their own delusions can the situation resolve itself favorably. Each day's teachings conclude with prayers for their brethren—both friend and oppressor—who still suffer, followed by a dedication of the merit gained to the speedy end of their suffering. In the words of the Tibetan prayer: "By their rough actions masses of cruel ones are bringing down ruin on themselves and on others. They are drunk with demonic delusions. Forge the glorious unity of friendship among them, these objects of compassion, and with love and mercy help them acquire the wisdom Eye to see what is right and what is wrong."

The cultivation of altruism remains the essential and pivotal goal of Buddhist practice and the essence of the Dalai Lama's own practice. He explains: "The essential teaching of Buddha Dharma is *Bodhicitta*—which means firm determination to achieve Buddhahood for the benefit of others that is on the basis of *Karuna* and *Maitreya*. I am developing that mind as a result of the last 30 years' effort, and somehow I am gaining experience. The other one is wisdom, which is *shunyata*—what shunyata is and understanding about that—and I am gaining experience.

"Without training you cannot utilize even your little finger properly. Once you train it properly, even a small finger can do big things. The mind feels very difficult sometimes—almost impossible —but through gradual training, step-by-step, you can do these things. It is one of the good qualities of human consciousness, frequently a troublemaker, but if you train it properly, that will be very nice and useful, like a real jewel."

To a mind thus cultivated, the precision and logic of modern science and technology holds a strong attraction. It has been a passion since childhood, when the adolescent Dalai Lama took apart watches, film projectors, and Tibet's three cars. He is an expert at and enjoys tinkering with mechanical things. Discussing the role of science, he states: "Scientific research is very important. The general Buddhist attitude is that we must accept reason; if a certain thing we cannot believe by reason as a fact or something, then we must accept the fact rather than the certain thing described in the scripture. For example, the Buddha himself says you must accept certain things through your own investigations, your own use and logic and reason, not out of faith."

The Dalai Lama in word and deed seeks to demonstrate how ethics and noble principles have been obscured by the shadow of self-interest, particularly in the political sphere. The instruments of our political culture have destroyed the ideals and concepts meant to further human welfare. He questions the popular assumption that religion and ethics have no place in politics and that religious people should seclude themselves as hermits. Ethics is as crucial to a politician as it is to a religious practitioner. Such human qualities as morality, compassion, decency, and wisdom have been the foundations of all great civilizations.

Rather than be divided by politics, His Holiness states: "So the other alternative is we try to develop a real human feeling. No matter what the differences to ideology or distance—all are human beings; all have to live together on this planet. On this level there should be more contact, more exchanges. Even disagreements are human, so the human dimension is still there. On that basis, we should make an understanding; that way you can achieve mutual trust. Then you can talk."

In recent years the Chinese have adopted a more subtle strategy to overcome Tibet. Due to attractive incentives, there has been a massive influx of Chinese into the harsh terrain of Tibet. In the northeast, for example, in the Koknoor region, where the Dalai Lama was born, there are now an estimated 3.5 million Chinese compared to 500,000 Tibetans.

His Holiness explains his own place in this ongoing struggle: "The Tibetan problem is the problem of six million human souls, not that of the Dalai Lama institution. The Dalai Lama is not so important; the important thing is that the nation must remain. In the future, it will remain. Happiness and the right of the nation are very important. The institution of the Dalai Lama . . . that comes and goes; that depends on the actual circumstances. If people feel that there should be another Dalai Lama, then I will appear. As my own incarnation, I will be there. As long as the suffering of any sentient being is there, I will serve as much as I can—this is my determination; this is not something extraordinary. All the persons who sincerely practice the Buddha's teaching, that is their way of thinking. I may be reborn as an American, as a Canadian, as a Tibetan, as an Indian—I don't know."

The Dalai Lama's role as a preeminent Buddhist monk is today almost universally acknowledged among the different schools of

Buddhism. While the battle between Marxist, or more lately, Western, materialism in China and Buddhist spiritualism—between the power of the gun and the power of wisdom and compassion—now simmers, the Dalai Lama himself reaches out to a world increasingly responsive to his personality, teaching, and message—if not to his political cause.

He explains: "Major religions of the world carry more or less the same teachings, the same messages. I always look at what is the real purpose of these different teachings, these different philosophies; I have found that all are meant for entire humanity. All are focusing or aiming at the same aim . . . however, because there are so many mental dispositions among humans, one religion may not be suitable for everyone. Under the circumstances, one thing we should keep in our mind is closer relations and better understanding. Then we will develop mutual respect."

The Dalai Lama has not sought one common faith for all people. He has instead reached out to the common ground of all religions, the quest for happiness. His disarming personality demonstrates the joy and laughter in the journey. Buddhism, never a missionary religion, is carried on his smiling face.

His Holiness suggests that we abandon religious divisiveness: "Small, small differences between this church or that church or this faith or that faith are very minor. Always the main goal, the supreme thing, is very important. Forget these small things; try to make a common effort for the bigger goal.

"I feel the ultimate aim is society's nirvana—of that nirvana, my definition is: completely peaceful, harmony, no hatred for each other. All people need to be concerned about their brothers and sisters—with less selfishness and no quarrels. Even if there is some disagreement, let's solve it by human understanding. . . . No racial problems, no ideology problems. Ideology is a private business. If someone believes a certain ideology is the best means to achieve happiness—that is his right to pursue that thing; another person has the right to a different ideology or a different faith. . . . They should not interfere with each other, but understand that both are human beings, members of the human family. Both want happiness and do not want suffering. Both have the right to be happy.

Under these circumstances, they remain as a brother, a sister. Now that is my dream."

In the finely balanced mixture of spirituality and politics, what room is there left for the man, the monk. He constantly surprises, questions, or overturns old habits—shifts the entrenched certainties. In the middle of a solemn Nobel lecture, he can pause, wave to a familiar face in the audience, and resume listening as if nothing has happened; he can shed tears when touched by the work of Baba Amte, break out into infectious laughter at his inability to express himself in English, or admit "I don't know" when he doesn't have an answer to the innumerable questions he is confronted with. The Dalai Lama carries his erudition and insights with an easy, comfortable grace.

The Buddha's teachings, as the Dalai Lama's today, are a call to the "more" of life, not to the ending of it and not to the running away from a relative and imperfect world. The transient world must die, but what attains enlightenment and achieves nirvana when the misery-causing self is dead? The answer is man, but to many, the Dalai Lama is more God than man.

THE DALAI LAMA
REINCARNATION INSTITUTION;
THE CURRENT, GREAT FOURTEENTH;
AND HIS ROLES AND TEACHINGS

by Robert A. F. Thurman

(Some passages in this chapter are adapted from previous writings in *Rigpa* magazine, T. Morgan's *A Simple Monk,* and *BlackBook* magazine, always under author's copyright.)

The Institution

The Dalai Lama reincarnation lineage is traced back to a Brahman boy who met Shakyamuni Buddha near the tree of enlightenment at Bodh Gaya and offered him a crystal rosary. Many incarnations in India are mentioned in the history of the lineage, up until the first Tibetan incarnation—the ordained lay Buddhist teacher Dromtönpa (1004–1064 C.E.), who was the Bengali master Atisha's foremost disciple and the founder of Reting Monastery and the Kadam order.

The evolutionary theory of karma existed from Buddhism's beginnings; and the concept of conscious, voluntary reincarnation (in contrast to involuntary, instinct-driven rebirth) developed quite early. The Buddha himself is presented as popularizing the principle in his Jataka and Avadana stories that illustrate the multilife-continuum perspective. Throughout history, small children in Buddhist cultures have routinely astounded parents, relatives, and neighbors by announcing that they were in fact merely the rebirth of such-and-such-a-deceased-person known to everybody. It is thus interesting that only in Tibet, as far as we know, did formal reincarnation lineages become institutionalized as a way of preserving traditions of leadership and authority, in religious settings primarily, but also eventually in the political arena.

This clearly was connected to the scale of monasticization that occurred in Tibet, unparalleled in any other country on Earth, under the aegis of any religion. Monastics are vocationally celibate, so blood lineage eventually became too weak a consideration in choosing leaders and was replaced by a commonly accepted notion of individual spiritual evolution in continuing reincarnations. Beginning as an institutional factor in the 13th century, reincarnation pedigree by the 17th century had become the dominant consideration in Tibetans' choosing their leaders.

His Holiness the Victor Karmapa was the first of such formal reincarnations, as far as we know. His earliest incarnation, Dusum Khyenpa (1110–1193), wrote a letter before he passed away in which he foretold his reincarnation in specific circumstances, a prediction realized ten years after his death with the birth of the second Karmapa lama, Karma Pakshi (1203–1283), who soon asked to be taken back to his monastery at Tsurpu to continue his teachings. The Karmapa reincarnations have continued to develop their institution and perform great service to the people of Tibet and now the whole world. The current 17th Victor Karmapa, Ogyen Trinley Dorje (1985–), has recently escaped from Chinese-occupied Tibet and is living in Dharamsala near the Dalai Lama, showing every promise of becoming another major teacher of the Dharma.

The second important reincarnation institution was that of the Dalai Lamas. It began formally in 1475 with the birth of Gendun Gyatso, who soon declared himself the reincarnation of the famous Gendun Drubpa (1391–1474) and expressed the wish to return to his disciples at the Tashi Lhunpo Monastery, which he had built during the last 25 years of his previous life. He was accepted as the true reincarnation by his parents, tutors, and attendants and was taken in glory back to the monastery. However, the ruling abbots of that large monastic university were clearly reluctant to formalize his recognition by handing the young boy the head position. So at a certain point in his studies, he took advantage of this blessing in disguise, escaped from his duties of office, and spent a number of years in intermittent retreat with the great teacher of the Kalachakra Tantra, Khedrup Norzang Gyatso.

During this time, the young reincarnation built the important monastery of Chokorgyal in the sacred area near the Ode Gungyel Mountain, where Tsong Khapa (1357–1419), his spiritual grandfather, had taken his own six-year retreat in the 1390s, and he made a special bond with the fierce protector goddess Shri Devi, whose sacred soul-lake lay hidden nearby. Eventually Gendun Gyatso's reincarnation status as the main teacher of the Gelukpa order was established beyond question, his principal seat located in the Ganden Palace at Drepung Monastery as well as in Tashi Lhunpo.

The third reincarnation was Sonam Gyatso (1543–1588), who was invited to northeast Tibet to the encampment of Altan Khan, a major Mongolian ruler. On this occasion, a major step was taken in converting the Mongols to Buddhism, building on the changes they had undergone when Kublai Khan ruled in China 300 years earlier. During the festive atmosphere of this transformative event, the Mongol Khan dubbed Sonam Gyatso the "Oceanic" ("Dalai") Lama (*gyatso* means "ocean" in Tibetan), and he became known as the "Third" in acknowledgment of his conscious connection to Gendun Drubpa and Gendun Gyatso. Sonam Gyatso did the great work of teaching and founding monasteries among the Mongols and the Amdo people in northeast Tibet, but still had no direct political responsibility in central Tibet.

The Fourth Dalai Lama was Yonten Gyatso (1589–1617), who was not Tibetan but was reincarnated among the Mongolians as a grandson of Altan Khan himself. He immeasurably strengthened the bond between the Mongolians and the Tibetans, returning while still quite young to central Tibet and his seat at Drepung Monastery.

It was the Fifth Dalai Lama, Losang Gyatso (1617–1682), who presided over the momentous changes of the 17th century that were to produce Tibet's modern form of society. During the mid-16th century, there had been intermittent conflict between the secular rulers of southern Tibet and those of the central region, which some historians have attributed to sectarian conflict between the Karmapa Lamas and their followers and the Gelukpa Lamas and their followers. But it is more accurate to recognize this to be the result of a clash between the secular warlord rulers of feudal Tibet and the continually increasing monastic institutions and spiritual leaders of all the Buddhist orders.

In all Buddhist (and Christian) societies throughout history, monasticism and militarism have opposed each other as institutional competitors for land, resources, and man- and womanpower. Whenever and wherever monasticism dominated, militarism was weakened. When warlords or a single emperor dominated and increased their militaristic activities, monastic institutions were purged, their resources confiscated, and their monks turned into warriors. The 15th and 16th centuries in Tibet saw a vast increase in monasticism, reaching a point by 1600 where aristocratic rulers saw their authority and resources dwindle to what they considered a danger point. Their basic opponent was not a sect or leader, but the whole new "mass-monastic" (a term I use for this unique Tibetan social development) social system itself.

The most powerful secular leader of the time was the King of Tsang, and of course he had to use an important religious leader for legitimacy in the eyes of a people more and more interested in spiritual pursuits and less and less in feudal power struggles. He chose the young Karmapa Lama H.H. Choying Gyatso (1604–1674), who was young and just growing up at the time. The King of Tsang proclaimed himself that lama's disciple in order to sanctify his aggressive intention to maintain his secular power, and then he set about trying to break the hold of mass monasticism on the Tibetans.

The Dalai Lama institution—which had up to that point declined to enter the political arena, devoting itself to the continual expansion of the monastic universities and their demilitarized lifestyle—reached out for its defense to its Mongolian patrons, who came into Tibet and defeated the warlord coalition. Then, in 1642, the Fifth Dalai Lama took an unprecedented step: he assumed political responsibility for the whole country, demilitarized and bureaucratized the secular warlords, defeudalized the ownership of land and the networks of relationships between people at all levels, and formalized mass monasticism as the official social system of Tibet, what is called the "Dharma-state coordination" system (*Chos-srid zung-'brel*).

This unprecedented arrangement is not to be confused with the "church-state unity," which led to intensive religious persecution in Europe and so was remedied in America by the constitutional separation of church and state. *Dharma* means "teaching"—the Buddha teaching of personal liberation and scientific enlightenment—not "religion," "church," or even "religious belief." So Dharma-state coordination intends that the central purpose of the national life be the evolutionary education of all citizens, more like "university-state unity" than "church-state unity."

Furthermore, Buddhists are not monotheistic, so the ruler is not thought to represent an inscrutable, omnipotent, authoritarian God, but rather to be himself a selfless, intercessory angel of a bodhisattva. As a Buddhist monk, the monastic ruler holds solemn vows of gentleness, poverty, chastity, and honesty. Hence, he is dedicated to the principles of nonviolence, economic minimalism, support of the freedom and education of individuals, and selfless service. He thus was preferred by the Tibetan people at this time over a warlord king with his armies, coercive demand for labor service, and self-aggrandizing ambitions for his dynastic progeny. This new Tibetan society was unique on the planet then and still is now; and therefore terms such as *feudal, theocratic,* and even *traditional* or *premodern* are not accurate in describing it.

The Fifth Dalai Lama embarked on the building of the Potala, symbol of the new Ganden Palace government, a remarkable fusion of royal palace, monastic establishment, Tantric mandala, and celestial paradise. He patronized the building of more monasteries for all the orders, not only the Gelukpa order, the leadership of which he abdicated to the senior abbot of Ganden Monastery so that he could represent the people of all religious orders. He gave the former warlord families bureaucratic ranks and salaries for service to the government, after depriving most of them of their feudal rights over their own lands and peasants—most important, the right to maintain a private army.

He gave land and sustenance not only to all Buddhist orders, but he protected the followers of the Bon religion, offered land to the Muslim residents of Lhasa to build mosques and allowed them to worship freely, and gave his permission and support to Christian missionary activities. Reaching out from Tibet, he made a pact to keep the peace in inner Asia with the newly triumphant Manchu rulers of China (1644–1911) and discouraged the Mongols from rebuilding their empire, inspiring them effectively to pursue the demilitarized Buddhistic lifestyle that Tibet was adopting.

The Great Fifth died in 1682, but his regent concealed his death for more than a decade, owing to a long delay in official recognition of the secretly discovered reincarnation, who was kept incognito with his family in a prisonlike atmosphere. Due perhaps to his oppressive upbringing, the Sixth Dalai Lama turned away from his monastic avocation and refused his state responsibilities. This caused considerable upset among his Mongolian and Tibetan followers, which led to his deposition and deportation, a dangerous civil conflict, and eventual Manchu intervention in the affairs of Tibet. After some time, the Seventh Dalai Lama restored the institution somewhat, his turn toward a focus on spiritual teaching empowering his cabinet and laying the foundation for a national assembly.

From the Eighth through the Twelfth Dalai Lamas, Tibet remained stable and peaceful, although static in governance, with the main innovations in many fields being developed in eastern Tibet and Mongolia, far from the complacent conservatism of the central authorities. The Manchu rulers of China also became less supportive of Tibet once the Mongol threat was reduced due to the pacifying effect of Buddhism, and the era of European imperialism brought the British and the Russians, for whom Buddhism was a complete enigma, into play around Tibet.

The Thirteenth Dalai Lama (1876–1933) was the first Dalai Lama to assume the full power of his office since the Seventh. His life's work was to respond to the pressures on Tibet from the decaying Manchu empire, czarist Russia, the British Raj, the nationalist Chinese, and finally the Russian and Chinese Communists. He tried to develop Tibet economically so that it could stand up to industrial militarism. He declared formal independence from the protected relationship Tibet had enjoyed with the Manchu empire, tried to develop a national defense force, and even made gestures toward joining the League of Nations and introducing Tibetan civilization to the world. Although he was supported in this by the leaders of the British Raj in India, the British home government's Realpolitik policy in dealing with the Manchus and then the Chinese nationalists caused London to frustrate his every effort to gain official recognition for Tibet from the nations of the world.

From within, also, his own conservative monastic leadership frustrated his efforts to create a modernized secular school system, build up a viable defense force, and develop even a modest industrial infrastructure. After hearing detailed reports of the fate of Mongolian Buddhists at the hands of Russian Communists in the early 1930s, he made statements to the effect that he was going to pass away a decade ahead of schedule in order to reincarnate and grow up soon enough to help Tibet when it, too, was submerged under the Red Tide of Communism he predicted would emerge from China. In 1933 he passed away.

The Fourteenth Dalai Lama is well known and has already earned the title "Great Fourteenth," due to his profound inner development and his magnificent works of teaching, writing, political leadership, and social engagement. He has resolutely proclaimed his intention to abdicate from the political responsibilities of the Dalai Lama institution once a dialogue is resumed with a less imperialistic and more pragmatic Chinese government that makes it possible for the fate of Tibet to be resolved in a just and reasonable way.

In conversation he has firmly rejected my proposal for a "constitutional *lamarchy*," so it is clear he considers that his duty will change once the occupation and exile has ended and a viable Tibetan democracy has begun to function in a free Tibet. I still wonder if there is a way to continue the noble experiment begun by the Great Fifth and create a "spiritual democracy," rather than just conform to the American and Indian pattern of secular democracy, wherein the god Mammon tends to take over. This spiritual democracy would obviously not elevate any particular religion, order, or sect as the "state church," yet it would educate the people to adopt a higher level of ethics—a higher level of spiritual education both in mind and in science—and would help balance the material and the spiritual for the people of the new Tibet.

Tibet could then assume its rightful role in the world as a center for nonviolence studies, methodologies to implement social justice, environmentalist methodology, scientific yet natural healing arts, and spiritual education and development. The Dalai Lama institution, perhaps, according to the wishes of the Great Fourteenth, could become relatively free of political responsibilities and could flourish as a source of spiritual teaching for the larger world. Future Dalai Lamas would follow in his footsteps and appeal to followers of all religions, not only Buddhists, and inspire them to curb the dangerous tendencies toward religious intolerance and ideological fanaticism and promote the beneficial elements of their venerable faiths.

The Great Fourteenth—Personal Development

I will recount some aspects of my early meetings with the Great Fourteenth over the last four decades. This might be helpful to sketch his personal development because I am one of the few non-Tibetans who has known His Holiness continuously over such a long period.

His Holiness is a giant of spiritual development, a living exemplar of the best qualities of a Buddhist monk: an inspired practitioner and teacher of the ethical, religious, and philosophical paths of the bodhisattva; and an elegant and energetic wielder of the vajra scepter of the Tantric adept. He is also, of course, a conscious reincarnation of Avalokiteshvara, the bodhisattva of universal compassion. As such, it might seem that his great attainments and vast deeds in this lifetime have spontaneously emerged from his practice in previous lives, as if he had done nothing special to develop himself during this life.

If we think that way, we might feel he is so far beyond our capacity that although we might enjoy his presence, learn from his teaching, and feel great devotion to him, it would be hard to emulate him. This would not please His Holiness at all. When we are relying on a *kalyanamitra* (in Tibetan, *dge bai bshes gnyen* or *geshe*), a Buddhist spiritual friend, propitiation through devotion and service through actions are important, but it is far more important to actualize his teachings by putting them into practice in our own lives. A significant point often made about Shakyamuni Buddha is that he was not some sort of primal divinity, a buddha from the beginning. He was human like us—and even an animal—in many previous lives. He struggled with passions and flaws, misunderstandings and inabilities, just as we do. Yet he practiced the Dharma; finally overcame all inadequacies; and ultimately became the shining, perfect Buddha who showed us the way to freedom, love, and happiness.

When I first met His Holiness in a personal audience, he was a young man of 29. We met in the audience room at his hotel in Sarnath, India, where he was the guest of honor at the 1964 congress of the World Fellowship of Buddhists. I remember a feeling of tense guardedness about him, a sense of his being from far away and high above and not quite relaxed in his surroundings. I also remember his friendliness toward me, especially when he heard me speak in clear Tibetan, which I could already manage to some degree. I was presented to him as a beginning student of Buddhism (around two years into it by then with my first spiritual friend, the Mongolian geshe Ngawang Wangyal) who wanted to study under his tutelage and if possible become a Buddhist monk. He said that I should come to him again in Dharamsala after the conference was over, and he would see how my studies should proceed. Then he swept out into the autumn sunshine to go to the dais set up near the great stupa of the Buddha's First Teaching to give his speech at the conference.

I don't remember the speech very well, as he gave it through an interpreter and it sounded strained and formal. His Holiness had a hard task before him. In those years, he was beginning to introduce Tibetan Buddhism to an international Buddhist audience that regarded (unfortunately, many still do) Tibetan Buddhism as "Lamaism," a provincial corruption of real Buddhism, where they thought the real thing was Theravada or Mahayana. Only the relatively few Shingon Buddhists of Japan really respected Buddhist Tantra, and even they were a bit intimidated by the Unexcelled Yoga Tantras, the supreme forte of the Tibetan Buddhists. But there is no doubt that even then His Holiness in person commanded great respect, and his combination of being a simple Buddhist monk as well as a sincere and dedicated spokesperson for his suffering people was effective in moving people's hearts slowly but surely.

During the next year, I remained largely unaware (at 23, I was blissfully unaware of a lot of things, even though I was all fired up to get enlightened!) of my great good fortune in meeting His Holiness regularly, almost every week, to discuss my studies and progress—as well as quite a few other things, as it turned out. His Holiness at that time lived above McLeod Ganj, in Svarg Ashram. When we would meet, our conversations followed an invariable pattern: First, His Holiness would listen briefly to my recital of what I had been learning from my regular teachers (he had assigned me to his senior tutor Kyabje Ling Rinpoche and to the abbot of Namgyal Monastery). Then I would address a few questions to him, especially on my favorite topic of that time: the Madhyamika philosophy of voidness and relativity.

His Holiness would always have a few good points to make, counter-questions, and observations, but then he would refer me to my assigned teachers and embark on asking me questions about the many things *he* was keenly interested in. He would ask about Darwin and Freud, Einstein and Jefferson, and life in the Americas and in Europe. I would answer as best I could, coining new words in Tibetan for some concepts—the subconscious, the id, relativity, natural selection, and so forth—and using English terms in other cases.

Trying to explain complex subjects to His Holiness's brilliant and eagerly inquiring mind was quite a challenge, and it caused me to rethink many of my own ideas. I am afraid I disappointed His Holiness on subjects connected with the hard sciences, since I had been an English major and a would-be poet, with strong philosophical and psychological leanings. But we had a fine time, often annoying his tutors and secretaries by spending too long talking, perhaps taking time away from his other duties. His Holiness seemed slightly stressed to me, lonely, and a little sad, although basically energetic and cheery. I was so intent on Buddhist philosophy and contemplation, and I knew so little about Tibet and the sufferings of his people at the hands of the Chinese Communists, that I could not really understand his situation. And I had very little idea what a tremendous blessing those meetings were for me.

Eventually I was ordained, and some time after that I returned to the U.S. to live in the monastery in New Jersey. As the '60s heated up with the war protests and civil rights movement, I was drawn back into society through peers, and by early '67 resigned my monkhood and returned to lay life. I am afraid His Holiness was strongly disappointed with me for quite a while after that.

I returned to my university and went on to graduate school in Buddhist studies, reaching the dissertation stage in 1970. Again I came to Dharamsala to see His Holiness, who by then had moved down into more adequate quarters near the newly constructed central cathedral.

My dissertation topic was a translation and study of Jey Lama Tsong Khapa's *Essence of True Eloquence* (Tibetan: *Drang Nges Legs Bshad Snying po*), which Geshe Wangyal unexpectedly directed me to undertake just as I was departing for India. This turned out to be His Holiness's favorite philosophical work, and in fact I discovered among my hastily packed books a modern printing of that very text he had presciently given to me back in 1965. When I was in his presence, it only took a few moments to break the ice of awkwardness of the departed monk returning as a married layman with two children. He generously blessed my wife and family and gave us serious admonitions to keep our relationship stable and healthy. Once he had discovered what I was working on for my dissertation (I blamed Geshe Wangyal for launching me on such a difficult work), he assigned me to a teacher as before and then invited me to a series of discussions with him on this text and the philosophical issues it addresses.

During this second series of conversations in 1971, I noticed an astonishing change in His Holiness that was very inspiring: He had come alive philosophically. No longer did he refer questions to other teachers. He had many points to make about Tsong Khapa's treatise, considered his most difficult. He cited numerous passages by heart, and he was lucid and lyrical in explaining the deep impact and extensive ramifications of the fine points, especially the critical differences between the dialecticist and the dogmaticist approaches to the famous Madhyamika central way. Forgetting for a moment that he was the Dalai Lama and so should know it all naturally anyway, I found it breathtaking to observe the powerful philosophical insight that shone through his infectious enthusiasm.

Our talks that year were so exciting that he decided to work with me to bring out a book on the central way in English, a project we started on. Unfortunately, I didn't get the manuscript until the last minute and couldn't complete the translation myself, as I had to get back to America for a teaching job, and another translator took over.

I spent the next eight years in the sword dance of overachievement that is required to attain tenure as a university professor nowadays. I had no chance to get back to Dharamsala, and His Holiness kept being denied visas to the U.S. as part of the oversolicitousness for Chinese feelings mandated by the Kissinger China policy. In '79, I got tenure and His Holiness got his first visa, thanks to Secretary of State Cyrus Vance. I had a year's sabbatical in India with the whole family. That fall, I was lucky enough to host His Holiness at Amherst and Harvard on his first trip and then travel on the same flight with him back to India to continue the sabbatical in Delhi and Dharamsala.

When His Holiness arrived in New York City on that trip, I couldn't believe the further change he seemed to have undergone. I remember having an early-morning dream vision of him that day, as if he were a giant Kalachakra Buddha couple, standing atop the Waldorf-Astoria, shining gloriously in that deity's particular luminescent pastel hues, the energy attracting a swarm of pinstripe-suited bees of diplomats, politicians, businesspeople, princes of the church, and other assorted bigwigs. During all that trip and the following year, I couldn't get over the rich power of his charismatic energy. He had always had the charisma of office—now he had ten times more charisma of person. Obviously he had been studying and practicing the Unexcelled Yoga Tantras, especially the Kalachakra Wheel of Time.

During that winter in India, we had our third series of conversations. His Holiness was now 44 years of age, having reached 20 years in exile. The period during the '70s (when Chinese pressure on governments restricted his world travel) had been put to good use—his sustained series of retreats, capping his 30 years of intense study of all levels of Buddha's teaching, brought him to a manifest fruition. One would like to believe that a Dalai Lama naturally has all knowledge, ability, and compassion. However, I can testify that there was a clear appearance of massive development through tremendous focused intelligence and untiring effort.

In these meetings, we discussed every topic under the sun. My interest was the Tantras, and His Holiness had many profound and helpful things to say. He still seemed interested in everything, especially history, politics, sociology, ethics, and what I might call the psychology of compassion. Our dialogues were hard to publish, since he made me talk too much answering his penetrating questions rather than talking more himself. What he had to say was much more interesting to everyone but himself.

In the decades since then, His Holiness has written many books, dialogued with many thinkers and authors, and given innumerable teachings and speeches. The constant progress I observed during those first 17 years still continues apace, still advancing by quantum leaps. Especially since around the time he won the Nobel Peace Prize in '89, his general talks—on kindness, the common human religion, nonviolence, disarmament, science, ecology and the environment, and comparative religion—are better, more moving, more lucid, and more powerful in understanding and passion. I can honestly say that I have never found a single one of his speeches to be mere repetition canned like a politician's message. Although he has some primary themes, each time he brings something new and fresh to them, such as another example from his ongoing readings and conversations, or a point made in a more compelling way. So it seems that his reincarnation continuum makes possible an endless advancement, growth, and enrichment of his skill in liberative arts.

The Great Fourteenth—Roles and Teachings

"A simple Buddhist monk," or "just a simple Buddhist monk!"—His Holiness often uses these phrases, and people usually smile and think that he is being too modest, striking a pose of studied humility and earnestly contradicting his enormous charisma, radiant good humor, and flashing intelligence. Doth he protest too much? In his remarkable interview with Spalding Gray, he reveals just how much he really means it.

Gray asks him if he ever has erotic dreams or is tempted by worldly desires, which Gray protests are the very stuff of his own life. The Dalai Lama responds quite thoughtfully, revealing that such imagery can emerge in the dream time, but he guards against ceding control to it by remembering that he is a Buddhist monk and retreating to the fortress of his renunciation. He goes on to mention that sometimes he dreams of aggression, finding himself in confrontations with knives or guns, but again reflects on his deepest identity as a simple Buddhist monk and withdraws from the patterns of hostility. Even in his dreams he never thinks, *I am the Dalai Lama!* This is truly remarkable.

The Dalai Lama does have multiple identities. He is a human being, of course, a male, the descendant of farmers, herdsmen, and strong working women of the province of Amdo in far northeastern Tibet, born right on the border with Mongolia to the north, China to the east, and Turkestan to the northwest. He is a Tibetan, of the Amdo region, his family naturally speaking a thick eastern dialect, and he is also familiar with central Tibetan and even conversant from childhood with the provincial Chinese of the Seeling district. Although his mother had no idea that he was the Dalai Lama, she dreamed of his incarnation as coming to her from the southwest in the form of a bright blue dragon, escorted by two playful green snow lions! He often says that green is his favorite color.

His next identity is that of a Buddhist monk—a person who has taken and maintains vows of personal nonviolence, poverty, celibacy, and spiritual honesty; and who spends most of his waking energy in the pursuit of a perfect enlightenment believed to last for all time, to satisfy the self with unimaginable fullness, and to benefit countless other beings with selfless compassion. Simplicity is a cardinal virtue of a monk; it minimizes his distractions and maximizes his using his most essential vital energies in evolutionary development. As a monk, he works on dissolving habitual egotism, including rigidity of his human, sexual, and national identities. He lives close to the bone and strives to be a universal being.

He also constantly creates—he calls it "shaping his motivation"—his working identity as a bodhisattva, a messianically driven being who has dedicated all his lives to the attainment of perfect enlightenment, complete wisdom, and inexhaustible compassion in order to be able to help all other beings find freedom from suffering. Although others consider him the incarnation of Avalokiteshvara, the quintessentially divine bodhisattva of compassion—and he certainly seems to have grown into manifesting that august personage—he clearly does not hold on to such a self-image. He does say that his religion is the common human religion of kindness, love, compassion, and universal responsibility.

He once was asked whom on the planet he considered his spiritual peers. He thought a moment and then answered with unmistakable sincerity, as if he had just rediscovered this fact afresh, that "actually every person in the world is my spiritual peer!"—that he was just like each of them. As the Transcendent Wisdom Sutras declare again and again, he who thinks to himself, "I am a bodhisattva!" that one is not a bodhisattva. Only one who sees no bodhisattva, who sees no being, that one is a bodhisattva with true compassion for all beings.

He daily labors to lead his people and fulfill his responsibility to preserve and rule his nation, one that has been under a genocidal pressure for more than half a century, in such mortal peril that Tibetans should be on the endangered-humans list. He is a statesman, a politician, a diplomat, a personnel manager, and a chief executive officer. He maintains these duties in exile as a refugee.

He is a committed scholar and a prolific writer, researching deeply the philosophical, psychological, and religious literature of his sophisticated civilization as well as exploring the modern sciences and literatures. He studies incessantly with a variety of tutors and teaches extensively, both advanced students in the Tibetan Buddhist monastic community and the entire Tibetan populace, as well as an ever-growing public of spiritual seekers around the world. He speaks to all with clarity and sincerity, with a good sense of humor and an unfailing optimism.

He is also an accomplished Vajra Master, teacher of the esoteric ritual and contemplative practices that his people consider the crown jewels of the Indian Buddhist tradition that they inherited and have done so much to preserve, refine, and extend. His precise knowledge of the architecture of the sacred mandala environment and of the details of elaborate ritual arts and procedures, his graceful gestures, magnificent chanting, and eloquent elucidation of the profound and poignant significance of the advanced contemplative practices leave even his veteran disciples amazed.

And finally, he is a peacemaker for the world, a Nobel laureate, an inspirer of world leaders—both political and religious—not to settle for the harmful by-products of blind institutional momentum, but to take responsibility for the poor and the oppressed, to use good sense and goodwill to solve the problems that beset our world, and not to give in to despair and cynicism and hide behind their powers and privileges. He is ready to be a good friend to everyone, even those who have harmed him or others, and he patiently offers the alternative of constructive dialogue as balm for violence and prejudice.

In his philosophical and ethical thought, His Holiness has powerfully emerged as a world leader with a compelling vision for a viable planetary community. Calling for a spiritual and ethical revolution, he is even a bit ahead of his time, a fact exquisitely ironic for those who assume he speaks from an "underdeveloped" civilization outside of the progressive modern stream.

His central thesis is that human nature itself mandates kindness and love, altruism being the key to happiness. Compassion is not just sentimentality, but rather an intelligent and effective method of living the good life and attaining real happiness: It is not only a spiritual good; it is a biological necessity for human beings. This fact of nature dictates an ethic of compassion and universal responsibility on the social level. The postmodern planetary crisis requires a spiritual and ethical response as a survival necessity. His main idea is that, given broad adoption of more spiritual outlooks and more ethical actions, the planet can continue to be livable down the coming centuries—things can go well for humanity in the future.

The second major theme His Holiness articulates in recent speeches and writings is that spirituality is broader than any specific form of religiosity and is essential for individual happiness and for keeping the world livable. He discourages an agenda of making anyone become a Buddhist and condemns all competition among religious institutions. In keeping with this, he argues that ethical principles are more universal than specific religious prescriptions. He elevates nonviolence as essential to overcoming the human-made disasters of conflict and wars and always calls for dialogue to resolve tensions. He insists that such idealism is not as unrealistic as some modern secular theories of psyche and society have made it out to be.

His prophetic voice has begun to emerge with a powerful critique of material progress and soulless mechanical technology. In his important recent *Ethics for the New Millennium,* he says:

> Although I never imagined that material wealth alone could ever overcome suffering, looking at the developed world from Tibet, a country materially always very poor, I must admit that I thought wealth would have gone further toward reducing suffering than is actually the case. I expected that with physical hardship much reduced, as it is for the majority living in the

industrially developed countries, happiness would be much easier to achieve. . . . Instead, the extraordinary advancements of science and technology seem to have achieved little more than numerical improvement . . . progress has meant hardly anything more than greater numbers of opulent houses in more cities, with more cars driving between them. Certainly there has been a reduction in some types of suffering, including especially certain illnesses. But it seems to me that there has been no overall reduction.

Further, in his passionate call for a spiritual and ethical revolution, he argues adamantly for universal disarmament, sketching a series of systematic steps toward the total prevention of wars and war industries, likening war to a bonfire on which people are heaped like logs and poignantly recalling his own visits to Auschwitz and Hiroshima. In a tradition as old as the great Buddhist teacher Nagarjuna (c. 2nd century C.E.), he courageously denounces excess in luxurious living as leading to extreme gaps between the rich and poor and makes a clear appeal for altruism and universal responsibility in economic policy. He is practical and optimistic about globalization, but not the imbalanced kind that makes the rich richer and the poor poorer.

In spirituality, he follows the Indian emperor Ashoka (3rd century B.C.E.) in calling for religions to focus on personal practice over institutional aggrandizement, tolerant pluralism over bigoted exclusivism. He insists on the priority of spirituality and ethics in personal practice over doctrinal purity and ritual formalism. He shows a willingness to dispense with religion altogether if it only adds to the burdens people struggle with. He acknowledges the benefit of religion sincerely applied, however, and makes the ingenious suggestion that to singularity in personal faith should be added pluralism in social practice.

In sum, were world leaders to take the teachings of this Nobel Peace Prize laureate more seriously, we could be sure that this 21st century would not be a repeat of the war-torn, holocaust-ridden 20th century, but would be an era of peace, reconciliation, environmental restoration, economic sufficiency, and spiritual progress for all humankind, with the added benefit of increased kindness to animals. The amazing thing is that in spite of the recent turn to violence, with terrorism and wars on terrorism superseding progress toward peace on many fronts, His Holiness remains unperturbed in his faith in human nature, undaunted in his call for nonviolence and dialogue, and positive in his outlook.

This refusal to give in to despair has an even greater power of example when we remember that it comes from the leader of Tibet, a nation and a people that has suffered so much genocide, mass destruction, and ongoing oppression. Thus, he embodies his intelligent teachings of non-retaliation, peace, understanding, and dialogue; and truly makes the idealistic seem realistic, reveals the optimal as the practical!

May he continue on without interruption as long as he feels comfortable! May his deep wish for the liberation of his special charges—the noble, long-suffering people of Tibet—soon be miraculously fulfilled, to the astonishment of all! And may his inexhaustible, compassionate effort for all peoples, including the Chinese, also come to fruition as he becomes the Dalai Lama who serves as an Oceanic Teacher for the whole world . . . leading its nations back to harmony with nature, and justice and peace with each other; and its individuals to freedom, wisdom, and happiness for themselves and all other beings!

A JOURNEY

by Isabel Hilton

I felt a quiet sense of achievement as the Jeep rounded the final bend and the little village of Taktser came into view. It clung to the side of a sunlit mountain, 9,000 feet above sea level in what is now called Qinghai, the Tibetan province of Amdo. It was here that His Holiness the 14th Dalai Lama was born. It was not a place the Chinese authorities wanted people to visit. But from the first occasion on which I met the Dalai Lama—in Dharamsala in 1994—his extraordinary life had intrigued me. That meeting had set my own life onto a different and unexpected track. Now I was determined to see the place where the Dalai Lama's story—in this incarnation at least—had begun.

There had been no encouragement in Xining, the provincial capital of Qinghai, to pursue this idea, despite the fact that the village figured in the official Chinese-language guidebook to the area. The birthplace of the Dalai Lama was, I read, "a remote and beautiful village," and was listed as a tourist attraction, along with the bird sanctuary at Kokonor Lake, the great Tibetan monastery of Kumbum, and the birthplace of the tenth Panchen Lama (the second-highest-ranking lama after the Dalai Lama), which was rendered equally difficult to visit. I carried the guidebook around like a talisman, my protection against the suspicious local officials who seemed to be under instructions to discourage anyone from trying to reach it.

The exact status of Taktser was a small indicator of the difficulties the Chinese government faced in trying to maintain a coherent account of their policies in Tibet. On the one hand, Beijing argued that Tibet, along with the rest of the People's Republic, enjoyed religious freedom, and at the same time, that the Tibetan people were happy under Chinese rule—contented members of the motherland's cheerful family of nations.

But on the other hand, the persistence of the allegiance and affection that Tibetans felt toward their exiled spiritual leader was an embarrassment to Beijing and sat uneasily with China's long-running campaign of vilification against the Dalai Lama. The leader of Tibetan Buddhism, according to Beijing, is an enemy of the state; a "splittist"; and, most bizarre of all, a man of doubtful spiritual credentials. To have his birthplace become a place of pilgrimage, as it surely would if access to it was unimpeded, would be deeply embarrassing to Beijing.

All this gives the Dalai Lama's birthplace a somewhat ambiguous status as an official tourist attraction. The solution is to list the village in the guidebooks, but to ensure that it is never "convenient" for anyone actually to reach it. None of the coach parties that tramp through the showcase monasteries of Qinghai—feeding both the local economy and the illusion that Buddhism is thriving under benevolent government protection—make the trip to Taktser. If you want to get there, you have to go alone.

I had been staying in Xining—once a walled city at one end of the great camel route west . . . now, after decades of modernization and "improvement," a dreary, dusty town from which any past romance had been erased. On the streets of Xining, it is evident that Qinghai is still home to that mosaic of border peoples—Tibetan, Mongolian, Golok, Tu, and others—who have been brought under Chinese rule since the 19th century. But today most of the passersby are Han Chinese, whose migration here is one element in the policy of assimilation. Once, this part of Qinghai marked the eastern edge of cultural and ethnic Tibet. It is the Tibetan province of Amdo, and both the 14th Dalai Lama and the

10th Panchen Lama were born in the vicinity. Several centuries ago, Tsong Khapa, the great reformer of Tibetan Buddhism and the founder of the Gelukpa school, was also born here, at a place commemorated in Kumbum Monastery.

Today, the Tibetans appear as a minority in Qinghai, of no more importance than the others in a province that is assuming the monotone gray cultural aspect imposed by the People's Republic. Follow the religious trail, though, and Qinghai seems like a palimpsest: just beneath the surface, obscured but not erased, the map of Tibetan culture begins to show through.

When I first met the Dalai Lama, I had no idea that the encounter would send my life off in a different direction—or that, several years later, I would be dodging local Chinese scrutiny to make this sentimental pilgrimage to his birthplace. It was not that I had suffered a sudden religious conversion. I had gone to Dharamsala in February 1994 simply to interview him for a BBC television documentary on the life and death of the German activist Petra Kelly. I had studied in China in the '70s but had never been to Tibet, and although I had once attended one of His Holiness's teachings in London, I was not in search of a new faith—either religious or political.

Perhaps it was coincidence, then, that on that visit to Dharamsala, I would get so involved in a Tibetan story that I gave up other pursuits to explore it. The story was the search for the late Panchen Lama's incarnation—a subject that presented itself to me with such force that, the Petra Kelly documentary completed, I decided to follow the process through to its conclusion. I took leave from my job and began to plan a book and a film. Telling the story, though, was conditional on the confidence and support of the Dalai Lama. To my great relief, he agreed to help and was to prove true to the commitment.

It was a delicate proposition: the process was secret and needed to be for many reasons. But having agreed to the proposal, the Dalai Lama was more than frank. As the undertaking unfolded, I realized that as well as following the twists and turns of the Panchen Lama process, I was also being afforded an opportunity to watch the Dalai Lama's handling of an issue that was to test to the limit the slender diplomatic resources of his government in exile and to pose a problem of leadership that would have enormous implications for the future.

The work meant many visits to Dharamsala and many interviews. There were meetings elsewhere—in Switzerland and Germany, and in London—all squeezed into an impossible schedule. For me, it was an eye-opening experience, watching one man deal with competing problems: the requirements of his religious followers, his political responsibilities toward Tibetans inside and outside Tibet, the diplomatic complexities of trying to maintain a dialogue with Beijing, the burden of satisfying not only his Tibetan following but the heterodox expectations of a worldwide audience—all this, as I soon realized, with remarkably little in the way of administrative backup.

It was a burden that I was aware we were adding to by imposing the tiresome requirements of filming, and I would not have been surprised if he had grown exasperated. But if he did, he disguised it, and when a conversation resumed after an interval of several weeks, he always began, with uncanny precision, at exactly the point at which we had left off on the last occasion.

The subject of our discussions was often harrowing. It turned out to be a difficult year: The Chinese government had sanctioned a search, led by the head of the Tashi Lhunpo Monastery in Shigatse, Chadrel Rinpoche. But Beijing would not admit the Dalai Lama's participation and were determined to use the process to reaffirm their claim to historical as well as actual supremacy. Chadrel was trying to juggle the competing demands of his religious conscience and his political masters: He wanted the Dalai Lama to make the final identification, but hoped that this would pass unnoticed until the Chinese government had given their approval to the boy. He also wanted the 11th Panchen Lama to be brought up at Tashi Lhunpo.

His Holiness, he told me, thought that was only fair—after all, in recent history the Panchen Lama had lived in Tibet while the Dalai Lama lived in exile. And while many in the exile community would be disappointed, he was conscious of his responsibility to the Panchen Lama's many followers in Tibet. In late January 1995 the boy was identified from a smuggled list; and, in Dharamsala, the Dalai Lama had no choice but to wait for the process in Tibet to run its course.

It was an agonizing few months: Chadrel had been summoned to Beijing, and all efforts to contact him came to nothing. Months went by with no news, bar the rumors that a lottery was to be held. Finally, the Dalai Lama decided to announce in June that the Panchen Lama's reincarnation—as Gedhun Choekyi Nyima—had been identified. It precipitated a crisis both in Beijing and in Tibet. Gedhun Choekyi Nyima disappeared, Chadrel was arrested, and Beijing began to coerce the Tibetan religious establishment into accepting a different candidate whose name would be drawn from the object that Beijing had decided symbolized the Qing emperors' sovereignty—the Golden Urn.

It was hardly a happy or a successful outcome, and I am often asked whether the Dalai Lama should have made that announcement when he did. At the time, I argued against it, since Beijing's reaction was all too predictable. Today, though, I think he had little alternative but to make the announcement. If he had not, there was an imminent danger that a lottery ceremony would be held in Tibet and a different name announced. There was nothing the Dalai Lama could do to prevent it, and to be seen as reacting to the news from Beijing—especially if the wrong candidate was selected—would have been unconvincing.

For many of his followers, the realization that the Dalai Lama's candidate was still in Tibet—and at the mercy of Beijing's fury—came as a shock. Ideally, the boy would have been spirited out of the country to be unveiled in exile. But reality was less kind. I had begun to realize how narrow the Dalai Lama's room for maneuvering was and to appreciate how skillfully he operates, despite his constraints. Like the Pope, the Dalai Lama commands no military divisions. All he has is his moral and spiritual authority, the devotion of his followers, and whatever influence he can conjure from his position as a religious leader. This, of course, is not a negligible hand to play, but nor is it one that carries any guarantees of political success in the short term.

By late October of 1995, the process was nearing its end: Months of coercion had left religious leaders in Tibet with little alternative but to bow to Beijing's pressure, and a meeting was in preparation that would bring that stage of the process to a conclusion. I was in Qinghai, researching the life of the tenth Panchen Lama and trying, for more personal reasons, to visit Taktser. As the months had gone by, I had become steadily more intrigued by the extraordinary life the Dalai Lama had led—one that began in traditions that had hardly changed since the 18th century but that was to lead to exile and a remarkable adaptation to the demands of the current century. Not only had the Dalai Lama survived as a political and spiritual leader, he had become a globally recognizable figure and a tireless voice for his people's cause. It can hardly have been the future imagined by the search parties who made their way to Taktser in the mid-'30s, looking for a house with oddly shaped guttering that matched the vision revealed in Lhamo Latso Lake.

I took a rattling public bus that headed south from Xining toward Ping An, a crossroads town that figured as the nearest point of departure to Taktser.

In the marketplace, the taxi drivers looked at me bemused and shook their heads. "You need a Jeep," they said. The Jeep driver shook his head, too. He did not mind taking the job, he said, but he didn't know where it was.

An old man among the crowd of curious bystanders that had begun to gather chimed in. He knew where it was, he said. In return for a lift, he would show us.

It was a beautiful autumn day as we drove out of Ping An on a metaled road that ran along a river valley. The valley bottom was lush, fertile ground, mostly bare in this autumn season—freshly plowed brown earth in tiny terraced fields lined with close-planted silver birch and poplar trees. On either side, the hills rose steeply, the higher slopes weathered bare to the deep red rock. We sped through mud-brick villages, scatterings of houses with the decorated gateways, and strings of prayer flags that marked Tibetan homes.

We dropped the old man off at one of the villages and, following the route he indicated, left the valley bottom and began to climb, now glimpsing the austere and compelling beauty of the snowcapped mountains that rose behind the gentler hills. Finally, we struck out on a muddy dirt road that climbed precipitously into the mountains. Two hours later, we reached the village.

As I climbed out of the Jeep, a knot of people stared at me as though I had descended from Mars. "The Dalai Lama's house?" I inquired. They gestured up a steep path to a whitewashed house at the top of the village. I climbed the path and, skirting an unfriendly but fortunately tethered dog, stepped through a decorated doorway into the paved courtyard.

The house had been freshly painted, and a flagpole stood in the center of the courtyard, flanked by two incense burners. It was silent and deserted. I climbed a wooden staircase to the first floor and stood on the flat roof, admiring the breathtaking view. When I turned back, I was startled to see that a man had appeared noiselessly behind me. He was about 50 and was looking at me warily.

"Who are you?" he asked.

"I'm from England," I said, hoping no further explanation would be demanded. "I have come to see where the Dalai Lama was born."

"Did you come by yourself?" he asked, looking around anxiously for clues as to my status in the official range of permitted visitors. I reassured him that I was alone.

He seemed puzzled, but on the whole, pleasantly surprised. He was, he said, the caretaker. I guessed that he was weighing whether he should send me packing or show me around. After a pause, he added quietly, "I am related to the Dalai Lama." I asked if he had met his illustrious relative. He had, he said, in Dharamsala, the Dalai Lama's exile home. He smiled sadly at the memory.

The house was empty but well tended. "It has been rebuilt," said my guide. "It was completely destroyed in the Cultural Revolution." The caretaker told me that he had once lived next door, but his house, too, had been destroyed in the Cultural Revolution. "It used to be like this one," he explained, "but they pulled it down, flattened it completely." He showed me some roofless mud walls, the remains of his former home. The government, though, had paid for the Dalai Lama's family house to be rebuilt in a brief period of relaxation of official hostilities toward His Holiness in the late '70s. "They knocked it down," said the caretaker. "Then they rebuilt it."

I imagined the Red Guards rampaging through the now-peaceful courtyard, the caretaker himself captive of the mob, paraded with a dunce cap before being put to some humiliating labor. As though to dispel bad memories, he took up his keys and began to unlock the rooms. Inside were simple shrines to the members of what, in other circumstances, would have been the ruling family of Tibet. He pointed to the Tibetan inscription on a large framed photograph of the Dalai Lama. "He wrote it himself," he said, and translated it for me. "Though I am far away," it said, "and cannot be with you, the people of Hung Nai are always in my heart." In front of the photograph, white *katags* had been laid.

As we walked through the house, I admired the freshly painted decoration on the roof beams "It's very beautiful," I commented to my melancholy guide.

"Do you think so?" he replied. "I don't. It's not beautiful enough for the Dalai Lama. If he were here, it would be so much more beautiful."

He was a man full of sadness, unable to speak openly of the lost world in which kinship with the Dalai Lama would have marked him out for honor rather than political disgrace and humiliation. Now he was the teacher at the local school. There were 15 children, he told me, and he had to teach them in Chinese.

I asked if he remembered the Dalai Lama. "I wasn't born when he left," he replied, "but I remember him coming to visit. I was a classmate of Ngari Rinpoche."

I knew Ngari Rinpoche, the Dalai Lama's younger brother who now ran a guesthouse in Dharamsala. I tried to imagine him in this remote village where, but for the vagaries of reincarnation, he, too, might have lived out his days.

"You know you are supposed to get permission to come here," the caretaker said, as we sat over a cup of butter tea. "I told the driver," he continued, "that *they* will be angry if they find out." There was no need to elaborate, and my driver smiled anxiously.

"Do many people come here?" I asked.

"Not many," the caretaker answered.

"Do many foreigners come here?"

He laughed and shook his head. My driver was beginning to fidget, perhaps turning over the possible consequences of this visit in his mind.

I rose to leave. "Do you think the Dalai Lama will ever come back?" the caretaker asked me.

I said, as gently as I could, that I didn't know, but it seemed complicated. A mist had descended on the village as we had been chatting, and he apologized for the unfriendly weather. "When it's clear," he said, "you can see how beautiful the Dalai Lama's birthplace really is."

"It's very peaceful," I said.

He pulled a face. "The mountains are too high," he replied, "and the road is too long."

I climbed into the Jeep and looked back for a final farewell. The caretaker was standing sadly in front of the house. As the Jeep pulled out of the village, a row of impassive figures, hands in pockets, appeared on top of the high bank that overlooked the road. They watched, silhouetted against the sky, as we began the long slithering journey down the mud road and back to Ping An. I wondered how many of them had been there in the Cultural Revolution, foot soldiers in the mob who had tried to erase the traces of the Dalai Lama's birthplace. In my pocket there was a handful of the bright red earth, scooped up in a last-minute impulse. I thought of taking it to Dharamsala the next time I went and offering it to His Holiness, but I never did: it was not, I thought upon reflection, the kind of nostalgia that he indulged in.

When I returned to Beijing two weeks later, the Panchen Lama crisis was reaching a climax. Tibet's religious leaders were locked up in a hotel in Beijing to give the appearance of approval to the Golden Urn ceremony that would take place in Lhasa within a few more days. I was only an observer of this process, yet it was impossible to avoid the emotions it aroused: to witness the coercion of a community of faith by a political force that held its beliefs and traditions in contempt made me both angry and sad. It was also clear that the process was a rehearsal for the moment when a new Dalai Lama would be sought.

According to a report from the Chinese news agency Xinhua, Raidi, the chairman of the Standing Committee of the TAR People's Congress, recently told a group of Hong Kong reporters: "After the passing of the 14th Dalai Lama, we will find the reincarnated child, according to historical conventions and religious rituals that were formed hundreds of years ago."

These traditions, which underwent frequent revisions during the search for the Panchen Lama, will conclude, as the search for the Panchen Lama did, with Beijing's insistence on the use of the Golden Urn lottery. There is little that Tibetans can do to prevent such an outcome if Beijing remains determined to impose it. But my own conclusion at the end of this painful story was that the appearance of victory can be deceptive. Beijing can force a religious leader on a people, but even the might of the People's Liberation Army (PLA) cannot make people believe what they do not choose to.

Mao's millenarian Communism is already dead, and his successors have ditched all of his most treasured beliefs, with the exception of his resentful nationalism and his vocation for conquest. For the Dalai Lama, the search for the Panchen Lama was one of many episodes that could be read as defeat—events to which he must respond with compassion, regardless of personal emotions.

But if I were to try to sum up what I had learned from observing the Panchen Lama process, it would be an appreciation of the long view. Buddhism has already outlasted Communism and endured, despite the appalling suffering of so many of its practitioners in the last five decades. The 14th Dalai Lama has said that he may be the last. If he contemplates the end of the institution of the Dalai Lama with equanimity, perhaps it is in part because the experience of the last five decades has demonstrated that political ideologies may come and go, but the teachings that have been at the center of his life as a spiritual practitioner and teacher have survived.

WRITING WITH HIS HOLINESS

by Alexander Norman

Although some of the greatest names in English literature began their careers writing in others' names, ghostwriting is generally regarded as a rather disreputable discipline. Indeed, many would argue that the term *discipline* is overdignified for a genre popularly associated with film-, pop-, and sport-star autobiographies.

Actually, many if not most political memoirs are ghostwritten, too. Those of Ronald Reagan, Margaret Thatcher, and, farther back, Golda Meir spring to mind. Yet there is some justice in this negative view. On the one hand, the subject of the star memoir is often rendered improbably articulate simply as a means to cull money out of credulous readers. On the other, even in the case of such a distinguished name as that of Sir Thomas More, writing in the name of his friend and patron Henry VIII, it cannot be denied that the two were collaborating in an act of literary legerdemain.

Within the Tibetan Buddhist literary tradition, there is only one attested example of passages of autobiography having been written by someone other than the actual author (in Heruka's sequence of Milarepa's poems). There are, however, people who argue that the whole body of Mahayana literature is no more than pseudepigrapha—writings misattributed to the Buddha and others for the purpose of establishing their authority. And it is a fact that His Holiness the Dalai Lama's first autobiography, *My Land and My People,* was ghostwritten by a well-known English writer, the late David Howarth, and not, as has been suggested, actually penned by the Dalai Lama himself.

Nevertheless, the great majority of the abundant autobiographical writings of Tibetan masters are entirely authentic, even if we do allow for a degree of tidying and editing by close disciples. It is, therefore, with some hesitation that I speak about His Holiness from the perspective of someone who has ghostwritten two of his books. It will entail making some confessions.

The first of these is that I could not claim to be a close disciple. I am not a Buddhist. Besides, no true disciple would take a fee for his services. As a professional writer, I have a relationship with His Holiness that is inevitably tainted with self-interest. Second, I do not speak Tibetan—the *sine qua non* for any real understanding of Tibetan life and thought according to Professor Michael Aris— let alone that I am no more than functionally literate in Tibetan. Finally, my formal qualifications for undertaking the two projects are almost nonexistent. My literary background, such as it is, is journalistic, not academic.

Together, these factors would seem to offer quite good reasons for hesitation. Yet I am highly conscious of my great good fortune and of the privilege I have enjoyed working so closely with the Dalai Lama over an extended period. Given that I have had an opportunity that many might envy, I take it as duty to tell a bit about the work, as well as to say something about what I have learned from it concerning His Holiness.

My first meeting with the Dalai Lama occurred during March 1988, when I traveled to Dharamsala to interview him on behalf of *The Spectator,* the English political journal. The very first impression I had upon entering the audience chamber was that His Holiness was not there. I remember being slightly disconcerted when, apparently out of nowhere, he came up to greet me. My second impression was of his strong physical presence. Here was no ethereal holy man, no airy sprite. Here was someone who, in another life, might have made a useful rugby player—out on the wing, perhaps. And with his ready laughter—so vigorous (yet far from dissolute) as it welled up, so startling (yet so full of conviction) in its final soprano flourish—he put me in mind of an earthy cherub, such as a more naturalistic Raphael might have painted.

Such are my memories of the first of a great many meetings during the years that have since elapsed. (I once calculated that *Freedom in Exile* occupied around 150 hours spent one-on-one with His Holiness over a period of 18 months, albeit that included interpreters. Actually there were generally four of us. *Ethics for the New Millennium* took about the same, but over a longer period.)

Nine months after that first meeting, I was back in Dharamsala to begin work on the autobiography. How this came about is unimportant here. Suffice it to say that from my perspective it was more a matter of good luck than good judgment. There followed three of the most heady and exciting months of my working life.

It has been observed that merely to meet the Dalai Lama is to be swept up in a romance that is almost impossible not to succumb to. I make no claim to being an exception to this rule. In some ways it is even more difficult now to remain levelheaded than it was back then. Although by the end of the 1980s the village of McLeod Ganj, where His Holiness resides, was just beginning its transformation from senescent ex-colonial hill station to today's international tourist destination, it still retained an air of genteel charm. There was little traffic and only a handful of hotels and teahouses. There was but one public telephone offering international calls. E-mail, satellite television, and the rest lay safely in the future.

Nothing but the growing stature of the Dalai Lama offered any indication of the revolution to come. And if as a visitor in those days you were a Westerner, you found yourself a member of an enchanted community and were valued, it seemed, just for being yourself. Often you would be greeted by Tibetans—so many of them monks, it was true—with a nod, almost a little bow, and a smile. All this has changed. And although the majority of Tibetans are as friendly as ever, the sheer volume of visitors over the years has made them somewhat more discriminating than formerly. Yet the Dalai Lama's private compound has altered little over the intervening years. The contrast between "the world" and this sanctuary is thus greater than ever.

To enter, you must first be frisked and vetted by the guards at the gate. Glancing back, you may note to your sneaking satisfaction the faces of one or two bystanders betraying a look of curiosity mixed with envy. (How beautiful is life for the Elect!) But once inside, registering the air of unhurried order, of discipline and high purpose, you dismiss the thought as unworthy. Ushered into a waiting room just inside the gate, you have some time to collect yourself.

In the distance stand the flashing peaks of the Dhauladhar mountain range, heralds of the mighty Himalayas and of the great Tibetan plateau itself. In the foreground, beyond the lower courtyard, lies a well-tended garden surrounded by a rhododendron grove. And the air—you can almost taste it on your tongue. Jasmine and orange, apple and rose jostle for your attention as a wisp of juniper burned in offering to the gods drifts over from a nearby shrine room.

A few minutes later, a young official, smartly turned out in traditional Tibetan *chuba* worn over gray flannels and well-polished shoes, leads you across the courtyard and up a flight of steps. To your right you half-notice a neat group of buildings on a lower level, forming three sides of a square around an area of lawn. In the middle stands a monk conversing with another official. You climb a second short flight leading into a well-proportioned building of colonial pattern. This, you gather, is the location of His Holiness's audience chamber.

You now enter what is obviously an anteroom, the windows of which look onto a veranda festooned with baskets of perennial pinks. Flowerpots stand stacked against the outer wall. Looking around the room, you become aware of an array of display cabinets crowded variously with Tibetan religious statuary and a collection of awards and citations honoring the Dalai Lama.

Next, you notice the silence. It seems so studied as somehow to drown out the exuberant, daylong chatter of birds outside. Perhaps it is broken by the crash and flurry of an ape bursting along the branches of a tree to land on top of a building. Then a call goes up from one of the Indian bodyguards, and you hear a stone skittering across its corrugated-iron roof. Then a pause; then the birds again. But again their song is caught up in the silence.

Suddenly a door opens. You hear laughter as an Indian family, showily dressed, passes through the room on their way out, the children chattering excitedly. And now it is your turn to meet the earthly manifestation of the god of compassion! The god of love! To spend an hour alone in his company! Two! Four! A day! Who would not be swept off their feet?

Well, of course, not everyone feels quite this way, or at least it is only that part of them that hopes for spontaneous enlightenment that does. Naturally, the cynics say that it is all a façade, while the realists clutch doubt to their breasts.

Whatever my own feelings, there was never much scope for them to get out of hand. Notwithstanding the informality of our meetings, it was always clear that His Holiness's aim was to impart the necessary information as quickly as possible. We had little small talk.

For my benefit, the interviews for *Freedom in Exile* were conducted largely in English, although His Holiness would frequently lapse into Tibetan for minutes at a time. In that event, either Kasur (then Kalon) Tenzin Geyche Tethong or Tendzin Choegyal, both of whom attended the majority of sessions as interpreters, would translate. If appropriate, the other would then add to or qualify the initial rendering in English. (And indeed His Holiness might himself then comment further in English.) Both of them were educated at English public schools in India, so their grasp of the language was complete—added to which, for the same reason, their use of it was charmingly seasoned with the idiom of the late-colonial era.

So far as method is concerned, my approach to gathering material for the autobiography was to treat the whole exercise as a single extended interview. I would familiarize myself with the broad outline of the various episodes of His Holiness's life, but only with a view to coming up with questions that would serve as prompts. To have been provocative would have skewed the narrative. The critical point was that the telling should come entirely from him. My primary role at this stage was thus to act as amanuensis. When the raw material was down on paper (having been both transcribed from tapes and worked up from notes taken down simultaneously), the plan was to knead the resulting text into prose that retained, so far as possible, His Holiness's own distinctive vocabulary and turns of phrase.

The Dalai Lama's English, as anyone who has heard it will testify, is impressionistic, one might even say *pointilliste*. On account of this, the work of reduction, of converting the material from digital to analog, so to speak, was by far the most challenging part of the undertaking. Always my intention was to infiltrate as few additional words as it seemed possible to get away with. (Even so, I now consider that I allowed myself rather too much license. For a start, there should have been much more sparing use of the first-person singular. The use of adjectives is also a bit wanton in places.)

Thinking back to that time, I recall the very first occasion on which we sat down to discuss the autobiography. His Holiness began by asking me whether I considered that another book about him was really worthwhile. At least three biographies had been published recently. I was naturally somewhat taken aback by this, as his own office had already signed a publisher's contract. I replied that since this was to be his autobiography, it would be a very different order of book than anything that had been written since *My Land and My People*. Evidently this was sufficiently reassuring, as I was summoned back the next day for the first dedicated interview.

From the beginning, His Holiness was cooperative in every way, to say nothing of his affability. It quickly became evident that he has a well-developed sense of the ridiculous. A particular source of amused incredulity were the extravagant lengths to which ceremony was taken in the Tibet of his youth. It was clear, too, that he is supremely patient with others and ready to see their point of view.

What was not in evidence, however, was anything to corroborate some of the more startling claims made about him. Some say he is omniscient; others that as a highly realized spiritual master, he is able to read people's minds. There are, of course, those who will say that great spiritual masters reveal their true nature to others only according to the capacity of the individual. (This idea, very current in Tibetan Buddhism, is strikingly reminiscent of the Docetists who, during the 2nd century A.D., argued that Christ could not in any ultimate sense have been "God made flesh." They argued that what people would have apprehended had they seen Jesus would have differed according to their spiritual capacity.)

Perhaps they are right. Nonetheless, I must say that, save perhaps for one incident, my impressions of His Holiness as our acquaintance grew were nothing out of the ordinary.

Because the majority of interviews were incorporated into His Holiness's schedule on an ad hoc basis, I was on occasion able to catch glimpses of his private life. One thing that concerned me at first was the fact that he did not appear to socialize much with friends. Like its Christian counterpart, Tibetan Buddhist monasticism may be ascetic in some respects, but the importance of recreation and conviviality is not ignored. Yet it struck me that His Holiness seemed to have almost no leisure time. He does not spend days out with his family, as most monks do. There are no long, relaxed meals with members of his private office. Of course he will chat with his staff. He is close to one of his surviving brothers. He receives various older members of his entourage from time to time. But none of this appeared to add up to much more than the occasional pleasant conversation. I wondered whether he did not sometimes feel rather cut off and lonely. Yet one could not hope to meet anyone more outgoing or more at ease with himself.

What I began to see was that the Dalai Lama is a man of prayer before all else. This is the most important part of his work. In a sense, much of his active (as opposed to his contemplative) life is recreation. Meeting people from all walks of life, traveling, talking to journalists and reporters—this is where he socializes and enjoys himself. And as soon as these activities are over—sometimes as soon as he can extricate himself (people do tend to ask the same questions a lot of the time)—he resumes his central practice, that of prayer (*gom* in Tibetan, literally "familiarization" but generally translated as "meditation").

Thus, when abroad, he is not like most of the rest of us, who return to our hotel after a long day and, flinging ourselves down on the bed, switch on the television, raid the minibar, and call up room service. Instead, his first priority is meditation. Indeed, whether at home or abroad, much of his waking day is spent this way. When he arrives at his office, generally at 8 in the morning, he will have spent three hours in prayer and *lectio divina,* studying scripture. There was even a period while we were finalizing the manuscript of *Freedom in Exile* when he was rising at three o'clock in order to have some special devotions finished by the time we began work. (Normally he gets up at a more leisurely four o'clock.)

The one slightly unusual experience I recall from this time occurred on a trip to Ahmadabad. His Holiness had suggested that I come, too, so that when he had any spare time, he could fit in an interview. On one occasion, I was shown into his room while he was still meditating cross-legged on the bed. I remember being struck by how small he suddenly looked, tiny even, like an animated altar statue. At the same time, I sensed an immense power— which evaporated only when he ceased his prayer some moments later.

It was a fleeting impression only and easy to overlook. Yet set in the context of a conversation I had later with a friend who is a deacon of the Catholic Church, it is perhaps worthy of mention. One day the priest, whom this friend assisted, had received the stigmata of Christ. As the deacon entered the room, he was thrown to the ground by what he described as an immense power. I have sometimes wondered whether what I sensed as the Dalai Lama's "spiritual energy" might not have been a pale, perhaps more controlled, manifestation of the same power.

A more concrete insight into His Holiness's character came on another occasion when, after a press conference in his hotel suite, I happened upon him straightening up the chairs that had just been vacated—not, I think, out of fastidiousness, but just because it needed to be done. Yet there were any number of people on hand whom he could have directed to the task. No doubt there are other figures of world renown who straighten chairs. But they are surely in a minority. Fewer still would actually interrupt an interview on camera to see to the welfare of a young bird that had fallen from its nest, as I saw happen on another occasion. And I doubt whether any others at all are ever to be found sitting at a window in their private quarters sorrowing over the dumb stupidity of a cloud of insects tumbling past on a current of warm air.

Having completed the necessary interviews for *Freedom in Exile,* I spent a year preparing a draft manuscript. This I took out to Dharamsala during the spring of 1989. There it was read and vetted by various members of the Dalai Lama's staff. I felt at that point that probably 90 percent of the work was done, that the changes required by these readers would bring it up to 98 percent, and that a final session or two with His Holiness would elevate it to the required standard. How wrong I was.

After taking delivery of a longish, but not particularly challenging, list of corrections and suggested alterations, I was called to see His Holiness. He wanted to know how I had gotten on, whether I had experienced any particular difficulties, and whether it was true that we already had publishers in a dozen countries. It was true, I replied. This, it seemed, both pleased him and surprised him a little. As to the work itself, I'd gotten on fine, but yes, I had one or two further queries. I forget now what they were, but I explained their substance to him.

I seem to remember him nodding and then remaining silent for a few moments. We were alone. "Tomorrow then. Eight o'clock," he said, brightening. "Come here and bring the book."

The next day I returned as instructed. "So," he began, "read it." I was stupefied. "Yes, go on. Read it to me."

The following two weeks passed in something of a frenzy. Each day I went up to His Holiness's residence to go through the manuscript, in the company of Tenzin Geychee Tethong and Tendzin Choegyal, as before, for eight, nine, even on one or two occasions, ten hours at a stretch. Every sentence was considered, each phrase scrutinized, and single words subjected to lengthy inquisition. Sometimes I would be drawn into quite heated debates over the use of particular terms. Often I would concede, but occasionally I refused to yield. Whenever this happened, my judgment was accepted. One instance (although not actually a contentious one) occurred in connection with my desire to use the word *mendacious* in a particular context. Although His Holiness was unfamiliar with the term, I felt it was especially appropriate at that point, and he allowed it. (I wish I could find it now to see whether it still seems right.)

When finally we came to the end, I walked away with alterations, additions, corrections, and sundry emendations accounting for fully a third of the manuscript. Hardly a page was not covered with scrawl. That was not the very end of the process, however. Just before the book went to press—three months late and barely six weeks before publication—it was checked again by Tenzin Geychee and Geshe Thupten Jinpa, the latter reading it from a specifically Buddhist perspective.

The work sessions with His Holiness for *Ethics for the New Millennium* followed broadly the same pattern. This book was published in the U.K. under the somewhat fey title (my fault) of *Ancient Wisdom, Modern World*—it really should have been called just *Ethics* everywhere. It was altogether a much more difficult enterprise, however. The book is half the length of *Freedom in Exile,* yet it took more than three times as long to write. As with the autobiography, there were the initial material-gathering sessions, followed by an extended period when we went through the manuscript as a team.

One difference in our method was that to save His Holiness's time, rather than have his every utterance translated into English then and there, he would sometimes explain a point to Thupten Jinpa (who collaborated on the project throughout), which the latter would then pass on to me when we came to transcribe the tapes later. Also, I adopted a more adversarial role during the preliminary discussions: it seemed essential often to play the devil's advocate in order to head off some of the objections likely to be posed by a Western readership.

As well as further deepening our acquaintance, working on *Ethics* gave me a much better appreciation of the Dalai Lama's intellect. I have to admit that it soon became clear that his is superior to mine by a rather comfortable margin. There were many occasions when I found myself stammering to explain a point of view when challenging something he had said. He, on the other hand, hardly ever came out with an utterance that was less than fully formed. I often felt as if I was wearing lead boots next to his sneakers.

One particular observation from this time concerns the way in which His Holiness can be quite splendidly disconcerting. Too often I found myself jumping to conclusions, only to find them confounded a moment later. I had, for example, always assumed that Tibetans were, of necessity, highly conscious of the natural world, thanks both to their nomadic culture and to Buddhism's reverence for all forms of life. Not at all, he said. Tibetans were entirely ignorant in these matters. It had simply never occurred to anyone that there could be such a thing as pollution. But that does not mean they did not themselves pollute the environment. It was just that the conditions prevailing in Tibet (wide-open spaces and very dry air) meant that it had little impact.

Similarly, I gathered that at a science conference His Holiness attended, he had caused consternation by telling the panel that he could imagine instances where it might be justifiable to use animals in experiments designed to further (human) medical science. (I noticed that in the transcript he used the plural "instances," but in the book published subsequently, this was changed to the singular: "an instance." Was this censorship?)

One of His Holiness's most attractive characteristics is his disinclination to offer value judgments unless specifically asked for them, and even then to be supremely careful in doing so. There are doubtless many good reasons for this. One is surely connected to his understanding of his role as Dalai Lama. He is, he insists, "just an ordinary human being," although it is doubtful whether many people take this at face value. Few would travel thousands of miles to glimpse, line up for hours to meet, or even listen to a stranger they thought merely to be an ordinary human being. Similarly, he maintains that he is not a religious leader but "just a simple Buddhist monk." Again, this is not the general perception. Yet it would help explain his reluctance to offer opinions.

Another reason for His Holiness's reluctance to speak out on certain issues is very likely connected to the Buddhist view of mission. A Buddhist teacher does not teach unless requested to do so. Nor does he (or to a much lesser extent, she) teach unless convinced of the motives of the supplicant. The bully-boy tactics of certain evangelical Christian missionaries in Mongolia are viewed with horror by many Tibetans, the Dalai Lama included.

Yet another factor is no doubt the Western tendency to resolve everything into clear-cut, either-or dilemmas. This seems rather unsubtle to the Tibetan mind. And where this seems likely to lead to intractable argument, His Holiness prefers to remain detached, knowing that often the aim is to push him into a corner.

This does not mean that he has no strong views. Moreover, he can be quick to state these unequivocally. I recall on one occasion telling him about some deep Green extremist who advocated that the world's population be reduced to a billion. His immediate response was to say that this person should set a good example and lead the way.

Similarly, I have observed many occasions when he was so distressed by something he had seen or heard that the very thought of it robbed him of speech. Then he would sit quietly for a moment or two, sometimes longer (offering a prayer?), sometimes taking off his glasses to wipe his eyes before continuing. A discussion about human-embryo experimentation and the possibility of growing human body parts in subhuman creatures created for the purpose was one such occasion.

I wonder, though, whether this reluctance to pontificate is not in large part the reason for the recent, rather disturbing, emergence of a sort of ersatz Dalai Lama living in the public eye. This is the Dalai Lama of "cool," the Dalai Lama as friend to everyone—although most notably to a clutch of entertainment-world royalty—a spiritual hero who offers comfort to the victim in us all. This is the Dalai Lama of the Dalai Lama industry (an industry I must have helped create) of countless books, articles, videos, television appearances, and even two major feature films—the Dalai Lama as New Age icon, a religious leader who is popularly understood to reassure without requiring repentance, to console without demanding contrition.

At first sight, this looks like innocuous sentimentalization. But is such sentimentalization ever really innocuous? The problem with turning the Dalai Lama into the uniquely spiritual being of popular imagination is that it enables us to ignore anything he says that troubles us (such as his insistence that the economic disparity between North and South is immoral). It becomes the utterance of someone we cannot identify with other than superficially.

Yet one does not need to know him well to guess that the Dalai Lama is someone who would sooner bless than curse his enemies, someone who gives the same consideration to all others alike, someone who pays no regard to social standing. Just by listening carefully, one can tell that here is someone who, to the utmost of his ability, seeks to be at peace with everyone—someone who is patient, who is kind, who is neither boastful nor conceited, who is never rude nor seeks his own advantage—that here is someone who neither takes offense nor stores up grievances. On the contrary, he is evidently ready always to make allowances, to trust, to hope, and, in adversity, to endure whatever trials come. (In saying this, I am of course plagiarizing St. Paul. No one has better described what it means to be spiritual than he.)

If, then, we merely adore the Dalai Lama, the danger is that we will overlook the fact that spirituality consists precisely in the exercise of virtue. Worse, there is every likelihood we will miss the most remarkable thing of all—which is that, just as he says, he is an ordinary human being. But therein lies our hope.

MAKING KINDNESS
STAND TO REASON

by Pico Iyer

Although the Dalai Lama is increasingly famous as a speaker, his real gift, you quickly notice, is listening. And even though he is most celebrated in the West these days for his ability to talk to halls large enough to stage a Bon Jovi concert, his special strength is to address 20,000 people—Buddhists and grandmothers and kids alike—as if he were talking to each one alone, in the language the person can best understand. The Dalai Lama's maxims are collected and packaged now as books to carry in your handbag, as calendar items, and as advertising slogans . . . but the heart of the man exists, I think, in silence. In his deepest self, he is that being who sits alone each day at dawn, eyes closed, reciting prayers with all his heart for his Chinese oppressors, his Tibetan people, and all sentient beings.

Yet the curiosity of the 14th Dalai Lama's life—one of the things that has made it seem at once a parable and a kind of koan—is that he has had to pursue his spiritual destiny for more than half a century almost entirely in the world . . . and, in fact, in a political world whose god is Machiavelli. His story is an all-but-timeless riddle about the relation of means to ends: in order to protect six million people and to preserve a rare and long-protected culture that is years away from extinction, he has had to pose for endless photos with models and let his speeches be broadcast on the floors of London dance clubs.

To some extent, he has had to enter right into the madness and vanity of the Celebrity Age in order to fulfill his monastic duties. The question that he carries with him everywhere he goes is the simple one of whether the world cannot be avoided and whether it will scar him before he elevates it: in three centuries, no Ocean of Wisdom, Holder of the White Lotus, and Protector of the Land of Snows has ever also served as guest editor of French *Vogue*.

I went to visit the Dalai Lama in Dharamsala not long ago, as I have done at regular intervals since my teens. I took the rickety Indian Airlines flight from Delhi to Amritsar, itself often a restricted war zone (because it houses the Sikh stronghold of the Golden Temple), and from there took a five-hour taxi ride up into the foothills of the Himalayas. As I approached the distant settlement on a ridge above a little town—the roads so jam-packed with scooters and bicycles and cows that often we could hardly move (for security reasons, the Dalai Lama has to drive for ten hours along such roads every time he wishes to take a flight)—Dharamsala came into view now and then, and then disappeared, like a promise of liberation or someplace that didn't really exist. Most of the time—the car collapsing on a mountain road, a group of villagers assembling to push it hopefully forward, night falling, and each turn seeming to be taking us farther and farther away from the distant string of lights—I felt sure we'd never get there.

As soon as you arrive at the dusty, bedraggled place, however, you realize that you are very far from a fairy tale, in the realm of suffering and old age and death. Windows are broken, and paths half-paved in the rainy little village where the Dalai Lama has made his home for more than half his life now; even the happy cries and songs of the orphans at the Tibetan Children's Village on one side of town have a slightly wistful air as the sun sets behind the nearby mountains.

When you call the Dalai Lama's office, you will hear that "all circuits are busy" or that the five-digit number changed yesterday. Sometimes my calls got cut off in midsentence, amid a blur of static; sometimes I got put on hold—for all eternity, it seemed—to the tune of "London Bridge Is Falling Down."

It is, therefore, perhaps the perfect paradoxical setting for a humble monk who lives alone when he is not being sought out by Goldie Hawn or Harrison Ford. In the antechamber to his living room—after you've been checked by a Tibetan guard and then an Indian one—you sit under a certificate of honorary citizenship from Orange County, an award from the Rotary Club of Dharamsala, and a plaque commemorating an honorary professorship from Kalmyk State University. Ceremonial masks, Hindu deities, and pietàs shine down on you. On one wall is a huge blown-up photo of the Tibetan capital of Lhasa, showing that the palace where the Dalai Lama once lived is now ringed by discos, brothels, and a new Chinese prison, with armed soldiers stationed upon the city's rooftops.

The Dalai Lama has a singular gift for seeing the blessing in everything and is seemingly unfazed by all the madness that swirls around him; he is always thoroughly human and always thoroughly himself. Sometimes as you wait to see him, his exuberant new friend, a very puppyish German shepherd, runs into the room and starts jumping over a group of startled Tibetan monks here for a serious discussion, licking the faces of the Buddhist teachers before romping off into the garden again. Sometimes a pair of English hippies sits there, since the Dalai Lama is ready to take advice and instruction from anyone (and is aware—such is the poignancy of his life—that even the most disorganized traveler may know more about contemporary Tibet and the state of his people than he does). As a photographer asks him to take off his glasses, pose with this hat, sit this way or that, His Holiness seizes the chance to ask him about what he saw when he photographed uprisings in Lhasa many years before.

As I sit across from him in his room with its large windows looking out on pine-covered slopes and the valley below—*thangkas* all around us on the walls—the Dalai Lama makes himself comfortable, cross-legged in his armchair, and serves me tea. He always notices that my cup is empty before I do. He often rocks back and forth as he speaks: the habit acquired, one realizes, over decades of grueling hours-long meditation sessions, frequently in the cold. And part of his disarming power (the result, no doubt, of all that meditation and the dialectics of which he is a master) is that he launches stronger criticism against himself than even his fiercest enemies might.

When first he met Shoko Asahara, he tells me one day (referring to the man who later planned the planting of deadly sarin gas in the Tokyo subway system), he was genuinely moved by the man's seeming devotion to the Buddha: tears would come into the Japanese teacher's eyes when he spoke of Buddha. But to endorse Asahara, as he did, was, the Dalai Lama quickly says, "a mistake. Due to ignorance! So, this proves"—and he breaks into his full-throated laugh—"I'm not a Living Buddha!"

Another day, talking about the problems of present-day Tibet, he refers to the fact that there are "too many prostrations there," and then, erupting into gales of infectious laughter again, he realizes that he should have said "too much prostitution" (although, in fact, as he knows, "too many prostrations" may actually constitute a deeper problem). He'd love to delegate some responsibility to his deputies, he says frankly, "but even if some of my cabinet ministers wanted to give public talks, nobody would come."

The result is that it all comes down to him. The Dalai Lama is rightly famous for his unstoppable warmth, his optimism, and his forbearance—"the happiest man in the world," as one journalist friend calls him—yet his life has seen more difficulty and sadness than that of anyone I know. He's representing the interests of 6 million largely unworldly and disenfranchised people against a nation of 1.2 billion whom nearly all the world is trying to court. He's the guest of a huge nation with problems of its own that would be very grateful if he just kept quiet. He travels the world constantly (on a yellow refugee's "identity certificate") and, although regarded by most as a leader equivalent to Mother Teresa or the Pope, is formally as ostracized as Muammar al-Gadhafi or Kim Jong II. He is excited when meeting Britain's queen mother—because he remembers, from when he was young, seeing news clips of her tending to the poor of London during the Blitz—but the world is more excited when he meets actress Sharon Stone.

And so a serious spiritual leader is treated as a celebrity; and a doctor of metaphysics is sought out by everyone, from every culture, who has a problem in his life. As a monk, he seems more than happy to offer what he can, as much as he can, but none of it helps him toward the liberation of his people. I ask him one day about how Tibet is likely to be compromised or distorted by its complicity with the mass media, and he looks back at me shrewdly and with a penetrating gaze. "If there are people who use Tibetans or the Tibetan situation for their own purposes," he says, "or if they associate with some publicity for their own benefit, there's very little we can do. But the important thing is for us not to be involved in this publicity or associate with these people for our own interests."

The razor-sharp reasoning is typical, even if it doesn't quite address the conundrum in which he finds himself. For precisely in order to satisfy his inner and outer mandate, the Dalai Lama is obliged to traffic in the world incessantly. He has to listen to a reporter asking him how he'd like to be remembered—which is, in the Buddhist context, akin to asking the Pope what he thinks of actress/singer Jennifer Lopez ("I really lost my temper," he tells me of the question, "though I didn't show it"). He has to answer for every scandal that touches any of the many often highly suspect Tibetans and Tibetan groups around the world. And he has to endure and address every controversy that arises when his image is used by Apple computers, or younger Tibetans deride him as an out-of-it peacenik who's done nothing to help Tibet for 50 years.

As we spoke day after day in the radiant fall afternoons—young monks practicing ritual debates outside his front door; the snowcaps shining in the distance; and the hopes of Tibet poignantly, palpably, in the air around the ragged town of exiles—the time the Dalai Lama most lit up, in some respects, was when he spoke of a group of Catholic monks he'd run into in France who live in complete isolation for years on end and "remain almost like prisoners" as they meditate. "Wonderful!" he pronounced, leaving it to his visitor to deduce that left to his own devices, that's how he'd like to be.

At this point, after two autobiographies and two major Hollywood films telling his story, the otherworldly contours of the Dalai Lama's life are well known: his birth in a cowshed in rural

Tibet in what was locally known as the Wood Hog Year (1935); his discovery by a search party of monks, who'd been led to him by a vision in a sacred lake; the tests administered to a two-year-old who, mysteriously, greeted the monks from far-off Lhasa as their leader, and in their distant dialect. Yet what the mixture of folktale and Shakespearean drama doesn't always catch is that the single dominant theme of his life, a Buddhist might say, is loss.

To someone who reads the world in terms of temporal glory, it's a stirring story of a four-year-old peasant boy ascending the Lion Throne to rule one of the most exotic treasures on Earth. To someone who really lives the philosophy for which the Dalai Lama stands, it could play out in a different key. At two, he lost the peace of his quiet life in a wood-and-stone house where he slept in the kitchen. At four, he lost his home, and his freedom to be a real person, when he was pronounced king. Soon thereafter, he lost something of his family, too, and most of his ties with the world at large as he embarked on a formidable 16-year course of monastic studies and was forced, at the age of six, to choose a regent.

The Dalai Lama has written with typical warmth about his otherworldly boyhood in the cold thousand-roomed Potala Palace, where he played games with the palace sweepers, rigged up a hand-cranked projector on which he could watch *Tarzan* movies and *Henry V*, and clobbered his only real playmate—his immediate elder brother, Lobsang Samten—in the knowledge that no one would be quick to punish a boy regarded as an incarnation of the god of compassion (and a king, to boot).

Yet the overwhelming feature of his childhood was its loneliness. Often, he recalls, he would go out onto the rooftop of his palace and watch the other little boys of Lhasa playing in the street. Every time his brother left, he recalls "standing at the window, watching, my heart full of sorrow as he disappeared into the distance."

The Dalai Lama has never pretended that he does not have a human side, and although it is that side that exults in everything that comes his way, it is also that which cannot fail to grieve at times. When the Chinese, newly united by Mao Tse-tung, attacked Tibet's eastern frontiers in 1950, the 15-year-old boy was forced hurriedly to take over the temporal as well as the spiritual leadership of his country, and so lost his boyhood (if not his innocence) and his last vestiges of freedom. In his teens, he was traveling to Beijing, overriding the wishes of his fearful people, to negotiate with Mao and Chou En-lai; and not long thereafter, he became only the second Dalai Lama to leave Tibet, when it seemed his life might be in peril.

At 24, a few days after he finally completed his doctoral studies and shone in an oral in front of thousands of appraising monks, he lost his home for good: The "Wish-Fulfilling Gem," as he is known to Tibetans, had to dress up as a soldier and flee across the highest mountains on Earth, dodging Chinese planes, seated on a hybrid yak. The drama of that loss lives inside him still. I asked him one sunny afternoon about the saddest moment in his life, and he told me that he was moved to tears usually only when he talked of Buddha or thought of compassion—or heard, as he sometimes does every day, the stories and appeals of the terrified refugees who've stolen out of Tibet to come and see him.

Generally, he said in his firm, prudent way, "sadness, I think, is comparatively manageable." But before he spoke of any of that, he looked into the distance and recalled how "I left the Norbulingka Palace that late night, and some of my close friends and one dog I left behind. Then, just when I was crossing the border into India, I remember my final farewell, mainly to my bodyguards. They were deliberately facing the Chinese, and when they bade me farewell, they were determined to return. So that means"—his eyes were close to misting over now—"they were facing death or something like that." In the decades since then, he's never seen the land he was born to rule.

I, too, remember that drama: the fairy-tale flight of the boy-king from the Forbidden Kingdom was the first world event that made an impression on me when I was growing up; and a little later when my father went to India to greet the newly arrived Tibetan, he came back with a picture of the monk as a little boy, which the Dalai Lama had given him when he talked of his own three-year-old in Oxford. Since then, like many of us, I've run into him everywhere I go, it seems—at Harvard, in New York, in the hills of Malibu, in Japan—and have had the even stranger experience of seeing him somehow infiltrate the most unlikely worlds: my graduate-school professor of Virginia Woolf suddenly came into my life again as editor of a book of the Dalai Lama's talks about the gospel; at the Olympics, a longtime friend and sportswriter for *The New York Times* started reminiscing about how he covered the Dalai Lama on the Tibetan's first U.S. tour, in 1979, and found him great because he was so humble.

"It sounds like he considers you part of the family," a friend once said when I told her that the Dalai Lama and his equally mischievous younger brother call me Pinocchio. But really, his gift is for regarding all of the world as part of his family.

At the same time, the world itself has not always been very interested in the details of his faraway country and a tradition that seems to belong to another world. When Tibet appealed to the newly formed United Nations for help against China, it was Britain and India, its two ostensible sponsors, who argued against even hearing the motion. And as recently as the 1980s, I remember his press conferences in New York being almost deserted; when I once organized a lunch for him with a group of editors, one of them called up a couple of days before to call it off, because no one really wanted to come in to the office on a Monday just to chat with a Tibetan monk.

When I first visited him in Dharamsala, in 1974, I really did feel as if I were looking in on one of the deposed emperors of China or Vietnam, sitting in a far-off exile. As we sat drinking tea in his modest, colorful cottage, clouds passed through the room from the rains outside—all we could see through the large windows was mist and gray—and it felt as if we were truly sitting in the heavens, at least a mile above anything that felt real.

Yet one of the paradoxes of the Dalai Lama's life—a paradox to answer the koan that has been his fulfillment of a spiritual duty in the world—is that it was, it seems, his monastic training that allowed him to be so focused and charismatic a presence in the world. In his early years in India, the Dalai Lama used the world's neglect of him to organize his exiled community and to write his country's constitution (in part to allow for his own impeachment).

Even exile could be a hidden blessing, he was saying (and showing his compatriots): It freed him from the age-old protocol that so shackled him in Tibet, and it brought the forever-feuding groups of Tibet together in a common cause. Most of all, though, he used his free time to go on long meditation retreats, enjoying a solitude that could never have been his in Tibet (or, now, in Dharamsala).

Robert Thurman, the professor of Tibetan studies at Columbia (and father of Uma), remembers first meeting the Dalai Lama in 1964, when he, full of spiritual ambitions, cross-questioned the young Tibetan about *shunyata,* or voidness, while the Dalai Lama questioned him, no less eagerly, about Freud and the American bicameral system. "It was fun," Thurman says, using the word people often apply to the Dalai Lama. "We were young together." At the same time, the answers that the monk, only in his 20s then, gave to complex theological questions were less good, Thurman feels, than those offered by more senior monks.

When the Tibetan leader emerged from his retreats, though, and came out into the world—Thurman saw him on his first U.S. tour, in 1979—"I almost keeled over. His personal warmth and magnetism were so strong. In the past, of course, he had the ritual charisma of being the Dalai Lama, and he's always been charming and interesting and very witty. But now he's opened up some inner wellspring of energy and attention and intelligence. He was glorious."

And yet that air of responsibility—the word he always stresses in the same breath as compassion—has never left him. I remember going to see him the day after he won the Nobel Prize, when he happened to be staying (as is so typical of his life) in a suburban ranch house in Newport Beach. What struck me at the time was that as soon as he saw me, he whisked me (as he would no doubt have whisked any visitor) into a little room and spent his first few minutes looking for a chair in which I would be comfortable—as if *I* were the new Nobel laureate and he the intrusive journalist.

But what I also remember from that moment was that even as the world was feting him—congratulatory telegrams and faxes pouring into the rec room downstairs—he couldn't let himself off the hook. "Sometimes," he confessed, "I wonder whether my efforts really have an effect. I sometimes feel that unless there is a bigger movement, the bigger issues will not change. But how to start this bigger movement? Originally, it must come from individual initiative."

The only way, he concluded, was through "constant effort, tireless effort, pursuing clear goals with sincere effort." Every time he left a room, he said, he tried to switch off the light. "In a way, it's silly. But if another person follows my example, then a hundred persons, there is an effect. It is the only way. The bigger nations and more powerful leaders are not taking care. So we poor human beings must make the effort."

Meeting him now, I find him a lot more businesslike than he was in those days (and, of course, much more fluent in English); when TV crews come to interview him, he knows how to advise them on where to set up their cameras (and when we begin talking, he is quick to point out that my tape recorder is moving suspiciously fast). He's not less jolly than before, perhaps, but he does seem more determined to speak from the serious side of himself as the years go on and Tibet draws ever closer to oblivion. Where he used to greet me with an Indian namaste, now he does so with a handshake . . . although the Dalai Lama does not so much shake your hand as rub it within his own, as if to impart to it some of his warmth.

As we talk, though—every afternoon at 2 P.M., day after day—he takes off his glasses sometimes and rubs his eyes; his aides say that in recent years, for the first time ever, they've seen him exhausted, his head slumped back in his chair (this the man usually seen leaning into the conversation, as if to bring to it all his attention and beady-eyed vigor). He doesn't have much time for spiritual practice now, he tells me—only four hours a day (his duties increasing as he becomes a more senior monk). He still likes to do "some repair work, of watches and small instruments," and he still loves tending to his flowers; one of the longest and most animated answers he gives me comes when I ask after his "four small cats." But these days the only real break he can take comes listening to the BBC World Service, to which he cheerfully confesses himself addicted.

This is the tendency of an engaging, still-boyish character alight with curiosity, but it's also the confession of a man whose duties are almost entirely tied up with the dealings of the world on a minute-by-minute level. One thing the Dalai Lama is not is otherworldly. He can explain in precise detail why the Tibetan cause is weaker than that of the Palestinians, or how globalism is, at its best, advancing a kind of Buddhism in mufti. His references nearly always come from the day's most recent news, and he watches everything—from the fall of the Berlin wall to the tragedy in Rwanda—both to see how it illuminates some metaphysical theory and to see what other kind of teaching it can impart. Exile, indeed, has allowed him, he will tell you, to become a student of the world in a way that no earlier Dalai Lama could and to see a planet that previously he, and the Dalai Lamas before him, could glimpse only through the parted curtains of a palanquin.

The best aspect of his traveling is that he can schedule meetings with scientists and psychologists and Hopi leaders, all of whom, he believes, can help him refine his understanding of his own tradition. Buddhists can and should learn from Catholics, from physicists, even from Communists, he is quick to tell his startled followers—and if the words of the Buddha (let alone of the Dalai Lama) are not borne out by the evidence, they must be discarded instantly.

This is one reason why he seems much more interested in asking questions than in giving answers, and much more comfortable as a student (which he has been, in the context of Tibetan Buddhism, most of his life) than a teacher. It is also why I would say that his sovereign quality is alertness: watch the Dalai Lama enter a crowded auditorium or sit through a long monastic ceremony that has many others nodding off and you will notice him looking around keenly for what he can pick up—a friend to whom he can unselfconsciously wave, some little detail that will bring a smile to his face.

Alertness is the place where the slightly impish boy and the rigorously trained monk converge, and although the world at large most responds to his heart—the pleasure afforded by his beam and air of kindness and good nature—the specific core of him comes no less from his mind and the analytical faculties honed in one of the world's most sophisticated metaphysical technologies. It's not unusual, I've come to see by now, for the Dalai Lama to remember a sentence he's delivered to you some years before or to complete an answer he began 90 minutes ago, while lacing up his sturdy mountain boots. Sometimes in large gatherings he will pick out a face he last saw in Lhasa half a century before; once as we were talking, he suddenly remembered something an Englishman had said to him 20 years before—about the value of sometimes saying "I don't know"—and asked me, searchingly, what I thought of it.

Again, the irony here is that the mindfulness he's cultivated in meditation—on retreats and at the hands of pitilessly strict teachers—is what has helped him in his travels. Spiritual training—this is one of the lessons of his life and his example—has constant practical application in the world. Much of the time he's speaking to people who know nothing about Buddhism, who may even be hostile to it; and he's mastered the art of speaking simply and ecumenically from the heart, stressing, as he does, "spirituality without faith—simply being a good human being, a warmhearted person, a person with a sense of responsibility." Talking to his monks, he delivers philosophical lectures that few of the rest of us can begin to follow; speaking to the world, he realizes that the most important thing is not to run before you can walk. The title of a typical book of his mentions not "Enlightening" the heart, but simply "Lightening" it.

In a sense, he's turned his predicament to advantage in part by learning about Western religions, as well as meditation practices in other traditions, as earlier Dalai Lamas could seldom do. And he's also had to deal with a worldwide stampede toward a Buddhism for which it may not be ready (to such a point that more and more as the years go on, he tells Westerners not to become Buddhists, but just to stick to their own tradition, where there's less of a danger of mixed motives and certainly less likelihood of confusion). Listening to him speak everywhere from São Paulo to Chicago, Philip Glass says, "The word *Buddha* never came up. He talks about compassion; he talks about right living. And it's very powerful and persuasive to people because it's clear he's not there to convert them."

Pragmatism, in short, trumps dogmatism. And logic defers to nothing. "Out of 5.7 million people," he tells me one day, his eyes glittering with the delight of a student immersed in one of Tibet's ritual debates, "the majority of them are certainly not believers. We can't argue with them, tell them they should be believers. No! Impossible! And, realistically speaking, if the majority of humanity remain nonbelievers, it doesn't matter. No problem! The problem is that the majority have lost, or ignore, the deeper human values—compassion, a sense of responsibility. That is our big concern, for whenever there is a society or community without deeper human values, then not even one single human family can be a happy family."

Then—and it isn't hard to see the still-eager student playing his winning card—he goes on, "Even animals, from a Buddhist viewpoint, have the potential of showing affection toward their own children or their own babies—and also toward us. Dogs, cats, if we treat them nicely, openly, trustingly—they also respond. But without religion, they have no faith!" Therefore, he says triumphantly, kindness is more fundamental than belief.

Yet the deepest loss of all in the Dalai Lama's often-bright and blessing-filled life is that all the friends he's made worldwide, all the presidents and prime ministers he's won over, all the analytical reasoning with which he argues for compassion and responsibility have not really helped him at all in what is the main endeavor of his life: helping the people of Tibet and sustaining a Tibetan identity among a scattered population, six million of whom have not seen their leader for two generations and the other 140,000 of whom have not, in many cases, seen their homeland. Many of those who witness him flying across five continents in a year (in business class) and delivering lectures to sold-out halls don't know that he's working with a staff drawn from a population smaller than that of Warren, Michigan, and with a circle of advisors who'd never seen the world, or known much about it, before they were propelled into a premature exile.

A SIMPLE MONK

by Sulak Sivaraksa

His Holiness the Dalai Lama often introduces himself as "a simple monk," despite the fact that he is widely known as the Ocean of Wisdom—a head of state as well as a special spiritual leader of Vajrayana Buddhism—not to mention his unique position as an emanation of Chenrezig, the Avalokiteshvara bodhisattva of compassion.

I find the way His Holiness describes himself most meaningful and touching. This reflects not only humility itself, but it is also significantly truthful.

A few years ago, leaflets were circulated by Christians outside a large public meeting at Diamond Head, Honolulu, stressing the fact that the Dalai Lama refers to himself as only a simple monk. As a result, this raises the following questions: *What could he do? Why should people be attracted to—or even respect—him?* Instead, the people should turn to Jesus, who was not only the Son of God but also the Savior of the world.

On the other hand, both in public as well as in private, His Holiness has often praised Jesus, Mohammed, and all religious leaders. He encourages Christians and Jews to practice their own religions wisely and mindfully. If they want to add Buddhist meditation to their spiritual traditions, it is all right, provided that they do not belittle their own religions.

This reminds me of another simple monk, my own late teacher, Bhikkhu Buddhadasa, whom His Holiness also greatly admired. He asked all his followers to uphold three crucial points:

1. Try to understand the essential teachings of the Buddha and put them into practice as selflessly as possible.

2. Respect and honor our friends' religions, not regarding them as inferior to ours.

3. Unite with those of other faiths and nonbelievers so that together we can overcome greed, hatred, and delusion.

These are increasingly being manifested in consumerism, centralization of power, and modern education, which concentrates only on intellectualism and is devoid of wisdom and compassion.

Bhikkhu Buddhadasa dedicated himself to work as the servant *(dasa)* of the Buddha. Indeed, the Buddha himself was a simple monk. We may recall that when he was a prince, he reveled in all worldly pleasures, shielding himself from suffering in the world. Eventually, he managed to witness an old man, a sick man, a dead man, and a monk. Suddenly, it dawned on him that sickness and death are a part of life. He wanted to overcome the suffering of life. He felt that abandoning sensual pleasures and family life and becoming a simple mendicant might be a way. In fact, the Buddha-to-be was a wandering monk for six years before he could become truly awakened from greed, hatred, and delusion. His understanding was so thorough that there was no selfishness left behind. As a result, his wisdom was automatically transformed into compassion. That is the reason why we Buddhists call him the All Enlightened and the Compassionate One.

For us, being a simple monk (or a simple nun) is really essential for a human person to achieve the highest goal in life—overcoming suffering and being in the state of real happiness without depending on sensual or external conditions.

If we do not lead a simple life, we depend so heavily on many other factors that we have no time and energy left for deep concentration in order to be mindful—to understand the reality of physical phenomena as well as the mysteries of the universe. Scientific knowledge only helps us understand some aspects of the universe, often compartmentally. On the other hand, deep meditation without selfishness will help us realize the truth holistically.

Being a simple monk allows one to be less selfish more easily than a layperson attached to family life, because a simple monk is not tied down to sensual pleasure, which is like a double-edged dagger. It is a fact that every gain, honor, sensual happiness, or praise has its negative attribute: loss, dishonor, suffering, and denunciation, respectively. According to the Buddha, these are the eight worldly conditions. Whoever is attached to any of these will not be free from the cycles of birth and death.

Unfortunately, some monks who have left the mundane world to pursue the truth are still caught in one or more of the eight worldly conditions. Losing their simplicity and sometimes even obsessed with fame and wealth, they are monks only in name: They no longer lead a celibate or a noble life. Hence, some have even become hypocrites—fooling themselves and others. These so-called monks are worse than ordinary laypeople.

Morality or ethics is said to be the foundation of the successful development of human potentials. According to the teachings of the Buddha, living within the discipline of the vows of morality—commitments not to harm any living being with one's body or speech by not lying, not killing, not stealing, and so on—is the most effective way to accumulate the positive karmic energy or morality: literally a buildup of positive habits of mind, body, and speech.

Vows or commitments are viewed not as moralistic restrictions but as practical guidelines for life. There are sets of vows for laypeople, but those of monks and nuns are said to serve as the most potent way to live within the commitments of morality. Fully ordained monks, for example, have 227 vows.

Logically, then, the more vows we have and keep—that we use as the tools they are meant to be—the easier it is to develop our innate potential for love, kindness, patience, wisdom, and the rest. And it is common sense that one is more likely to succeed at something by devoting more time to it than less, and by living in an environment—internal and external—that totally supports the endeavor.

Put another way, the life of a monk (or a nun) deals with integrity, restraint, and chastity in matters related to the sexual instincts of the body. In this day and age of consumerism and materialism, most people do not see the virtue of those who lead completely celibate lives.

An English monk, Bhikkhu Jayasro, expresses this issue beautifully as follows:

> It's only through taking this impeccable standard that we can begin to understand the whole nature of sexuality. We begin to see its conditioned nature, how it arises and passes away. We begin to see the suffering inherent in any attachment to it, how impersonal it is, what feeds it, what gives power to it—whether it be physical conditions, foods, lack of sense restraint, or indulgence in imagination. We begin to see it as a conditioned phenomenon. But we can only have a distance from it, be able to reflect on it, and see it for what it is by refraining from its physical and verbal expressions.
>
> There is an important point about defilements here: that we have to pin them down on the mental level before we can let go of them. And the way we pin something down on the mental plane is that we refrain consciously or endure through the intention to express it physically or verbally. This is where the relationship between *sila, samadhi,* and *panna* becomes very clear. As long as we're still expressing sexual feelings physically or indulging in lascivious or careless speech about sexual matters, then we can never isolate it. It's moving; it's still receiving energy. We're still keeping it in motion; we're still feeding the flames. So we seek to counter the stream of craving. And to do that successfully, we must aspire to transcend sexuality altogether. It is that aspiration, as much as the actual restraint, that distinguishes the *samana* from the layperson.

So as celibate monks, we take a whole new stance toward our sexual feelings, toward women—half of the human race. We practice looking on women who are older than us as mothers; if they're just a few years older than us, as older sisters; if a few years younger than us, as younger sisters. We substitute whole-some perceptions of women for the sensual. This is a beautiful gift that we can give women. An attractive woman comes into the monastery, and we refrain from indulging in sexual percep-tions, sexual thoughts about that woman, and substitute it with wholesome reflections, whether it is consciously trying to per-ceive the woman as a sister or wishing that person freedom from suffering. Practicing *metta,* we reflect, "May they be well."

We offer women the gift of a wholesome response to them as human beings rather than following the instinctive attraction or obsession with their body or some aspect of their physical appearance. Through that intention, we experience an immedi-ate elevation from the blind instinctual level of our being to the uniquely human. It is a movement from the coarse to the refined. Indeed, the Pali word *brahmacariya,* which we translate into Eng-lish as celibacy, literally means "the way of the gods." In other words, within the human realm, a chaste life led voluntarily and with contentment is the most refined, sublime, and happy form of existence.

A simple monk endeavors to attain and uphold *upekkha,* which is tragically lacking in our richly violent world. *Upekkha* is the fourth stage of *brahmavihara,* the divine sentiments or sublime states of mind, and is generally defined as equanimity, neutrality, or poise. Venerable P. A. Payutto, a leading Thai monk, explains *upekkha* as follows: "Seeing things as they are with a mind that is even, steady, firm, and fair like a pair of scales; understanding that all beings experience good and evil in accordance with the causes they have created; [and the readiness] to judge, position oneself, and act in accordance with principle, reason, and equity."

Raising a good example, the Venerable Bhikku argued that *upekkha* is detachment—not bossing people around or interfering. It is compared to a carriage driver who, when the horses are run-ning smoothly and on course, sits quietly and alertly in his or her seat. In this sense, a more comprehensive definition of *upekkha,* drawn from *Visuddhimagga,* may be "passively watching when others are able to take responsibility for themselves, or when they deserve the results of the actions for which they are responsible."

A point that needs to be emphasized is that *upekkha* does not mean hermetic isolation, apathy, insensitivity, or criminal negligence—sitting on a fence and doing nothing. *Upekkha* calls for mindful (temporary) detachment in order to cultivate wisdom; the latter is a prerequisite for helping others with compassion and understanding.

In the Theravada tradition, there are ten stages of perfection, and the individual is recommended to practice them. *Upekkha* is the final stage. The first nine stages are:

1. *Dana:* giving, charity, generosity, and liberality

2. *Sila:* morality, good conduct—that is, respecting oneself and all sentient beings

3. *Nekkhama:* renunciation or trying to overcome sensual pleasures

4. *Panna:* wisdom, insight, and understanding

5. *Viriya:* energy, effort, and endeavor

6. *Khanti:* forbearance, tolerance, and endurance

7. *Sacca:* truthfulness

8. *Adhitthana:* resolution, determination

9. *Metta:* loving-kindness, friendliness

In this tradition, the ten stages of perfection are divided into three levels. The first is ordinary perfection or *parami.* In the case of *upekkha,* one becomes indifferent to praise and is not in the stranglehold of blame in the performance of one's duty. (Again, indifference to blame is not the same as being irresponsible for the negative consequences of one's action or inaction.) The second is superior perfection or *upaparami.* Here one is indifferent even when one is being harmed physically. Last is supreme perfection or *paramathaparami.* At this level, one is indifferent even when being tortured to death. In other words, through the supreme perfection, one would achieve the stage of awakening from selfishness to selflessness—the "I" is completely decentralized.

As pointed out above, *upekkha* is always the last, because one needs to cultivate loving-kindness first and foremost. The *Mettakaraniyasutta* makes this clear:

> He or she who wants to attain peace should [first] practice being upright, humble, and capable of good speech. He or she should know how to live simply and happily, with the senses calmed, without being covetous and carried away by the emotions of the majority. Let him or her decline from doing anything that will be disapproved of by the wise ones.

> [This is what he or she must contemplate.] May all people be happy and safe and may their hearts be filled with joy. May all living beings live in security and in peace—whether weak or strong, tall or short, big or small, visible or invisible, near or far away, already born or yet to be born. May all of them dwell in perfect tranquility. Let no one do harm to anyone. Let no one put the life of anyone in danger. Let no one, out of anger or malice, wish anyone any harm.

> Just as a mother loves and protects her child at the risk of her own life, we should cultivate Boundless Love and offer it to all living beings in the entire cosmos. We should let our Boundless Love pervade the whole universe, above, below, and across. Our love will know no obstacles; our hearts will be absolutely free from hatred and enmity. Whether standing or walking, sitting or lying down, as long as we are awake, we should maintain this mindfulness of love in our own hearts. This is the noblest way of living.

> Free from the wrong views, greed, and sensual desires . . . living beautifully and achieving Perfect Understanding, those who practice Boundless Love will certainly transcend Birth and Death.

In sum, a simple monk is someone who is ever humble, chaste, and mindful and practices Boundless Love. He leads a noble and celibate life. He wants so little for himself that all his time and energy are sacrificed for the happiness and welfare of other sentient beings. His happiness depends on his thoughts, speech, and actions being first and foremost for the well-being of others.

His life is so harmonious within himself, physically, mentally, and spiritually. And this harmony leads to harmonious relationships with other monks and nuns, as well as with laypeople. His lifestyle would influence that of the laity who try to imitate the monks' simple way of living mindfully. His lifestyle would also influence natural phenomena, making them more harmonious and wholesome. Even birds and bees would learn to be less harmful and more compassionate.

The simple living of a monk can contribute much to social welfare and environmental balance. Besides, a simple monk would have the time for learning various sciences, which would be useful to lead humans and other beings to overcome suffering. As these sciences are interrelated and necessary to prevent as well as to cure (not compartmentally or commercially) contemporary personal or social ills, they are advantageous indeed.

His Holiness has successfully held dialogues with leading scientists over the last few years. As a result, some of them have become more humble and have seen the value of the spiritual dimension in helping scientific knowledge transcend logic and materialism. Publications on these series of dialogues are most meaningful. Works by His Holiness himself or by those who have been inspired by him are likewise worthy.

Some social ills are so damaging and horrendous, such as the Chinese invasion of Tibet and all the dreadful events in that country. Yet to have a simple monk like His Holiness, as well as his followers, insisting that we all learn to love and empathize with the Chinese people and to forgive the Chinese government—which has committed acts of aggression out of ignorance or delusion, not to mention greed and hatred—is profoundly illuminating.

Even when a simple monk is tortured physically or mentally, he practices his mindfulness of loving-kindness and compassion. Although His Holiness has not been tortured physically, he is mutilated mentally every time he learns the hard fact that his subjects, monks, and nuns are being tortured mercilessly. Yet he bears this pain magnanimously. And he reminds us all that the only way to overcome suffering is to cultivate seeds of peace within and to work nonviolently and patiently.

Being a simple monk in exile for five decades, His Holiness has shown to the world that truth, beauty, and goodness are not only possible but also practical. One only has to witness the deeds of His Holiness and his followers. Even laypeople who follow in his footsteps lead a simple lifestyle based on compassion and nonviolence.

Although His Holiness is obliged to travel all over the world to meet people of all walks of life, as a simple monk he still manages to find the time to hold spiritual retreats, perform meaningful religious ceremonies, and teach young monks to walk the noble eightfold path of the Buddha.

I believe that the influence of His Holiness in the world is not due to his being a bodhisattva, a head of state in exile, or a spiritual leader of a large Buddhist community. Neither is it because he possesses supernatural powers. Rather, it is because he is a simple monk who wants so little for himself and devotes most of his time and energy to helping the people of the world who are being trammeled by greed, hatred, and delusion. Yet with good humor and humility, His Holiness, in bearing the tribulations of his people and his country, is showing to the world that truth, forgiveness, love, and compassion really have power.

Even religious leaders of other faiths—not to mention other heads of state, and leading people in almost all walks of life—admire him because he does not want to make converts. He only desires happiness and well-being for all; and he shows them that the best happiness depends on simplicity, truthfulness, and compassion. With seeds of peace within, a simple monk like His Holiness is in an excellent position to guide others who are aspiring for world peace, social justice, and environmental sustainability.

A Very Human . . .
Human Being

by Mary Craig

It was September 1989. The monsoon rains were belting down, and the Dharamsala roads had turned to mud as I made my way up to Thekchen Choeling for my first audience with the Dalai Lama. A few months earlier when I was searching for a subject for my next book, a friend had suggested Tibet. A crazy idea, I thought—a country at the back of beyond, with a language, religion, and culture I knew nothing whatsoever about. Although I had, of course, heard of the Dalai Lama, I must admit that my mental image was confused—owing more to dim memories of *Lost Horizon* than to reality. I had not heard of Dharamsala, nor of the large numbers of refugees there. Nor that it was where the Dalai Lama actually lived.

The idea took root, and—especially after I was promised an audience with His Holiness—I began to explore the possibility of going to Dharamsala to see for myself. I boned up on recent Tibetan history and was overwhelmed by the horrors of what I discovered about the Chinese occupation. Arriving in Dharamsala and given access to the refugees, I found myself weeping with rage and pity and disgust as their stories unfolded. When the time approached for my audience with the Dalai Lama, somehow it began to seem unnecessary and self-indulgent, a distraction from the terrible reality in which I had become immersed. It was sure to be a brief formal encounter, more an exercise in protocol than a meeting of minds.

How wrong I was! The Dalai Lama was welcoming, warm, and deeply impressive. Within moments I found myself thinking that here was the most radiantly human human being I had ever met. There was a no-nonsense earthiness about him, but also a deep serenity and inner peace. Far from being a stiff and formal occasion, it was a person-to-person encounter in which I felt both challenged and healed. This man, I told myself wonderingly, could read me like an open book, yet was completely accepting of what he found.

He expressed interest in my half-formed plan to write about the refugees, and soon the questions were tumbling out—mainly about the current situation in Tibet and about the danger of young Tibetans there turning to violence. That very morning he had attended the stormy opening session of a Tibetan Youth Congress sympathetic to the idea. Time sped by, my allotted 20 minutes becoming half an hour, then an hour, an hour and a half, and still we were in full spate. When it was over, we had our photos taken; there were gifts of signed books, scarves, and old coins; and it was like the parting of two old friends, with much pumping of hands and an invitation to come and visit next time I was in Dharamsala. Next time? With this meeting, any remaining doubts about the book had vanished. I was well and truly hooked.

The following May I was back, for a new crop of ever-more-harrowing interviews with the refugees. Once again I was to meet the Dalai Lama and looked forward to a repeat performance of the first time. I had yet to learn that no two meetings with him are ever the same; every encounter is a new learning experience.

In the anteroom, waiting his turn, was a little four-year-old lama, the recently discovered reincarnation of Ling Rinpoche, His Holiness's former tutor. An elderly monk was gently fussing over the child, making sure he knew what to do. As they left, the little boy gingerly put his hand in that of the older man.

A short time later, the child reappeared, wreathed in smiles, hand in hand this time with the Dalai Lama. The latter gave him an affectionate hug; bent down to adjust the boy's shoe strap; then stayed crouching down, waving, smiling, and blowing kisses like a loving father until Ling was out of sight. It was a scene of immense tenderness—and I will never forget it. Then His Holiness stood up and greeted my friend and me with such warmth that it nearly took our breath away. I felt again that here was a uniquely luminous person who could make you want to laugh aloud for the sheer job of being alive.

My companion was an American artist, Brigid Marlin, who had asked to paint a portrait of the Dalai Lama. As the Private Office had allocated her a mere 40 minutes for a portrait that would normally take several days, Brigid was understandably nervous. As I was supposed to talk to His Holiness and keep his face animated while she painted, I began by asking him about the Nobel Peace Prize he'd just received. "Well"—he smiled self-deprecatingly—"when I heard the rumor in the early evening, I was a little bit excited. But when I listened to the 8:30 news, there was no mention. So I thought, *Oh well, it was just a rumor,* and went to bed. Next morning I got up at 4 as usual and heard that it was true after all. But by then, no more excited." End of story.

He went on to talk about the new constitutional changes he was introducing to Dharamsala, about Tibet's relationship with China, and of how much he had admired Mao Tse-tung until disillusion had set in. It was riveting stuff, and I was swept up into it. Suddenly I realized that the time was up and that Brigid was on the verge of tears. His Holiness noticed, too. Walking over to inspect the sketchy beginnings of an oil painting, he teased her that his left eye looked too big.

"I've had no time," Brigid wailed, bursting into tears.

His Holiness gave her a sympathetic hug, went and sat down again, then held up a hand to tell her to wait. "I'm—just—wondering . . ." he said slowly, before sending an official to ask the next visitor if she would mind an artist sitting in on her audience.

When the visitor agreed, Brigid's emotions got the better of her. "Oh, I do love you!" she burst out. His Holiness hooted with mirth and prepared to greet the next arrival.

We both saw how he abstracted himself for a few moments, seeming to disappear somewhere deep inside himself, wiping the slate clean, as it were, so as to offer his undivided attention to the next arrival. As Brigid painted, I was a fly on the wall for the next couple of hours, observing how he could be different things to different people, paying each one the courtesy of total absorption in their concerns.

With an American girl who planned to start an electronic newsletter for the Tibetans in Tibet, he was the practical, well-informed man of the world, discussing costs, logistics, and sponsorships, exploring the merits and demerits of the scheme. Then—after he had dispatched the official a second time and once again collected himself—came a Swiss girl with a smart new exercise bike, a present from her father, a sports-shop owner who had been horrified to see a magazine picture of the Dalai Lama on a dilapidated old machine. Instantly, he dashed out to the corridor to see the bike, hitched up his robes, and began pedaling with the enthusiasm of a small boy.

Our unexpectedly extended visit had opened a window for us: that afternoon we saw several Dalai Lamas—loving father, compassionate friend, Nobel Prize winner unfazed by world renown, widely experienced politician, savvy businessman, and enthusiastic child.

My book *Tears of Blood* was almost finished when I returned the following year. The Dalai Lama had been overseas, but as he was due back any day, the flags and banners were fluttering expectantly. Dharamsala is only a shadow of itself when he is not there. Somehow his absence is palpable. I was disappointed, however, having heard that he was scheduled to leave again almost immediately and the audience list had been closed.

When I received news the next day that I would be allowed to see His Holiness after all, I was so excited that I slipped and fell in the mud—it was monsoon time again—and arrived at the residence with my arm in a sling. It didn't matter—we joked about it momentarily, but my thoughts were full of a young Tibetan woman

I'd just met who'd been used as a prostitute by the PLA and had later witnessed fellow Tibetans being experimented on in the hospital. I told His Holiness straightaway. He knew the girl and shared my horror and disgust, proceeding to tell me about an Amdo woman who had been told by a Chinese doctor that to fulfill his quota of abortions he had often killed healthy babies, telling the mothers they had been stillborn.

The ghastliness of it reduced us to silence—it was the first time I had seen him like this, visibly overcome by the appalling fate of his people. When I left, he held my hand for several minutes, thanking me for the work I was doing for Tibet. He draped the *khata* around my neck. "Here, you'd better have this," he said, finally breaking into the familiar chuckle. It was a very small Tibetan flag.

Tears of Blood came out in 1993, and the Dalai Lama gave me the green light for a second book on Tibet, a sort of family biography. When I returned in 1994, I was privileged to see him four times. Arriving at Thekchen Choeling for the last of these long audiences, I was introduced to a young woman in the anteroom. It was her first meeting with His Holiness, and she looked apprehensive.

"Don't be nervous," I said. "He's the most human person you could ever hope to meet."

She gave me a shocked glance. "He's a living Buddha!" she protested.

"Well, isn't that the same thing?" I asked her. To me, "living Buddha" means a spiritually enlightened being who shows in his own person what it means to be human and makes us want to follow his example.

Emerging from her audience, she looked transformed. We exchanged a few words in the corridor, arranging to meet later that day. Suddenly I looked up—there was His Holiness waiting at the far end of the corridor, doubled up with laughter. Embarrassed by my seeming discourtesy, I positively hurtled toward him, my white *khata* unfolding as I ran. "Oh, Your Holiness, I'm so sorry," I stammered, proffering the rumpled scarf. He went on laughing, tucking my arm in his, and we went into the audience room together.

I realized then how he relishes and thrives on informality. That afternoon as we talked about his infancy in Amdo, he reminisced about how his mother would carry him on her back everywhere she went, and if he wanted her to change direction, he would tug at her long earring. "Sometimes very hard indeed," he added cheerfully, leaning forward and yanking on my own earring for all he was worth. "Just like that!" We both dissolved into laughter, and later when I was leaving, he gave me a big friendly bear hug. I hugged him back.

In all my visits to the Dalai Lama—and he continued to delight and surprise me for a couple of years more—I came to realize that what I most valued in him was his genuine humility and his refusal, in spite of everything, to hate the Chinese. He sees himself as a simple monk and dreams of ending his days in a remote monastery in Tibet.

He once talked to me about a monk he'd met who after more than 20 years in a Chinese prison, insisted that the worst danger he had faced was the fear of losing compassion for his torturers. "Isn't that wonderful?" asked His Holiness with an admiration I both understood and shared. "I feel sure that in his place, I'd have let rage engulf me. Or I'd have given in and told them what they wanted to hear." He showed the same humility in speaking of the tenth Panchen Lama, describing him as "a true freedom fighter" whose courage he could not ever have matched. Perhaps it is because he is so accepting of his own perceived frailties that one feels so secure with him.

Both books (and a third one, too) are long since published. I have not returned to Dharamsala, and I may never see him again except at the end of a long reception line in London. You don't just drop in on His Holiness the Dalai Lama. His time is parceled out carefully, and there is an endless list of those whose need to see him is greater than mine. Why should I complain? I had my hour in the sun—many hours, in fact. For almost a decade I had the unbelievable privilege of encountering a multifaceted, very special human being, in whose presence I felt more of a human being myself. For that I shall always be grateful.

A PORTRAIT OF THE DALAI LAMA

by Matthieu Ricard

At the foothills of the dark and imposing Himalayan peaks, Dharamsala, an Indian village, is sleeping peacefully. A few lights shine at the top of a wooded hill. The 14th Dalai Lama gets up. It is 3:30 in the morning. This is how the day of one of the most remarkable people of our time starts, with prayer and meditation. Wherever he may be, in whatever circumstances, every day in the morning the spiritual and temporal head of the Tibetan people meditates for four hours. It is a meditation that is, above all, a profound prayer for the good of all beings.

The room is a simple one, with varnished wood paneling, devoid of the usual rich decorations of the Tibetan temples. A statue of the Buddha, the photographs of his spiritual masters, and some sacred books are kept on a small altar. At around six o'clock, the Dalai Lama has a hearty breakfast while listening to the news on the BBC, since, like all Buddhist monks, he does not eat in the evening. Then he continues to meditate until eight or nine o'clock.

Come what may, the Dalai Lama maintains this discipline that gives him the strength he so deeply needs to untiringly pursue his activity for the Tibetan cause. When in 1989 he received the Nobel Peace Prize, journalists rushed early in the morning to be the first to obtain the reactions of the Tibetan leader. The only response they could get from the courteous and discreet monk who for the past 30 years has been faithfully tending to the needs of the Dalai Lama, was: "He has not yet gotten the news. We never disturb him when he is praying."

To conclude his meditation, the Dalai Lama goes to a room where some precious relics brought from Tibet are kept. Among them is a life-size statue of the Buddha sculpted out of sandalwood that was given to him by his followers, who succeeded in saving it from destruction during the Chinese invasion. The Dalai Lama bows down a hundred times in front of this sacred image, which for him is the Buddha in person; this is the humble homage he offers not to a god but to Awakening, the Supreme Knowledge.

"At around 9, I go to my office if I have to meet people," says the Dalai Lama. "Otherwise, I work on some texts. I refresh my memory about writings that I studied in the past, and I reflect more deeply upon the commentaries of the great masters of various schools of Tibetan Buddhism. I reflect upon the teachings, and I do some meditation. At around 2 in the afternoon, I eat my lunch. Then, till five o'clock, I look after current affairs. I meet the elected ones of the Tibetan people, the ministers of the government in exile and other functionaries, and I meet visitors. At around six o'clock, I have tea. If I am hungry, I take the permission of Buddha to eat some biscuits [laughter].

"Finally I do my evening prayers, and I sleep at around nine o'clock. It is the best part of the day! I sleep soundly till 3:30 the next morning."

Meeting the numerous visitors who have arrived from Tibet is a particularly poignant moment. To see the Dalai Lama at least once in their lives, Tendzin, his wife, and two children have crossed snowy passes at a height of more than 16,000 feet, eluding the Chinese army, which controls the borders and denies Tibetans permission to go to India. Some of Tendzin's companions have had to amputate their frozen toes. But they are finally here, abundant tears flowing down their cheeks, trying their best to contain their emotions so as to reply to the Dalai Lama, who in his beautifully resonant voice is inquiring about their personal odyssey and the situation in Tibet.

He asks Guedun, a monk who has been tortured several times during his 20 years in prison: "Did you ever experience fear?"

Bowing his head, the monk answers, "My greatest fear was to feel hatred toward my torturers."

The residence of the Dalai Lama overlooks the vast Indian plains, which unfold to infinity under his windows. To the north, some majestic peaks remind us that Tibet is just a few hundred miles away as the crow flies, beyond the imposing mountain range that circles the "roof of the world." The country of snow, so near yet so far, is out of reach for the Dalai Lama as long as its inhabitants are denied the basic liberties.

A subdued atmosphere and a beneficial peace surround this residence. Everyone talks softly, conscious of the vanity of superfluous words and of the inexorable march of time, this precious gift that ebbs away at every moment of our lives. Not a single gratuitous gesture or word—this golden silence is punctuated only with the rippling sound of the benevolent laughter of Kundun, the "Presence," as the Tibetans lovingly and respectfully call the Dalai Lama—he who is never absent when you are in front of him and always present when you are far away from him. Sometimes this joyful laughter is replaced by a silent smile when the Dalai Lama goes into retreat for a month or a few weeks each year. His only words then are prayers, which he communicates through gestures or in writing. The retreat is a fertile alliance of an inward-looking contemplation and compassion, which shines forth effortlessly to the outside world.

A typical day for the Dalai Lama at his residence seems to be simple and tranquil. However, for several months of the year, this orderly schedule is disrupted because of his wide travels and the teachings he gives in India or abroad to crowds that sometimes number several hundreds of thousands. The need to respond to everyone's aspirations and to support the cause of Tibet creates for this untiring peace pilgrim a busy schedule allowing little respite. In spite of this, Kundun maintains an unchanging serenity, an unchanging sincerity. For everyone—whether a visitor or a passerby met at the airport—he is totally and immediately present, with a look of overflowing goodness that penetrates your heart to leave a smile there before discreetly disappearing.

Goodness should not, however, be mistaken for weakness, so when the opportunity appears, the power of the orator suddenly wakes up. To the Parisian bar that welcomed him very warmly, he made the following statement: "My struggle for the Tibetan people is not one of those battles at the end of which there is a victor and a vanquished or, more often than not, two vanquished. What I endeavor to obtain with all my might is the victory of truth."

He often explains how the main objectives of all his travels are to promote human values and contribute to better interreligious understanding. For him it is obvious that an education that aims at developing the intelligence of the youth and at giving them a heavy load of information is not adequate. "Those who prepared the September 11, 2001, disaster went about it with a lot of intelligence. But they used this intelligence to prepare an act as unthinkable as that of using an aircraft full of people as a bomb to kill other human beings." He underscores that it is therefore imperative to help the youth develop human qualities that will enable them to use their intelligence in a wise and altruistic way.

According to the Dalai Lama, it is equally essential to realize that it is our mind that experiences happiness and suffering; in hoping to find happiness outside ourselves, we are going on the wrong track. In November 2001 during a visit to Portugal, where he noticed that the building sector was very active, he used a striking image to illustrate this point: "If someone who has just shifted to the hundredth floor of a luxurious apartment is unhappy within himself, the only thing he will be looking for is a window from where he can fling himself." It is, therefore, essential to find happiness within ourselves and to realize that our happiness is intimately linked to that of others.

All this does not exclude humor or simplicity. How often have I seen him, just after having bade good-bye to a president or a minister, go and shake hands with the doorman in his box or with the telephone operator behind her glass window and mischievously give a tap on the back of the rigid republican guard with his sword and superb uniform, who in turn is surprised but happy that someone is treating him like a person. When Danielle Mitterrand, wife of the erstwhile French president, came to visit the Dalai Lama in Dharamsala, he took her around. In front of a big statue of the Buddha that is in a temple of the monastery, the Dalai Lama respectfully pointed at the statue and said: "My boss."

His message is always the same, and he does not tire of repeating it to those who want to hear it: "Every person, even a hostile one, is like me, a living being who faces suffering and aspires to happiness; he has every right to be spared suffering and attain happiness. This reflection makes us feel deeply concerned by others' happiness, be they a friend or an enemy. This is the basis of authentic compassion."

The inexplicable power of compassion becomes clearest during surprise visits. I remember one night at the end of a meeting with young students at the University of Bordeaux, while the Dalai Lama was moving through a compact crowd of those who did not find places in the amphitheater, there was an old couple on the side, not daring to join the jostling crowd. The husband was standing behind his frail wife, who was sitting in a wheelchair. The ever-alert gaze of the Dalai Lama fell on them; he cut through the crowd to go and hold the old lady's hands in his and looked at her from close range, smilingly, without any words except the inexpressible ones of limitless love. After these few moments, which seemed to be an eternity, the old man said to his wife, "You see, he is a saint."

On another occasion, at the Amnesty International concert at Bercy, Paris, in December 1999, the Dalai Lama, who was a surprise guest, stepped onto the brightly lit stage between two rock songs, and 15,000 young people got up as one and offered a formidable ovation to the apostle of nonviolence. They then listened in silence, which is unusual at such places, to his warm words to them. After he spoke, once again a resounding ovation came from the hall. How does one explain such unanimity, such a heartfelt response coming from an unprepared crowd? It's reminiscent of Gandhi, Martin Luther King . . . this crowd had fathomed the depth of his heart.

When you ask the Dalai Lama why he elicits such reactions of warmth, he answers, "I do not have any special quality. Maybe it is because all my life I have meditated with all the strength of my mind upon love and compassion."

One of the most powerful interactions of the Dalai Lama with others is certainly when he teaches. There is no fiery rhetoric, but a calm and profound philosophy (combined with down-to-earth advice and a solid sense of humor) on how to become a better human being. The Dalai Lama's way of teaching is extremely sensible and practical. Yet, because the simple things he says are the distillation of his lifelong authentic spiritual practice and direct experience, they are never banal. When he tells you that a good heart is the most precious quality you can develop, it never sounds like a cliché, because he himself has such an immense heart.

Sometimes he may read out a verse:

May I be a guard for those who are protectorless,
A guide for those who journey on the road.
For those who wish to go across the water,
May I be a boat, a raft, a bridge.
May I be an isle for those who yearn for landfall,
And a lamp for those who long for light;
For those who need a resting place, a bed;
For all who need a servant, may I be their slave.
Like the earth and the pervading elements,
Enduring as the sky itself endures,
For boundless multitudes of living beings,
May I be their ground and sustenance.
Thus for everything that lives,
As far as are the limits of the sky,
May I provide their livelihood and nourishment
Until they pass beyond the bonds of suffering.

The reading of such a verse can bring tears to the Dalai Lama's eyes. He stops and waits silently, unassumingly, until he can speak again. There is no hint of showmanship in this quiet display of feeling.

At other times, when he is illustrating his commentary with anecdotes or remarking on something unusual in the crowd, he may break into sonorous and spontaneous laughter with the uninhibited freedom of someone who is detached from worldly preoccupations. This reminds me of a verse of the 19th-century Tibetan yogi Shabkar:

> *Look at my delighted laughter!*
> *The delight of a vast, free mind!*
> *The experience of lightness of being*
> *As when emerging from a narrow gorge*
> *Onto a high, wide mountain pass!*
> *Look how, free from mistaking things as real,*
> *I am blissful, and yet more blissful,*
> *Enjoying the realm of primordial wakefulness!*

When His Holiness gives expanded teachings, such as the initiation of the Tantra of the Wheel of Time, or *Kalachakra,* immense crowds gather to listen to him silently. In 1985 and in 2002 when he gave the Kalachakra in Bodh Gaya, the place where the Buddha became enlightened, more than 200,000 devotees gathered to attend the teachings, including the main spiritual masters of the different Tibetan Buddhist traditions. Several thousand people managed to come down from Tibet. They braved the border guards to escape the relentless repression of the Communist regime for a while, crossing the high snowy passes in hazardous journeys that cost a few their lives.

It was an amazing sight to watch them, seated in the first rows, their dreams fulfilled beyond imagination—not only being able to get a furtive glance at their beloved leader and spiritual master, but also being able to sit all day long for a week right in front of him! In the warm Indian climate, they were still wearing their felt boots, sheepskin coats, and torn down jackets that hardly protected them from the biting cold during their journey. Their eyes looked at things in quite a different way than those of the Tibetans who had been refugees in India for decades. Everything was new to them, especially freedom. Amid this attentive audience, there were faces of astonishing character and beauty, their gazes as clear as the sky as they looked at the Dalai Lama with a fervor that welled up from their very bones.

And at the end of the day, the Dalai Lama will conclude with the prayer that he says inspires every moment of his life:

> *As long as space endures,*
> *As long as beings exist,*
> *May I too remain*
> *To dispel the misery of the world.*

(Reproduced from *Buddhist Himalayas,* Matthieu Ricard and Olivier and Danielle Follmi, Éditions de La Martinière, Paris 2002.)

THE OCEAN OF WISDOM
AS HUMAN AND SPIRITUAL PRESENCE

by Brother Wayne Teasdale

It is not easy to write about the Dalai Lama, and specifically, Tenzin Gyatso, the 14th Dalai Lama. He is a rare and unique spiritual teacher. There is always the tendency to slip into hyperbole in praising his extraordinary, divine-like position and qualities, and the whole aura surrounding this "simple monk"; or into the opposite extreme of hiding behind a dry, scholarly objectivity that is often skeptical. Here, like the Buddha, I will try to walk a middle path. Personally, I am convinced that there are certain figures, saints, and bodhisattvas about whom it's not really possible to exaggerate. Such are Mahatma Gandhi, Thomas Merton (the Trappist sage), Mother Teresa, and Tenzin Gyatso.

When we encounter great holiness in anyone, there is evident a superhuman degree of virtue and sensitivity, a transcendence of self-concern, an availability and responsiveness to others. The preceding figures all possess these qualities. As an example in the Dalai Lama's life—an example so characteristic of who he is beyond his position—let me offer an instance from one of his many visits to the U.S.

Some years ago at Harvard University, there was a special conversation going on between His Holiness and three or four professors before a huge audience that included a film crew. The first professor to speak was hogging the limelight, and he went on and on, way past his allotted time. As his talking became excessive and there was no sign he would stop, the other professors, fearing their own time would be used up, became impatient, and their impatience then turned to indignation and anger.

Through it all, His Holiness patiently, calmly, attentively, and with a smile listened to the man. His Holiness's sensitivity was such that he knew this person needed to feel that he was being heard. He needed attention and affirmation. His Holiness's compassion was in responding to the professor's deeper agenda instead of descending into resentment, frustration, and anger, as the other participants were doing. He chose quite spontaneously to respond compassionately, even if it meant a slight inconvenience to others. This little story is typical of His Holiness and illustrates the nature of his sensitivity.

In what follows, I would like to explore His Holiness's commitment to interreligious dialogue, which is really a dialogue of life itself, not a stiff, formal activity as it often is in academic forums. The first part of this chapter will consider the Dalai Lama's encounters with Thomas Merton and Bede Griffiths. Then I will share the first of my own meetings with His Holiness, meetings that essentially continued the line of experience and development initiated with Merton. After that, I will present some impressions of His Holiness that have occurred to me over time. The next section of the essay will examine His Holiness's interest in the integration of science, wisdom, and all the other areas of knowledge; and this will be done primarily within the context of the Synthesis Dialogues.

We will then move on to the Buddhist/Christian Monastic Dialogue and reflect on the prophetic dimension of this very valuable relationship. This reflection will then crystallize into what I call the *matrix* as a way to integrate the essential metaphysical, existential principles of Buddhism and Christianity. A brief section will look at the Tibetan issue and the Catholic Church. Finally, in the last section, I will reflect on the significance of the 14th Dalai Lama for this third millennial age.

Thomas Merton and Bede Griffiths

Tibet's first experience of Christians involved a mission of the Jesuits to the "roof of the world," as Tibet is known, in the latter part of the 17th century with the arrival of Father Desiderio. He had learned Tibetan and written a work in that difficult and little-known language. Of course, the Jesuits were engaging in missionary activity, and their methods were innovative and even visionary. They tended to be way ahead of their time because they respected the cultures they worked and lived in and eventually came to modify their evangelical objectives with the realization that in China, India, Japan, Tibet, and so forth, they were dealing with very advanced systems of wisdom.

This realization certainly also characterizes the outlook of Thomas Merton, especially in the last years of his life. He had been absorbing Eastern wisdom on a deep level long before his fateful trip to Asia in the autumn of 1968. Thomas Merton had only three audiences with His Holiness in Dharamsala in November of that year. This was the whole extent of their relationship in terms of time. His Holiness said later that he never realized Christians were spiritual until he met Merton. Here was a Christian monk completely unlike any Christian the Dalai Lama had ever met before; he was nothing like the missionaries of the time, most of whom were bent on conversion of Buddhists, Hindus, Muslims, and so on.

His Holiness discerned in this Trappist monk from Kentucky a Christian *geshe,* a profoundly learned man in matters of spirituality, comparative religion, and culture. He found an openness in Merton rarely seen in other Christians. Thomas Merton discovered in His Holiness a brother and fellow monk, equally open and very curious about Catholic monastic life and practice. The two men liked each other immensely and looked forward to a wonderful friendship, one that now awaits its unfolding in eternity.

Father Louis, which was Merton's monastic name, and His Holiness talked about everything. They shared their experience of monastic life in their respective traditions, looking at various practices, the education or formation of monks and nuns, their ways of prayer and meditation, and their sacred texts. They reflected deeply on the differences and similarities between Buddhism and Christian faith. They discussed the horrific tragedy of the Tibetan people before the barbaric practices of China, the diaspora of the Tibetan exiles, and the focus on securing and preserving their culture and tradition in India. They also talked about the Vietnam War, the superpower rivalry, the civil rights movement in the U.S., and the antiwar movement in Europe and America.

His Holiness and Thomas Merton made a deep impression on each other, and the impact of Merton on the Dalai Lama was considerable. He often speaks of this literary genius, this American monk, with affection and wistfulness. In a wonderful documentary on Merton's life released in the early '80s, His Holiness was interviewed by the filmmakers. They asked him about his experience of the Christian monk. His Holiness spoke affectionately of him on that occasion, and then, with profound emotion and in a higher pitch of voice, he remarked, "If Thomas Merton had lived, we would have done something for peace together."

The Dalai Lama met with Bede Griffiths on three occasions, as in Merton's case, but these encounters were spaced by years. They were together twice in India at conferences in which both were participating. But their most telling conversation occurred in Australia in the early '90s. Both were visiting this continent "Down Under" and happened across each other's path. It was an eventful exchange. Each was completely relaxed and open to the other. They discussed many theological and mystical teachings of each tradition. Although I never knew Merton, I did know Bede and had a 20-year friendship with him.

At the time of their third encounter, Father Bede was greatly interested in Dzogchen. He told me of this wonderful meeting with His Holiness, and His Holiness also told me of it. He said to me, "Bede Griffiths is a great teacher!" Father Bede and the Dalai Lama shared a lot of mutual respect, and had Bede lived longer, they might have achieved something of importance together. Bede's knowledge of Hinduism and Buddhism was far greater than that of Thomas Merton, but both were Christian prophets drinking from the well of Eastern wisdom and reinvigorating Western contemplation. Both had a similar mission, but with different circumstances.

First Encounters and Impressions of the Dalai Lama

Passing through Britain for a month's rest after a long period in India, I had a fascinating experience with His Holiness. This happened for the first time in April 1988 at the residence of Basil Cardinal Hume, O.S.B., the archbishop of Westminster and Catholic patriarch of England. Although I had seen His Holiness at St. Patrick's Cathedral in New York City in 1979 when I was a graduate student at Fordham University, it was not until this event in London in 1988 that we actually met for the first time. Cardinal Hume was a Benedictine monk who had also been an abbot before being named patriarch of England. He had an interest in a dialogue and welcomed a Catholic/Tibetan monastic exchange.

I was invited to this historic dialogue. There were 20 of us— Christian and Buddhist monks, with a few nuns—seated around an oval table. His Holiness entered and was introduced by the abbot of Prinknash Abbey, which was Bede Griffiths's monastery before he went out to India in 1958. This gathering was an intimate situation, and from the very beginning, there was a strong rapport between His Holiness and me. After the 70-minute conversation, His Holiness came over to me with an extended hand. It was a warm and meaningful introduction.

Afterward, I followed up with a letter to Tenzin Geyche, his long and faithful secretary, a good friend, and before long found myself in Dharamsala in early January 1989. His Holiness and I had our second encounter at his place in the form of a two-hour conversation. It proved to be eventful, because it resulted in our collaboration in producing a document entitled "The Universal Declaration on Nonviolence"—a brief statement of one page that is a kind of declaration of independence between religion and war making. It was later ratified by His Holiness and Monastic Interreligious Dialogue (MID), the organization I represented. MID had taken responsibility for the document after I had written the first draft. Other members of MID and I refined its final form.

I have often felt, or had a sense, that the unique position I have been placed in continues the relationship with His Holiness, Tibetan Buddhism, and the Tibetan people that Thomas Merton initiated in modern times with his historic visit to Dharamsala in 1968. I have always remained conscious of His Holiness's words about doing something substantial for peace and have hoped that maybe I could contribute to that important aspiration. Although I'm certainly no Merton, I share with him an openness to the East; a keen interest in the Dharma and in Hinduism, Taoism, and Sufism; as well as the powerful hope for a lasting, just, and comprehensive planetwide peace—a peace that is more than simply the absence of conflict . . . one that reflects, as St. Augustine called it in his time, "the tranquility of order," a spiritual harmony animating an enlightened humankind, and a human civilization based on love and compassion. Such a peace is based on our ultimate potential, and that requires the engagement of our spiritual resources for self-transformation leading to social change grounded in awareness.

Over the years, His Holiness and I have seen each other a couple of times a year, and I am also a friend of his younger brother, the Ngari Rinpoche, and his family, as well as many other Tibetans. These encounters have become progressively more profound in depth and friendship. Many impressions have formed in my understanding of who the Dalai Lama is as a person.

I remember so well a visit with him after the 1993 Parliament of the World's Religions in Chicago. We sat together for two hours as he talked with others, participated in an interview, and shared stories with me. On that occasion I saw very clearly how Christlike he actually is, and I said to him: "I see Christ in you more than I have perceived Christ in most Christians!" I suppose I could have used different language to express this spiritual perception. Perhaps what I was really discerning was the sanctity, love, and compassion of this man.

Another impression that has taken root in my view of His Holiness is his gift for intuition—or we can say, for clairvoyance, even telepathy. This gift is not a light matter, and I view it as a by-product of spiritual realization. I have been in his presence so many times when I have become conscious of how completely he knows me and where I'm coming from or what I'm preoccupied with when I'm with him. He seems to draw me into a larger state of awareness, including me in his own. There is no need to say anything, since in these moments our communication is perfect, and words would only detract from what we experience and know and would possibly confuse the issue.

A further impression that has struck me is his intellectual profundity, his ability to understand virtually anything. His intellectual gifts, however, are not abstract abilities, but always in service to his quintessential humanity, his good-heartedness. His knowledge is always grounded in compassion and wisdom, and these are practical qualities, ones found in the saints of all traditions—or most of them. But there is so much more. In addition to the attributes outlined above, there is his sense of humor and playfulness, indomitable strengths that not even tragedy and suffering could eclipse. Basically, what I discern in his example is a highly developed humanism rooted in spiritual practice and extended to all sentient beings.

His Interest in the Integration of Knowledge

His Holiness has been interested in science and the other areas of knowledge for many years. He has attended many conferences around the world, attempting to discover the common ground between science and spirituality. Most of these meetings he has found disappointing for one reason or another. Usually they have fallen short of his expectations because—as he puts it—either the scientists were too "hard" or too "soft." By "hard," he means that they were closed to the spiritual dimension of life and adhered to a purely uncritical reductionist view of science, a view that really isn't very scientific at all! The problem with the "soft" scientists is that they are too quick to jump to a common ground or a spiritual view of science and the cosmos. The science in this case is suspect even though the soft scientist may actually be enlightened, and so wiser than the hard scientist, who tends to be close-minded and a materialist reductionist.

His Holiness has been, and is, intrigued with the notion of *synthesis,* the conscious attempt to find the common ground among all the areas of knowledge, as well as a grand unifying paradigm that harmonizes science, religion, spirituality, social justice, peace, and the environment. The work toward finding such a paradigm took form for the first time in Synthesis I, or the Dharamsala Dialogues, held in Dharamsala September 11–16, 1999. His Holiness participated in this significant gathering in which 110 people were present, 35 of whom were active synthesizers, while the remaining were observers and the media. The synthesizers represented all the major disciplines and areas of culture: physicists; mathematicians; biologists; astronomers; spiritual teachers; theologians; thinkers in commerce, government, diplomacy, and the environment; and activists in the struggle for the environment, the work for justice, and the promotion of peace.

This event was in many ways historic, not in what it achieved— since it was only a beginning, and so there were not dramatic results—but in the recognition of spirituality as the basis to integrate all knowledge in a practical value of transformation. In this recognition, there is an insight that all knowledge has to have a practical relationship to the improvement of our human nature and that of other sentient beings. Spirituality, the mystical life, provides such a unifying vision for knowledge and allows science and religion to have a more positive—indeed, friendly—collaboration. Mysticism being the most universal and all-encompassing, comprehensive, and ultimate wisdom, all other areas of knowledge must be implied in its range—or rather, its reality affects all the areas of knowledge, and none can contradict it. This is a major contribution to the process of finding common ground and synthesis itself.

Synthesis II convened in Trent, Italy, with His Holiness June 26–July 1, 2001. Around 30 synthesizers participated in this event in the beautiful surroundings of the Dolomite Mountains. This meeting was far more focused than the Dharamsala Dialogues, and insights emerged from the conversations that were encouraged. The important aim of this conference, and these dialogues, was simply to have a number of relevant discussions free of ego and hidden agendas, in a spirit of friendship and community in such a way that a tangible sense of communion surfaced and a new vision emerged from the various insights contributed.

The Buddhist/Christian Monastic Dialogue

Another important interest His Holiness shares with Western monks and nuns is the intermonastic dialogue, and this relationship—especially with the Tibetans and His Holiness—has been going on since Thomas Merton's visit to Dharamsala, although there had been contact between Christian monastics and members of the Zen and Theravadan traditions prior to Merton's journey to India. The connection with Catholic monastics is very dear to His Holiness's heart, and he has mentioned that to many people over the years, including me. The intermonastic dialogue is really moving into advanced stages, especially with the event that took place at the Parliament of the World's Religions in Chicago in 1993 and the Gethsemani Encounter at Merton's monastery in Kentucky in July 1996. April 2002 witnessed another round when Gethsemani II was convened, and the Dalai Lama again participated.

The Parliament dialogue lasted three hours, but its topic was highly specific—*Sunyata and Kenosis: The Rising of Universal Compassion in the Spiritual Journey*. Gethsemani I went on for several days and explored numerous topics of mutual interest, such as monastic life in each tradition, the role of the teacher, monastic education, mystical experience, meditation, and the like. Gethsemani I was profoundly historic and useful. It was a watershed in Catholic/Buddhist relations, and Gethsemani II was equally momentous.

The increasing importance of intermonastic relationships and interreligious dialogue can be seen in the appearance of the first *Encyclopedia of Monasticism*.[1] This two-volume work encompasses Hindu, Buddhist, Christian, and Jain monasticism and represents a needed contribution to a hitherto-neglected area. The intense conversations that are taking place, coupled with the intermonastic hospitality exchange initiated by the Monastic Interreligious

Dialogue (MID) in America (formerly known as the North American Board for East-West Dialogue) and His Holiness, no doubt have heightened interest in what is unfolding.

The intermonastic hospitality exchange between Catholic and Tibetan monastics has been going on since 1980 and has reached a level of great depth. From its very inception, the Dalai Lama has enthusiastically supported it, and he continues to do so. The exchange works in this manner: Four or five Tibetan monks and nuns will come to the United States and spend six months visiting a number of monasteries and convents of the Cistercian, Trappist, and Benedictine communities. The longest they would stay in one place might be three weeks to a month, with a minimum of a week. The Christian monks and nuns—again, four or five of them—would spend a similar amount of time in the great Tibetan monasteries in India. The Catholic groups would always visit His Holiness, who has eagerly followed and encouraged this wonderful program.

In either case—whether Tibetans coming to America or American monastics going to India to visit Tibetan monasteries—they would enter deeply into the monastic observance of each community they found themselves in. A reservoir of widsom has accumulated over the years from these extraordinary exchanges and has prepared the way for the quality and richness of dialogue and conversation that has transpired both at the Parliament of the World's Religions and at Gethsemani, to name two in recent years.

His Holiness always emphasizes the necessity of friendship as a basis for genuine dialogue, one that reaches a profound level of mutual recognition of each other's traditions, their equal authenticity, and their intrinsic complementarity . . . a recognition that in the case of Christianity and Buddhism, they complete each other. In his numerous relationships with Christians, as well as Hindus, Jains, and Jews, the Dalai Lama has followed his own teaching: He has made friends with people of other traditions, and from the openness and affection emanating from and surrounding these friendships, he converses with these individuals.

Such is my experience with him since the beginning of our friendship and collaboration. Because we are well disposed to each other—that is, because we are friends, spiritual friends with a strong bond—we are able to talk about any subject, even ones regarded as sensitive in each of our traditions. It is this kind of friendship that makes possible a very vital kind of work that is in service to humankind's ultimate destiny for liberation and salvation.

The Prophetic Vision of the Buddhist/Christian Relationship

This vital work is a prophetic collaboration that through the process of deep dialogue propels consciousness forward in each tradition and in a global, universal sense. From the open-ended character of the dialogue, something new will emerge for humankind and eventually, for all sentient beings. The tension between the two views, the working toward common ground and greater understanding, will generate a new awareness, a more enhanced view that unites what is truest in each tradition. This work may take centuries, even millennia, but there will come a day when Christianity and Buddhism will together offer a new vision to the world.[2]

During Synthesis I at Dharamsala, an idea occurred to me near the close of the conference, an insight I call a seed of synthesis, and it is related to the Buddhist/Christian dialogue and collaborative relationship. This seed of synthesis can be formulated in this way: the Divine as matrix of dependent arising. His Holiness was present for this and other "seeds" from among a number of the participants in the Dharamsala Dialogues. Let me elaborate here. I believe this integration of the two principal insights represents an embodiment of Divine Incarnate Wisdom.

The Divine as a matrix of dependent arising relates and unites the essential insight of each of these traditions. Dependent arising is the interconnection of all sentient beings; their intrinsic interdependence exists within the boundaries of the matrix of boundless consciousness, and this consciousness is the Divine itself. A matrix both defines and contains, and in the case of the Divine matrix, defines and contains the interconnection of all sentient beings. The Divine, in the Christian mystical experience, is the very connection or connectivity of all the sentient beings that co-arise together. It is infinite consciousness animated by Divine compassion and love. Consciousness as a loving, compassionate, merciful, kind intelligence and knowing connects all beings in a cosmic, ontological community. This is an insight that must be considered with great care.

There are many other points of common ground between the Buddhist and Christian traditions, and a number of these are being discussed in the intermonastic dialogue, in the forums of the Society for Buddhist-Christian Studies, and in hundreds of academic situations around the world. They are being thought about by individual practitioners and writers, pioneers of the spirit opening up new vistas of realization and universal culture. Again, His Holiness often leads the way by his openness and his own insights into where the common ground might be—as, for instance, when he met with Christians and reflected on the inner meaning of the Gospel.[3] Buddhists and Christians who are friends and engaged in ultimate levels of dialogue are servants of a great purpose larger than either's tradition, and they are responsible for this work because they have the consciousness that makes it possible. With their consciousness comes a burden of responsibility that they cannot shun or escape. His Holiness has a sense of this when he speaks of our universal responsibility.

Tibet, Monasticism, and the Catholic Church

For many years now, a number of us from the monastic world have stood in solidarity with His Holiness and the Tibetan people. We have tried and continue to try to awaken the Catholic Church to the moral responsibility it has to similarly support the Tibetan struggle, which is nonviolent and respectful of the People's Republic of China. In Catholic theology and culture, we like the term *conscientization* to refer to moral awakening to justice issues. We are engaged in such a labor of conscientization—not simply in the Church, but extending to all the other religions and the world at large.

His Holiness has been following this development with keen interest and realism. To date, we have not been successful in raising the level of concern in Rome on Tibet to a high-priority status. At the 1993 Parliament of the World's Religions, in the midst of the Buddhist/Christian Monastic Dialogue session, MID introduced the document "Resolution on Tibet." It was read and presented to His Holiness, who was present for the dialogue.[4] His Holiness was very pleased with this action, although it displeased the Vatican. Even though there are many in Rome who are interested in this matter, none are willing to speak out. So, we go 'round and 'round.

I believe there will come a day when this situation will change and the Church will come out vigorously, standing with the Tibetan people, but this will still take some time. I feel the time is much nearer than many think. We need to keep pushing—that is, raising the issue whenever opportunities present themselves—and be willing to converse with anyone willing to listen. Relentless pursuit of justice will eventually yield a rich harvest. I am convinced that the voice of the Catholic Church would provide the kind of support that would result in the concretization of humankind on the Tibetan tragedy.

The Significance of the Dalai Lama

There are many reasons why I feel unqualified to evaluate His Holiness's contribution to our planet and to suggest his historical significance. He is such a rare figure—he is unique and precious, and made so further by the circumstances of his people and the fascinating role he is playing as a global spiritual teacher. A number of attributes enhance his contribution and are extremely valuable in this new age that has just dawned.

The first is what I call his *spiritual humanism,* his ability to relate to all kinds of people, with or without any particular commitment to a tradition. He has seen clearly what's really important, and that has to do primarily with how we treat one another, including other sentient beings. In his book *Ethics for a New Millennium,*[5] His Holiness offers a vision of ethics that can be said to be a form of natural spirituality, a moral understanding that reveals those qualities in our human nature that are universal and are the basis not simply of ethics, but of the best of religion and spirituality. He is committed to presenting a practical guide to ethical life founded on the commonality of the human traits of compassion, love, kindness, and mercy to people who either do or do not belong to any of the world's religions. In this teaching, he offers solid advice to the whole of humanity.

His significance is as an icon of spiritual and human depth, a powerful presence gently but firmly advocating change, transformation of the heart, and justice for his people. His human and spiritual presence in our history is reinforced by a humble, accessible style of leadership, often conveyed with humor and laughter. The nature of his presence and his teaching is also revealed in who he is as a person, rather than his position. His generosity as a teacher benefits us all and has played an essential role in the lives of thousands of Westerners and millions of Tibetans. His Holiness's subtle teaching on universal responsibility represents something new and refreshing; it manages to steer clear of a provincial view or the pitfalls of nationalism and evokes what is deepest, most authentic in all of us. It appeals to our basic and common humanity. The Dalai Lama, like the Pope and other world spiritual leaders, is an eloquent voice of advocacy for the planet, and no other such leader has equaled his contribution to ecological awareness.

All in all, His Holiness is a person with farsighted vision. In this respect, like a circle, I'd like to return to that moment when we first met so many years ago in Britain. When he spoke on that occasion, he said something that has always stayed with me, making an indelible impression. He remarked, "We must keep our attention and determination fixed on the far horizon and not be distracted by what is unimportant." He is a master of that destiny toward which we are all moving. His ultimate significance concerns this destiny and his prophetic witness to it.

Endnotes

1. *Encyclopedia of Monasticism,* ed. William M. Johnston, 2 vols. (Chicago: Fitzroy Dearborn, 2000).

2. I have explored this relationship and its possible fruit in my book *The Mystic Heart: Discovering a Universal Spirituality in the World's Religions* (Novato, CA: New World Library, 1999).

3. The Dalai Lama, *The Good Heart: A Buddhist Perspective on the Teachings of Jesus* (Somerville, MA: Wisdom Publications, 1997).

4. For the text of this document, see: *A Source Book for Earth's Community of Religions,* ed. Joel Beversluis (Ada, MI: CoNexus Press, 1995), p. 171.

5. The Dalai Lama, *Ethics for the New Millennium* (New York: Riverhead, 1999).

10

THE BUDDHA OF COMPASSION IN OUR MIDST

by Nick Ribush

I am a very ordinary person, and it is humbling to have been requested to contribute a piece about His Holiness the Dalai Lama, especially in such august company. However, since other ordinary people may read this, perhaps they might find something of interest in the experience of a peer.

I first encountered Tibetan Buddhism at Kopan Monastery, Kathmandu, Nepal, toward the end of 1972. My first teachers were Lama Thubten Zopa Rinpoche and Lama Thubten Yeshe, who were just starting to introduce the Dharma to Westerners, an activity that continues swiftly to this day. I was immediately attracted to this path and have been trying to understand and practice it since.

From the start, Lama Yeshe and Lama Zopa Rinpoche manifested extraordinary respect for and devotion to His Holiness the Dalai Lama, and as a cynical Westerner from a predominantly materialistic and atheistic upbringing, I was struck by their attitude toward what I imagined was simply another human being.

I was able to meet His Holiness for the first time about 15 months later when, in January 1974, I went to Bodh Gaya, India, to attend the Kalachakra initiation he was to confer. I also planned to take novice ordination, along with nine other prospective Western monks and nuns. There were well over 100,000 people there, and we Westerners were lost in a vast and wonderful sea of Tibetans.

Out of his customary kindness, Lama Yeshe had requested that His Holiness perform the very first part of our ordination ceremony, where the last tuft of hair is snipped off the crown of one's otherwise freshly shaved head, recalling Siddhartha Gautama's own renunciation when he left his father's palace and set out on his quest for enlightenment. Accordingly, on the last day of the initiation, we lined up with everybody else to receive a blessing from His Holiness and view the mandala.

As we approached His Holiness, Lama Zopa Rinpoche pulled out a pair of scissors and explained who we were and what we wanted. His Holiness smiled, laughed out loud, and exclaimed, "I hope it lasts!" (In my case it did—not for life, as intended, but for only about 12 years.) That brief but warm encounter, that individual attention despite a million other things going on, was my first taste of His Holiness's astonishing kindness, compassion, focus, and love.

I met His Holiness a few more times in the next couple of years, mainly in the company of Lama Yeshe and Lama Zopa Rinpoche, when they would seek His Holiness's advice on their work in the West and report to him what had happened on their travels. In 1977, my mother visited me in India, and I took her to Dharamsala to meet His Holiness and his two tutors, Kyabje Ling Rinpoche and Kyabje Trijang Rinpoche. They were all amazingly kind, especially His Holiness, who gave my mother a 45-minute private interview (they let me in, too), patiently answering all her questions about past and future lives and the six realms of cyclic existence.

I have heard His Holiness described in many ways over the years. He always describes himself as a simple Buddhist monk, but to various writers he has been the god-king of Tibet; to the Chinese, a splittist; to most politicians, the true head of Tibet; to Dharma students everywhere, a great teacher and a perfect living example of what he teaches; and to the world at large, a Nobel laureate, a great statesman, the leading advocate of nonviolence and peace, the voice of Buddhism, and, in general, our best hope for the future. To the Tibetan people, His Holiness has always been the living manifestation of Chenrezig Avalokiteshvara, the Buddha of Compassion. I've often wondered what this means.

While never for a moment agreeing that he is indeed a manifestation of Avalokiteshvara, in his teachings at the Kalachakra initiation in Los Angeles in 1989, His Holiness described Avalokiteshvara as a deity, a bodhisattva, or a Buddha. As a deity, Avalokiteshvara is not a separate being but a manifestation of the compassion of all Buddhas, a quality of all enlightened beings. When a person striving for enlightenment attains his or her goal through practicing the yoga method of Avalokiteshvara, we can call that person an individual Avalokiteshvara. Also, the compassion of a particular Buddha, for example, Shakyamuni Buddha, can manifest as Avalokiteshvara.

As His Holiness Dudjom Rinpoche has explained, historically Tibetans claim to be descended from Avalokiteshvara, who in ancient times is said to have come to Tibet from his reputed abode in south India, Mount Potalaka; manifested as a monkey; and mated with an "ogress of the rocks." The first religious king, Songtsen Gampo (A.D. 617–650), is said to have been a manifestation of Avalokiteshvara. So, too, are Nyatri Tsenpo, the first human king to rule the whole of Tibet; Dromtönpa, translator for the great Atisha, who restored pure Buddhism to Tibet about a thousand years ago and founded the Kadam tradition; and all 14 Dalai Lamas, including, of course, the present one, His Holiness Tenzin Gyatso, the 14th Dalai Lama of Tibet.

Also, the mantra of Avalokiteshvara, OM MANI PADME HUM, is the "official" mantra of Tibet. Many Tibetans, both lay and ordained, recite it constantly, and it may be found painted and carved on rocks and stone tablets all over the Himalayas.

Thus, the practice of Avalokiteshvara is central to Tibetan Buddhism, and as a part of that, Tibetans regard their spiritual and temporal leader, the Dalai Lama, as the living embodiment of Avalokiteshvara and everything he represents.

The Buddha's intent was that all sentient beings attain enlightenment. In order to do so, they have to follow the path that leads to enlightenment; we have to make the effort ourselves—the infinite Buddhas cannot do it for us. In other words, we have to practice Mahayana Buddhism, and if we want to attain enlightenment as quickly as possible, we have to practice Vajrayana, the form that was practiced and preserved in Tibet.

His Holiness has also said that of all the Buddha's teachings, the most important is that of compassion; and of all the attributes of a Buddha, the best is again compassion. Even a Buddha's omniscience depends on this quality; it is only through the power of compassion that it is possible for the wisdom realizing emptiness to become the ultimate wisdom of a Buddha. Furthermore, the exalted activities of a Buddha arise through the union of pure mind and pure body. These, in turn, similarly depend upon the wisdom that is empowered by compassion. Thus, again, compassion is crucial.

As the great Indian pandit Chandrakirti declared, compassion is important at the beginning, in the middle, and at the end. All the great qualities of a Buddha have their root in compassion.

In praise of His Holiness, Lama Zopa Rinpoche addressed him in this way:

> Your Holiness is able to preserve the complete teaching of the Buddha, the three higher trainings of morality, meditation, and wisdom, the three baskets of teaching which are the essence of the Hinayana teaching and the foundation of the causal Mahayana Paramitayana path and the resultant secret Vajrayana, which flourished in the past in Tibet and now even outside Tibet.
>
> Because of that, you are able to produce continuously many hundreds of thousands of holy scholars and highly attained yogis, like stars in the sky. Even nowadays in different parts of the world, large numbers of people are able to receive many highly qualified practitioner-teachers from the monasteries of Sera, Ganden, and Drepung and also from the monasteries of the other Tibetan traditions. Thus, many Westerners are able to learn whatever they wish from them in depth and are able to make their lives meaningful by putting these teachings into practice, finding fulfillment in this way. They have so much opportunity to enjoy

peace and happiness and are able to direct their lives toward liberation and enlightenment, and this is increasing every year.

This is solely due to Your Holiness's kindness. This means that without Your Holiness, Buddhism would suffer, and it would be extremely difficult to continue the preservation of the entire Buddha Dharma. Without the teaching, sentient beings would suffer. The teaching of the Buddha is the only medicine to cease all the diseases of delusion and negative karma and their imprints. . . .

A special quality of Your Holiness that ordinary people can see and feel is that even though there might be some evil beings who criticize Your Holiness, differently from common people in the world and even other religious leaders, you only benefit them in return and you have greater compassion for them and cherish them most in your heart. You speak about their qualities and only pray for their well-being and temporary and ultimate happiness up to enlightenment. This means that there is no doubt that Your Holiness is a bodhisattva, the Compassion Buddha.

What are the activities of a Buddha? The main one is to reveal the teachings that lead to enlightenment to those who are open to them—that is, according to the karma of potential disciples. First, however, how does one become a Buddha? How does one become enlightened?

As I understand from the teachings of my own precious teacher, Lama Zopa Rinpoche, the principal cause of enlightenment is Bodhicitta, the determination to reach enlightenment for the sake of all sentient beings. Bodhicitta arises from great compassion, which is generated in dependence upon each and every sentient being. With great compassion, one not only feels the suffering of all sentient beings as one's own, but is also compelled to do something about it. This feeling only grows as one approaches enlightenment and remains with one forever, even after enlightenment. Therefore, a Buddha has no choice but to help sentient beings in whatever way possible.

Since sentient beings have to make the effort themselves, they need to be shown the path. Showing the path and inspiring others to follow it is a Buddha's main job. But, if one were a Buddha, how would one go about it?

One couldn't remain in the enlightened sphere of the Dharmakaya, because there, one could communicate only with other Buddhas. One could manifest in the Sambhogakaya, but only advanced bodhisattvas can be taught at that level. Instead, one would have to manifest in a form with which lower beings could communicate. However, very few sentient beings have the capacity, let alone the interest, to practice Dharma, so one would have to manifest among those who do—in other words, as a human.

Manifesting among humans, one could appear in some kind of miraculous form, like a rainbow body, but while that would attract attention, it wouldn't really be of that much benefit. People need to be inspired to follow the path to enlightenment by being able to see that they, too, can become enlightened. To inspire people in this way, one would have to manifest in a form they can relate to as a person. Then they can think, *I'm a person; she's a person. I can become like her.* In that way, they open themselves to the teaching. Thus, if the people on Earth at this time were open to benefit, one would manifest as a human teacher.

Watching His Holiness, even from afar, as I've had to do, one finds it easy to see how he could indeed be the living embodiment of an enlightened consciousness. He radiates love and compassion; everybody wants to be near him all the time. His wisdom is also clearly apparent—he can teach a range of students, from rank beginners to highly learned geshes, and advise the most sophisticated hermits in retreat. He takes responsibility not only for his land and his people—Tibet and the Tibetans—but also for the whole world, striving constantly to bring peace, reason, and understanding to as many as he possibly can. His Holiness travels tirelessly, meeting and inspiring world leaders, ordinary people, and Dharma students everywhere.

Day after day, His Holiness extends himself as much as any man on Earth, but all for the benefit of others. He is constantly traveling the world, teaching Dharma and giving initiations, holding audiences for all manner of visitors, meeting politicians, giving speeches and press conferences, appearing at this function or that, participating in conferences, and so forth. From morning to night, in Dharamsala and abroad, His Holiness runs from one appointment to the next, taking great responsibility every time—responsibility for the spiritual welfare of not only the sentient beings on this planet but also countless others throughout all of space, for peace on Earth, for the welfare of Tibetan refugees and the oppressed people in Tibet, and for the freedom of Tibet itself.

I don't see His Holiness all that often, perhaps a few days each year, but each time I feel exhausted just watching how busy he is, how constant are the demands on his time, and how amazing is the energy he puts into every person he meets.

His Holiness never forgets "unimportant" people, either. Once I was at an event where His Holiness was consecrating a stupa built by his elder brother Taktser Rinpoche. Everybody was lined up, three deep, along the path; I was at the back somewhere. I'd disrobed a year previously and hadn't seen His Holiness since that time. As he moved down the path, looking back and forth at the people on either side, he noticed me, slightly bent over, hands folded at my heart. In Tibetan, he called out, "What happened to being a monk?" or words to that effect, and swept on. I was amazed he would see me and remember who I was and that the last time we met, more than a year before, I was a monk. He also knew that I wasn't just wearing lay clothes but had actually disrobed.

Ten years later, His Holiness was visiting Brandeis University in Boston. Moving rapidly from one meeting to the next, His Holiness, surrounded by security, was walking through a crowd of people, smiling at everybody he could, when again he saw me bent over about 20 yards away. "Old friend," he called out, motioning me to come over. "Old friend!" I was so touched that in all this busyness, he would be so kind. And of course, it's not just me. His Holiness is like this with most people he knows, and he knows so many.

Surely His Holiness the Dalai Lama is the Buddha of Compassion. Who else would have the wisdom, power, and compassion to accomplish all that he does? Of course, I wouldn't even pretend to see or know but a fraction of what His Holiness does for others, but anybody who observes him with clear sight and an open mind will see more than an extraordinary person among us.

References

His Holiness the Dalai Lama, *The Thirty-seven Practices of the Bodhisattva*. (Audiotape.) Translated by Jeffrey Hopkins. Los Angeles: Thubten Dhargye Ling, 1989.

Dudjom Rinpoche, Jikdrel Yeshe Dorje. *The Nyingma School of Tibetan Buddhism*. Boston: Wisdom Publications, 1991.

Lama Zopa Rinpoche, "The Compassion Buddha is no other than Your Holiness." From the praise and request offered to His Holiness after the Kalachakra initiation in Sydney, Australia, September 1996. Reprinted in *Mandala* magazine, November–December 1996.

11

UNIVERSAL RESPONSIBILITY IN THE DALAI LAMA'S WORLDVIEW

by Bharati Puri

Among the debates on rights and responsibilities, which are both fascinating as well as interminable, is the argument offered by the Dalai Lama. Considered one of the foremost arbiters of human and environmental rights, the Dalai Lama determines to put forth those of human beings as inherent in the Buddhist notions of human "dignity" and "compassion" and conceptualizes them by postulating reciprocity of rights and responsibilities of all human beings. Although lacking a formal character, his thesis, springing from his Buddhist concerns, offers a normative understanding of the issue.*

The idea of "reciprocity" as found in Buddhist theory encapsulates as well as conceptualizes its theory of rights. Scholars who accept the concept of "human rights" as implicit in classical Buddhism contend that . . .

---

*Bharati Puri holds a doctorate from Jawaharlal Nehru University. This chapter is a part of her recently published doctoral thesis, "Engaged Buddhism in the Modern World: A Study of the Dalai Lama's Worldview" (2002), in which she has deconstructed the various Dalai Lama writings for the first time.

> . . . under Dharma, husbands and wives, kings and subjects, teachers and students, all have *reciprocal obligations* [italics added] which can be analyzed into rights and duties. We must qualify this conclusion, however, by noting that the requirements of Dharma are almost always expressed in the form of duties rather than rights. . . . Until rights as personal entitlements are recognized as a discrete but integral part of what is due under Dharma, the modern concept of rights cannot be said to be present.[1]

Even though Buddhist etymology does not categorically refer to "rights"—a concept, incidentally, with a long intellectual history in the Western philosophical tradition[2]—this does not mean that Buddhists cannot agree with the substance of the "human rights" discourse. Peter Harvey explains:

> Buddhists are sometimes unhappy using the language of "rights" as they may associate it with people "demanding their rights" in an aggressive, self-centred way, and may question whether talk of "inalienable rights" implies some unchanging, essential Self that "has" these, which is out of accord with Buddhism's teaching on the nature of selfhood. Nevertheless, as rights imply duties, Buddhists are happier talking directly about the duties themselves: about "universal duties," or, to use a phrase much used by the Dalai Lama, "universal responsibilities" . . . rather than "universal rights."[3]

Etymologically, the word *responsibility* comes from the verb *respond*, which means "to answer or reply"; responsibility must, therefore, involve answerability. A reference to the term *responsibility* is expressive of and concerned with every individual in the society, as well as the society itself,[4] and is therefore in accordance with the Dharmapada, which points out that the concept of "one world" is theoretically realized when we accept the sense of relatedness between one individual and another. The Dharmapada says: "So although the world may become large or small ultimately it is the relation between two individuals only. As soon as the second man is visualized, the concept of the world also arises. The second man, therefore, includes in him all the rest of individuals in the world."[5]

This ontological assumption essentially describes the existence of all beings in one—that is, in the other. Even if one does not come into contact with every individual in society, it is this relation that is its formative principle.[6] Reflected in contemporary writings, too, this assumption emphasizes the necessity of considering the effects of personal and social actions on others in the realms of speech and symbolic manipulation in the present information age and in the policies, programs, and products of large and small institutions. "'The others' affected by [these] actions must be understood not only as a unit, but as significant collectivities: families, neighbors, and workplace teams; social, ethnic, and economic groups; national and international populations; and, not least, just as biological species and ecosystems."[7]

The concept of *vasudhaiva kutumbakam,* which in Sanskrit literally means "to regard the whole world as one's family," the Kantian insistence on the universalization of the maxims of moral will, as well as the concern of Utilitarian philosophers with the ideal of the "common good," all go to reveal that as a concept, universal responsibility has been accorded a wide range of ethical reflection in the history of thought. A genuine sense of universal responsibility advocated by the Dalai Lama cannot arise from an individualism bred by an economic worldview.[8] Through universal responsibility, he attempts to articulate a "moral vision"[9] in which "universal connectedness" is emphasized. He sees in this unity a universal feeling of being linked with, and a responsibility toward, all people.[10]

First used by the Dalai Lama, the term *universal responsibility* has been put to more than just linguistic use and has become a rallying point for movements, as well as the foundational principle for institutions.[11] Defining this concept, he says: "True compassion is universal in scope. It is accompanied by a sense of universal responsibility. To act altruistically, concerned only for the welfare of others, with no selfish or ulterior motive, is to affirm a sense of universal responsibility."[12]

In the Tibetan language, the term closest to universal responsibility is *chisem,* which literally means "universal consciousness" (*chi,* "universal," and *sem,* "consciousness").[13] In a speech made at the Parliamentary Earth Summit, held under the auspices of the United Nations Conference on Environment and Development in Rio de Janeiro, Brazil, on June 7, 1992, the Dalai Lama said that universal responsibility is the real key to human survival.[14] "[It] is the best foundation for . . . world peace, the equitable use of our natural resources and, through concern for future generations, the proper care of the environment."[15] From the point of view of awareness, universal responsibility is not even a principle; it is an inherent aspect of everyone's deepest sense of being: "the principle of universal responsibility is what every person fundamentally is; we, by birth, embody it."[16]

Human dignity in Buddhism lies in the infinite potential or capacity of human nature for participating in goodness. Emerging from Buddhist philosophy, the Dalai Lama's *weltanschauung* is representative of the fundamental sameness of all human beings.[17] It is with such an understanding that he sees Buddhahood as "within the reach of all human beings." Carrying the argument further by seeking similarity between Buddhist thought and the Universal Declaration of Human Rights, he suggests that the U.N. declaration facilitates the advancement of human beings toward the "Buddhist goal." Other comparative studies of the Buddhist conceptualization of rights and the Universal Declaration of Human Rights discuss similar paradigms.[18]

The argument put forth by those who are opposed to the Universal Declaration of Human Rights is that this concept, produced from a Western imagination of individualism, attempts to impose international human-rights standards on all cultures as a form of imperialism. This has been criticized for various reasons.[19]

Samuel Huntington's controversial analysis explores how clashes between civilizations are the greatest threat to world peace and how an international order based on civilizations appears to be the best safeguard against war. His understanding of the Western ideas of individualism, liberalism, constitutionalism, human rights, equality, liberty, the rule of law, democracy, free markets, and the separation of church and state is that often these have little resonance in Islamic, Confucian, Japanese, Hindu, Buddhist, or Orthodox cultures. Furthermore, the Western efforts to propagate such ideas produce instead a reaction against "human rights imperialism" and "a reaffirmation of indigenous values."[20]

This, however, has been strongly criticized on the grounds that such a relativist thesis is not entirely convincing. "It assumes that there is a single set of Western, Islamic or Asian cultural values respectively. This is patently untrue. . . . Huntington's list—Confucian, Japanese, Hindu, Buddhist—refutes the popular catch-all of 'Asian' values. There are many traditions and beliefs, some of them hostile to each other, even within each of these."[21]

Those subscribing to the "Asian" view of human rights suggest that the standards laid down in the Universal Declaration of Human Rights are basically advocated by the West and that these "universal" human rights cannot be applied to Asia or other parts of the developing world—not simply because of differences in culture, but also owing to differences in economic development.[22] In addition, they argue that the Universal Declaration of Human Rights does not take into due consideration the equitable economic development of these regions.

Opposing such a view, the Dalai Lama insists that fundamental human rights are as important to the people of Asia as they are to those in Europe or the United States.[23] This is because all human beings—whatever their race, religion, sex, or political status—are basically the same by virtue of the fact that they share common human needs and concerns.[24] For this reason, he stresses not only the logical need to respect human rights worldwide, but more important, the need for a definition of these rights.[25] The Dalai Lama emphasizes that all human beings yearn for freedom, equality, and dignity. Since the Universal Declaration of Human Rights upholds all three of these beliefs, he agrees with it. This, in a way, also spells out his departure from his predominantly Buddhist position on the issue, although this stance can also be interpreted as strengthening the preceding arguments in which he unifies all human beings.

The Dalai Lama's position can be assessed on the basis of the understanding among Tibetan scholars of the trend in political economy that lays stress on economic gains rather than on national glory, a trend that has gained currency the world over.[26] The Dalai

Lama has completely understood the implications of this trend. Contrary to the position of the advocates of the Asian human rights on whether economic development can suffer due to human-rights protection, the Dalai Lama turns the argument around and suggests instead that it is with economic coercion, sometimes, that human rights may be protected.[27] He concludes: "The universal principles of equality of all human beings must take precedence."[28]

He reasons that individuals and nations can no longer resolve many of their problems by themselves and are forced to be *interdependent*. The principle of interdependence basically emphasizes and encourages a "growing" awareness in people about the responsibility they share as individuals vis-à-vis one another, and the responsibility they owe the planet where they live.[29] Such a thought process, in the Dalai Lama's thinking, is especially influenced by the Buddhist doctrine of *Pratityasamutpada*, or interdependence, which is considered the foundation of all teachings of the Buddha.[30]

Buddhism identifies the doctrine of Pratityasamutpada as that which leads to the cessation of all plurality. It is in this sense that the Dalai Lama says: "It is a major error, a 'root-error,' to isolate human life, to attribute to it an essence, in-itself."[31] This ensures that the dignity, growth, and evolution of the individual is not of great regard. In Buddhism, human dignity flows from the capacity of human nature to reach perfection, as demonstrated by the historical figure of the Buddha. Therefore, it is suggested that the Buddha is the living embodiment of human perfection. It is in his profound wisdom and compassion that he exemplifies the inherent qualities that can be cultivated with human dignity.[32]

In his attempt to fuse the metaphysics of Buddhism with consciously lived reality, the Dalai Lama has entirely reinterpreted the doctrine of karma, in which the active role of the human agency is emphasized. In this respect, perhaps, the Dalai Lama's formula fundamentally differs from Gandhi's, especially when seen in the context of karma and human rights. Where Gandhi considers an individual human condition as designated by the karmic law, the Dalai Lama goes a step further by making the individual larger than karma.

As a concept, karma is seminal to Buddhism. In Buddhism, the various manifestations of suffering, natural as well as unnatural, are taken to be its consequence.[33] Yet in the Dalai Lama's view, an individual cannot shirk the responsibility for finding him- or herself in a particular situation. He explains, "To say that every misfortune is the result of karma is tantamount to saying that we are totally powerless in life."[34] Going to the root of the word *karma*, the Dalai Lama sees it as denoting an active force, the inference being that the outcome of future events can be influenced by our actions. To suppose that karma is some sort of independent energy that determines the course of our whole lives, he suggests, is incorrect.

He questions, "Who creates *karma?*" and answers his own question in the following words:

> We ourselves. What we think, say, do, desire and omit creates *karma*. . . . In everything we do, there is cause and effect, cause and effect. In our daily lives the food we eat, the work we undertake, our relaxation are all functions of action: our action. This is *karma*. We cannot, therefore, throw up our hands whenever we find ourselves confronted by unavoidable suffering. . . . If this were correct, there would be no cause for hope.[35]

This stance exemplifies the difficult task that the Dalai Lama has chosen, of treading a middle way between the preservation of tradition and the necessity of progress.[36]

Envisioning the human condition on the principle that all human beings are essentially equal and each has an equal right to life, liberty, and happiness—regardless of economic condition, education, or religion—as the Dalai Lama does (and that karma ought not predetermine these), is a logical corollary to his Buddhist understanding that each human being is equal to every other by virtue of *being* a human being.[37]

However, a rational, authentic appeal of any discourse on rights lies in its "correct" application. Mrinal Miri brings this up in his theory of rights, where he strives to balance the freedom of human agency, besides rescuing human-rights discourse from absurd nominalism: "Human rights are rights, which belong to human beings, qua human beings, as beings who can exercise freedom through reason. Such rights, therefore, are unique to human beings and apply universally to all human beings."[38]

It is in this sense that the Dalai Lama argues that each human being can seek to live in a society where everyone is allowed free expression and each person can strive to be the best he or she can be.[39] However, he emphasizes: "To pursue one's own fulfillment at the expense of others would lead to chaos and anarchy. So what is required is a system whereby the pursuits of the individual are *balanced* [italics added] with the wider well-being of the community at large."[40] Without the motivation for striking a balance, violence could find a perfect situation to breed in. He reasons that universal responsibility is this balancing principle.

Nonviolence is the bedrock of the Dalai Lama's commitment to universal responsibility.[41] Buddhism is deeply associated with nonviolence and peace; both are strongly represented in its value system.[42] It is important in Buddhism to see humans as a part of the community of "sentient beings" in a conditioned world where suffering is endemic, and thus to kill or harm another being deliberately is to ignore the fragility and aspiration for happiness that one has in common with it.[43]

Buddhism also suggests that it is in understanding the impermanent nature of phenomena that one can eschew violence.[44] "Impermanence," as referred to in Buddhism, is radically different from violence. Even though impermanence stresses the phenomenon of "transitoriness"—which means that nothing is permanent and therefore could, by the very logic of its definition, suggest rectitude in resorting to violence—the difference between the two can be drawn by understanding that whereas impermanence is essentially based on the nature of phenomena, violence calls for a change brought about by a human agency and thereby becomes a violation of the "natural" law of change. In Buddhist thought, it is said: "Let the law of impermanence, not lawlessness of violence, determine the life-span of all that lives: individuals, species, cultures, the earth as a whole."[45]

The Buddhist law of impermanence supports nonviolence. "Non-violence," the Dalai Lama says, is "compassion in action."[46] Hence, responsibility when it refers to a compassionate concern for humankind is named *universal responsibility* in the Dalai Lama's thought. It can be defined as developing of the "sense" to work not merely for one's individual self, family, or nation, but for the benefit of all humankind.[47] This Buddhist approach, which concentrates on the individual, does not lose sight of a necessary corollary, which is a meaningful individual life interrelated with a lived social condition.[48] In an argument tautologous to this, he states that it is important to reassess the rights and responsibilities of individuals, peoples, and nations in the context of globalization and interdependence.[49]

It is his faith in interdependence that not only ensures a sense of respect for the rights of others, but also ensures that they are recognized above one's own. He suggests that a keen awareness of the interdependence phenomenon is only possible with the help of compassion. For the Dalai Lama, "the practice of compassion is not idealistic, but the most effective way to pursue the best interest of others as well as our own."[50] To experience genuine compassion is to develop a feeling of closeness to others, combined with a sense of responsibility for their welfare.[51] Enumerating the Buddhist belief in freedom, equality, and compassion for all as being fundamental to any discourse on rights,[52] he has consistently argued that the most important "moral quality" that individuals need to cultivate is compassion.[53]

While some philosophers restrict duties to the public sphere and establish the sanctity of the private, the most important thing about a discourse on rights grounded in compassion is that it has the capacity to address moral life in what liberals regard as the private domain.[54] The Dalai Lama's discourse on rights grounded in compassion[55] does not see true happiness emerging from limited concerns, but from developing love and compassion "for all sentient beings." His earnest wish is that all sentient beings can find happiness and compassion. This means that they can all be free of suffering.

This spirit finds a true echo in Tsong Khapa's words: ". . . the character of the great ones is limited to the benefit and happiness of others,"[56] and in Schopenhauer's explanation of this as a situation in which distinctions between individuals cease.[57] For the Dalai Lama, to begin with compassion is to have the good of others in one's heart or as one's motive for action. He ventures to give a social face to compassion and extends it from the individual to the society at large, and much in consonance with Schopenhauer, holds that differences between individuals are not real. Schopenhauer describes the apparent difference between persons by saying: "According to experience, the difference between my own person and another's appear to be absolute. The difference in space that separates me from him, separates me also from his weal and woe."[58] Again, he says, "My true inner being exists in every living thing as distinctly as it makes itself known in my self-consciousness only to me. . . . It is this that bursts through as compassion on which all genuine . . . virtue therefore depends,"[59] a vision that echoes the non-dualistic philosophy of the Advaita.

According to the Dalai Lama:

> Different philosophies and traditions have different interpretations of the meaning of love and compassion. . . . The Buddhist interpretation is that genuine compassion is based on a clear acceptance or recognition that others, like oneself, want happiness and have the right to overcome suffering. On that basis one develops some kind of concern about the welfare of others, irrespective of one's attitude to oneself. That is compassion.[60]

The Dalai Lama postulates that it is possible to have compassion without any physical proximity to the situation or person one is feeling compassionate toward.[61] A similar insight is encountered in the Tibetan Buddhist philosophy, where visualizing each sentient being as one's mother becomes a means to extend natural sympathy into universal compassion.

Arguments that concur with the Dalai Lama's position—that rights are not merely rights but are also duties, and that both rights as well as duties are interdependent[62]—would also suggest that at present there is no endogenous theory capable of unifying contemporary societies and no imposed or imported ideology that can be simply substituted for it. Therefore, some scholars have suggested the need for "a mutual fecundation of cultures."[63] For a concept to become universally valid, it is imperative for it to fulfill at least the condition that it should be the universal point of reference for any problems regarding human dignity. In what emerges as their criticism, they assert that "the culture which has given birth to the concept of Human Rights should also be called upon to become a universal culture."[64]

Even where scholars discount the concept of rights as a peculiarly Western notion, they explicitly affirm that the world should not renounce declaring or enforcing them. Rights are imperative, and a technological civilization without an assertion of rights amounts to the most inhuman situation imaginable. They insist, however, that room should be made for other traditions to develop and formulate their own "culture specific" views corresponding to or opposing Western rights, as otherwise it would be impossible for non-Western cultures to survive, let alone offer viable alternatives. It is here that the role of cross-cultural philosophical approach becomes important. *Human pluralism* must be recognized in principle, as also in practice, and an intermediary space must be found for mutual criticism that strives for "mutual fecundation" and enrichment.

Scholar Raimon Panikkar observes: "Perhaps such an interchange may help bring forth a new myth and eventually a more humane civilization. The dialogical dialogue appears as an unavoidable method."[65] It may be said here that the Dalai Lama has been constantly emphasizing the need for dialogue as paramount for establishing mutual understanding and harmony. A cross-cultural critique, on the whole, considers new perspectives for an internal criticism and sets the limits of validity of human rights. It offers at the same time two possibilities—of "enlarging its realm and of a mutual choice with other conceptions of man and reality."[66]

Arguments, however, counsel that claiming universal validity for human rights in the formulated sense, as of the Declaration of Human Rights . . .

. . . implies the belief that most of the peoples of the world today are engaged in much the same way as the Western nations in a process of transition from more or less mythical *Gemeinschaften*[67] (feudal principalities, self-governing cities, guilds, local communities, tribal institutions . . .) to a 'rationally' and 'contractually' organized 'modernity' as known to the Western industrialized world.[68]

As a vision and a response to these various debates, the Dalai Lama's interpretation of rights and responsibility can be seen as a plea for upholding and preserving the dignity of humankind, an ideal he foresees to be the necessary foundation for every society.[69] The connection he articulates between rights and responsibility is representative of his "engaged Buddhist ethic," wherein the individual does not debunk his or her social responsibility, and neither does the society undermine the humanity of an individual.

Endnotes

1. Damien Keown (ed.), *Contemporary Buddhist Ethics,* Richmond, Surrey, U.K.: Curzon Press, 2000, p. 63.

2. Richard Dagger, "Rights," in Terence Ball, et al. (eds.), *Political Innovation and Conceptual Change,* Cambridge, U.K.: Cambridge University Press, 1989, p. 297, as cited in Keown (ed.), pp. 59–60.

3. Peter Harvey, *An Introduction to Buddhist Ethics,* Cambridge, U.K.: Cambridge University Press, 2000, p. 119. Also see: *The Dalai Lama, a Policy of Kindness: An Anthology of Writings by and about the Dalai Lama,* compiled and edited by Sidney Piburn, Ithaca, NY: Snow Lion, 1990, pp. 111–115.

4. S. S. Barlingay, "Responsibility, Universality and Religion," in Ramesh Chandra Tewari and Krishna Nath (eds.), *Universal Responsibility: A Collection of Essays to Honor Tenzin Gyatso the XIVth Dalai Lama,* New Delhi: Foundation for Universal Responsibility of His Holiness the Dalai Lama and A "N" B Publishers Pvt. Ltd., 1996, p. 121.

5. Ibid., pp. 122–123.

6. Ibid., p. 121.

7. Christopher Queen (ed.), "Introduction: A New Buddhism," in *Engaged Buddhism in the West,* Somerville, MA: Wisdom Publications, 2000, p. 3.

8. Ramesh Chandra Tewari and Krishna Nath (eds.), *Universal Responsibility: A*

Collection of Essays to Honor Tenzin Gyatso the XIVth Dalai Lama, New Delhi: Foundation for Universal Responsibility of His Holiness the Dalai Lama and A "N" B Publishers Pvt. Ltd., 1996, p. xvii.

9. Matthew Kapstein, "Three Questions About Universal Responsibility," in Tewari and Nath (eds.), p. 213.

10. Tewari and Nath (eds.), p. xii.

11. (a) Ibid., p. xxiii. (b) An example can be given in the Foundation for Universal Responsibility of His Holiness the Dalai Lama in New Delhi: "The Foundation is not there to promote any one individual, political ideology or cause. It is rather to build bridges of cooperation and understanding." Geeti Sen and Rajiv Mehrotra, "Laughter and Compassion: His Holiness Tenzin Gyatso The XIVth Dalai Lama of Tibet in Conversation with Geeti Sen and Rajiv Mehrotra," *India International Center Quarterly* (New Delhi), vol. 18, no. 4, p. 127.

12. "Importance of Compassion in Human Life," *The Spirit of Tibet: Universal Heritage, Selected Speeches of HH The Dalai Lama XIV,* edited by A. A. Shiromany, New Delhi: Tibetan Parliamentary and Policy Research Center and Allied Publishers Ltd., 1995, p. 253.

13. His Holiness the Dalai Lama, "Universal Responsibility," *Ancient Wisdom, Modern World: Ethics for the New Millennium,* London: Abacus, 1999, p. 168.

14. "Speech At Parliamentary Earth Summit," in *The Spirit of Tibet: Universal Heritage, Selected Speeches of HH The Dalai Lama XIV,* edited by A. A. Shiromany, New Delhi: Tibetan Parliamentary and Policy Research Center and Allied Publishers Ltd., 1995, p. 299.

15. Ibid., p. 299.

16. Eleanor Rosch, "Portraits of the Mind in Cognitive Science and Meditation," in Tewari and Nath (eds.), p. 163.

17. His Holiness the Dalai Lama, "Asian Values and Democracy," *Tibetan Bulletin* (Dharamsala: Department of Information and International Relations, Central Tibetan Administration), vol. 3, no. 1, January–February 1999, p. 19.

18. L. P. N. Perera, *Buddhism and Human Rights: A Buddhist Commentary on the Universal Declaration of Human Rights,* Colombo, Sri Lanka: Karunaratne & Sons, 1991, p. 24.

19. "Asian countries" have propagated ten points justifying why human rights should not be raised or linked with trade and aid: sovereignty and human rights, internal matters, development, food, individual vs. Society, order, historical and religious background, socio-genic and cultural specifics, higher morality, and trade and aid. Lobsang Sengay Taksham, "Human Rights and Universality: Asian Excuses and Contradictions," *Tibetan Review* (Delhi), vol. XXX, no. 2, February 1995, pp. 12–16.

20. Samuel P. Huntington, "The Clash of Civilizations?" *Foreign Affairs,* vol. 72, 1993, pp. 40–41. The argument was explored further in Samuel P. Huntington, *The Clash of Civilizations and the Remaking of World Order,* New Delhi: Penguin, 1997, pp. 40–41; also see pp. 22–49.

21. "Controversies and Cultures," *The Economist* (London), December 5, 1998, p. 10.

22. Advocates of "Asian values" sometimes say that Asians place the "common good" before the individual, whereas the West accords priority to the individual. Mahathir Mohamad has listed the six most important societal values of the East Asians on the basis of a survey by David Hitchcock. They are enumerated as the following: (1) an orderly society, (2) societal harmony, (3) the accountability of public officials, (4) openness to new ideas, (5) freedom of expression, and (6) respect for authority. Mahathir Mohamad, "Let's Have Mutual Cultural Enrichment," *New Straits Times,* March 16, 1995, pp. 10–11.

Also see: Michael Freeman, "Human Rights, Asian Values, and the Clash of Civilization," *Issues and Studies* (Taipei: Institute of International Relations, National Chengchi University), vol. 34, no. 10, October 1998, p. 62.

Michael Freeman suggests that the comparable values held by the Americans are: (1) freedom of expression, (2) personal freedom, (3) the right of the individual, (4) open debate, (5) thinking for oneself, and (6) the accountability of public officials. Mahathir conclusively says that this makes it apparent that East Asians give priority to order-supporting values whereas Americans privilege rights-related values. Michael Freeman, "Human Rights, Democracy and 'Asian Values,'" *The Pacific Review,* vol. 9, no. 3, 1996, pp. 352–366.

Also see: David I. Hitchcock, *Asian Values and the United States: How Much Conflict,* Washington, D.C.: Center for Strategic and International Studies, 1994.

23. (a) His Holiness the Dalai Lama, *Speeches, Statements, Articles, Interviews: 1987 to June 1995,* Dharamsala: The Department of Information and International Relations, Gangchen Kyishong, 1995, p. 205. (b) His Holiness the Dalai Lama, "Asian Values and Democracy," *Tibetan Bulletin* (Dharamsala: Department of Information and International Relations, Central Tibetan Administration), vol. 3, no. 1, January–February, 1999, p. 20. (c) His Holiness the Dalai Lama, *Speech Delivered to New York Lawyers Alliance for World Security and Council of Foreign Relations,* New York City, April 27, 1994.

24. "Human Rights and Universal Responsibility, Vienna, Austria, June 15, 1993," *The Political Philosophy of His Holiness the XIV Dalai Lama: Selected Speeches and Writings,* edited by A. A. Shiromany, New Delhi: Tibetan Parliamentary and Policy Research Center and Friedrich-Naumann-Stiftung, 1998, p. 89.

25. (a) Ibid., p. 90. (b) His Holiness the Dalai Lama, *Speeches, Statements, Articles, Interviews: 1987 to June 1995,* Dharamsala: The Department of Information and International Relations, Central Tibetan Administration, Gangchen Kyishong, 1995, p. 205.

26. Dawa Nearby, "Tibetan Buffer Good for Both India and China," *Demilitarization of the Tibetan Plateau,* Dharamsala: The Department of Information and International Relations, 2000, p. 23.

27. "Interview to *The Economic Times,*" *The Political Philosophy of His Holiness the XIV Dalai Lama: Selected Speeches and Writings,* edited by A. A. Shiromany, New

Delhi: Tibetan Parliamentary and Policy Research Center and Friedrich-Naumann-Stiftung, p. 195.

28. His Holiness the Dalai Lama, *Speeches, Statements, Articles, Interviews: 1987 to June 1995,* Dharamsala: The Department of Information and International Relations, Central Tibetan Administration, Gangchen Kyishong, 1995, p. 206.

29. Ibid, p. 204.

30. Chandradhar Sharma, *A Critical Survey of Indian Philosophy,* Delhi: Motilal Banarsidass Publishers, 1987, pp. 72–75.

31. His Holiness the Dalai Lama and Jean-Claude Carrière, *The Power of Buddhism,* Dublin: Newleaf, (1994) 1996, p. 35.

32. *Encyclopedia of Applied Ethics,* vol. I, San Diego: Academic Press, 1998, p. 394.

33. There is a category of natural suffering—including phenomena like war, poverty, and crime—into which the Dalai Lama has incorporated contemporary issues such as illiteracy and certain diseases, also. The second category is of natural suffering like old age, sickness, and death. His Holiness the Dalai Lama, *Ancient Wisdom, Modern World: Ethics for the New Millennium,* London: Abacus, 2000, pp. 138, 141.

34. His Holiness the Dalai Lama, *Ancient Wisdom, Modern World: Ethics for the New Millennium,* London: Abacus, 2000, p.141.

35. Ibid., pp. 141–142.

36. Fredrick R. Hyde-Chambers, "Buddhism in Action: The Dalai Lama and the People of Tibet," *The Middle Way* (London), vol. 71, no. 1, May 1996, p. 9.

37. His Holiness the Dalai Lama, n.17, p. 19.

38. Mrinal Miri, "A Note on the Idea of Human Rights," *Journal of Indian Council of Philosophical Research* (New Delhi), vol. XVII, no. 2, January–April 2000, p. 160.

39. His Holiness the Dalai Lama, n.17, p. 19.

40. Ibid., p. 19.

41. *The Political Philosophy of His Holiness the XIV Dalai Lama: Selected Speeches and Writings,* edited by A. A. Shiromany, New Delhi: Tibetan Parliamentary and Policy Research Centre and Friedrich-Naumann-Stiftung, 1998, p. xxvi.

42. Peter Harvey, *An Introduction to Buddhist Ethics,* Cambridge, U.K.: Cambridge University Press, 2000, p. 239.

43. Ibid., pp. 185–186.

44. Some scholars have attempted to explain environmental issues from the Buddhist perspective by drawing a parallel from the Buddhist concept of impermanence: "Impermanence of Phenomena" is a tenet of Buddha's teaching. While teaching that we must accept transitoriness, he forbade willful killing. It was Buddha's injunction that in order to retain our environment, we must not kill and destroy beyond the capacity of Mother Earth. Doboom Tulku Lama, *The Buddhist Path to Enlightenment: Tibetan Buddhist Philosophy and Practice,* San Diego: Point Loma Publications, 1996, pp. 162–163.

45. Doboom Tulku Lama, *The Buddhist Path to Enlightenment: Tibetan Buddhist Philosophy and Practice,* San Diego: Point Loma Publications, 1996, p. 163.

46. His Holiness the Dalai Lama, *The Four Noble Truths,* New Delhi: Harper-Collins Publishers India, (1997) 1998, see pp. 130–150.

47. "No Substitute for Love," *The Political Philosophy of His Holiness the XIV Dalai Lama: Selected Speeches and Writings,* edited by A. A. Shiromany, New Delhi: Tibetan Parliamentary and Policy Research Centre and Friedrich-Naumann-Stiftung, 1998, p. 79.

48. His Holiness the Dalai Lama, n.17, p. 19.

49. "Speech on India's Role on Tibet," *The Political Philosophy of His Holiness the XIV Dalai Lama: Selected Speeches and Writings,* edited by A. A. Shiromany, New Delhi: Tibetan Parliamentary and Policy Research Centre and Friedrich-Naumann-Stiftung, 1998, p. 89.

50. "Human Rights and Universal Responsibility," n.24, p. 93.

51. "Importance of Compassion in Human Life," *The Spirit of Tibet: Universal Heritage, Selected Speeches and Writings of His Holiness the XIV Dalai Lama,* edited by A. A. Shiromany, New Delhi: Tibetan Parliamentary and Policy Research Centre and Allied Publishers Ltd., 1995, p. 252.

52. "Address to the U.S. Congress, U.S. Capitol Rotunda, April 18, 1999," *The Political Philosophy of His Holiness the XIV Dalai Lama: Selected Speeches and Writings,* edited by A. A. Shiromany, New Delhi: Tibetan Parliamentary and Policy Research Centre and Friedrich-Naumann-Stiftung, 1998, p. 64.

53. (a) Jay L. Garfield, "Human Rights and Compassion: Towards a Unified Moral Framework," in Tewari and Nath (eds.), p. 197. (b) His Holiness the Dalai Lama, *The Global Community and the Need for Universal Responsibility*, Boston: Wisdom Publications, 1992. (c) His Holiness the Dalai Lama, *Kindness, Clarity, and Insight,* edited by Jeffrey Hopkins and Elizabeth Napper, Jeffrey Hopkins, trans., Ithaca, NY: Snow Lion, 1984.

54. Annette C. Baier, *Moral Prejudices,* Cambridge, MA: Harvard University Press, 1964, p. 25; and see also: J. Tronto, *Moral Boundaries: A Political Argument for an Ethic of Care*, New York: Routledge, 1993.

55. His Holiness the Dalai Lama, *The Global Community and the Need for Universal Responsibility,* Boston: Wisdom Publications, 1992. It has been acknowledged (see Jay L. Garfield, "Human Rights and Compassion: Towards a Unified Moral Framework," in Tewari and Nath [eds.], p. 184) that there is a similarity in the arguments proposed by Baier (1964) and Tronto (1993) (for references of both Baier [1964] and Tronto [1993], see n.54).

56. Alex Wayman, *The Ethics of Tibet,* Albany: State University of New York Press, 1991, p. 26.

57. Arthur Schopenhauer, *On the Basis of Morality,* E. F. J. Payne, trans., Indianapolis: Bobbs-Merrill, 1965, p. 144.

58. Ibid., p. 205.

59. Ibid., p. 210.

60. His Holiness the Dalai Lama, *The Power of Compassion: A Collection of Lectures by His Holiness the XIV Dalai Lama,* Geshe Thupten Jinpa, trans., New Delhi: HarperCollins Publishers India, 1994, pp. 62–63.

61. Ibid., p. 67.

62. Henry J. Steiner and Philip Alston, *International Human Rights in Context: Law, Politics, Morals,* Oxford: Clarendon Press, 1996 (second edition), p. 208.

63. Ibid., p. 208.

64. Ibid., p. 208.

65. R. Panikkar, "Is the Notion of Human Rights a Western Concept?" *120 Diogenes 75* (1982), as cited in Henry J. Steiner and Philip Alston, *International Human Rights in Context: Law, Politics, Morals,* Oxford: Clarendon Press, 1996 (second edition), p. 209.

66. Ibid., p. 207.

67. *Gemeinsam* in German means "together, mutual, joint, common." Therefore, *Gemeinschaft* means "community." *Gemeinschaften* is the plural of community. See the Langenscheidt Editorial Staff, *Langenscheidt's German-English, English-German Dictionary,* New York: Pocket Books, (1952) 1970, p. 120.

68. Panikkar, n.65, p. 205.

69. His Holiness the Dalai Lama, "Universal Responsibility: Key to Human Survival" (Asian Human Rights Commission), **www.ahrck.net/solidarity/199903/v93-16.htm.**

12

Universal Responsibility and the Roots of Empathy and Compassion

by Daniel Goleman

His Holiness the 14th Dalai Lama, Tenzin Gyatso, who has lived in India since he led thousands of his people to freedom from Chinese oppression in 1959, is renowned as the recipient of the 1989 Nobel Peace Prize. He is respected worldwide as a spokesman for the compassionate and peaceful resolution of human conflict, as articulated in the principle of universal responsibility.

Less well known is his intense personal interest in the sciences; he has said that if he were not a monk, he would have liked to have been an engineer. As a youth in Lhasa, he was the one called upon to fix broken machinery in the Potala Palace, be it a clock or a car. That early interest in science burns as brightly today. In part, I believe, it's motivated by his instinct that scientific truths lend yet another base of support to his most basic beliefs, such as this principle of universal responsibility.

Over the last decade or so, I have had the privilege of convening or participating in a series of dialogues with His Holiness and scientists and scholars. These dialogues have been a rich source for finding the agreements between science and the spiritual views that support a philosophy of universal responsibility. The topics have been wide-ranging: the philosophical bases of physical reality; the nature of time, emotions, and health; neurophysiology and states of consciousness; and the nature of suffering. But an underlying, unifying theme has been the interconnectedness of phenomena, and particularly the web that ties together all life.

Throughout these discussions I have been struck by the attitude of His Holiness: one of openness, deep curiosity, keen insight, and a high level of scientific sophistication. Often, for example, a scientist would describe an experiment and its results—whether in neuroscience or quantum physics—and His Holiness would ask a question about whether such and such a proposition or some other possibility had been tested, only to have the scientist say, "Your Holiness, that is exactly the next experiment we want to do." He is, as it were, a natural scientist.

His attitude toward finding the truth is that of the true scientist: ideas and beliefs are hypotheses, to be investigated, explored, and tested. Where the weight of evidence lies, there is truth to be found. His openness extends even to his own faith, Buddhism. He has said that if some belief of Buddhism were to be tested scientifically and irrefutably shown to be false, then it would have to change. Indeed, he sees investigation of the truth as vital to the spirit of his religion. As he told one scientist, "From the Buddhist perspective, the more explanation and insight there is here, the better."

His Holiness's view that science and the life of the spirit are complementary was aptly summed up in his introductory remarks before a dialogue with neuroscientists at Harvard Medical School:

> Science has made tremendous progress in understanding and harnessing matter. Buddhism, on the other hand, has a profound philosophy and over the centuries has developed a systematic method of shaping and developing the mind. Whether we are scientists or spiritual practitioners our basic needs and aspirations are the same. Scientists may study mainly matter but they cannot ignore the human mind, or consciousness; spiritual

practitioners may be engaging mainly in developing the mind but they cannot completely ignore their physical needs. It is for this reason that I have always stressed the importance of combining both the mental and the material approach to achieving happiness for humankind.

The Roots of Empathy

In this spirit of seeing the complementarity of science and spirit, I would like to explore one of the taproots of universal responsibility as seen in my own field, psychology, in the development of children's sense of connectedness with others, of empathy, and of compassion. For the newborn infant, this feeling revolves around the sense of touch, the intimate contact of mother and baby. When infants are deprived of human touch, they fail to thrive. A therapy for premature infants involves having them picked up and gently stroked several times each day. Its effect in increased body weight and brain size is measurable—a finding His Holiness has cited many times in talking of the basic human need for connection.

From this base of intimate contact comes older infants' sense of rapport and attunement with their caretakers. When an infant smiles or laughs or utters sounds, the caretakers' response in turn begins to build a rudimentary feeling of being emotionally connected with others—the feeling that someone will respond appropriately, rather than one's communications falling into a void.

From this sense of emotional connectedness springs the earliest signs of altruism in toddlers around a year old. At this age there emerges a capacity psychologists call *sympathetic distress*. A toddler sees another fall down and start crying, and tears well up in her own eyes as she watches, as though it has been she herself who was hurt rather than the other child. In one study of sympathetic distress, for example, a typical incident occurred when a 15-month-old child got hurt and was crying, and his playmate tried to comfort him by offering him a favorite teddy bear. These small acts of caring are the beginnings of compassion, the early precursors of empathy.

Developmental psychologists have found that infants feel sympathetic distress even before they fully realize that they exist apart from other people. Even a few months after birth, infants react to disturbances in those around them, crying when they see another child's tears. By one year or so, they start to realize the misery is not their own but someone else's, although they still seem confused over what to do about it.

In the research of Martin L. Hoffman at New York University, for example, a one-year-old brought his own mother over to comfort a crying friend, ignoring the friend's mother, who was also in the room. This confusion is seen, too, when one-year-olds imitate the distress of others, possibly to better comprehend what they're feeling. For example, if another baby hurts her fingers, a one-year-old might put her own fingers in her mouth to see if she hurts, too. On seeing his mother cry, one baby wiped his own eyes even though he had no tears.

Such "motor mimicry," as it is called, is the original technical sense of the word *empathy,* as it was first used in the 1920s by E. B. Titchener, an American psychologist. This sense is slightly different from its original introduction into English from the Greek *empatheia,* "feeling into," a term used initially by theoreticians of aesthetics for the ability to perceive the subjective experience of another person. Titchener's theory was that empathy stemmed from a sort of physical imitation of the distress of another, which then evokes the same feelings in oneself. He sought a word that would be distinct from *sympathy,* which can be felt for the general plight of someone else with no sharing whatsoever of what that other person is feeling.

Motor mimicry fades from toddlers' repertoire at around two and a half years, at which point they realize that someone else's pain is different from their own, and are better able to comfort them. A typical incident from a mother's diary is as follows.

> A neighbour's baby cries . . . and Jenny approaches and tries to give him some cookies. She follows him around and begins to whimper to herself. She then tries to stroke his hair, but he pulls away. . . . He calms down, but Jenny still looks worried. She continues to bring him toys and to pat his head and shoulders.

At this point in their development, toddlers begin to diverge from one another in their overall sensitivity to other people's emotional upsets, with some—like Jenny—keenly aware and others tuning out.

A series of studies by Marian Radke-Yarrow and Carolyn Zahn-Waxler at the National Institutes of Mental Health showed that a large part of this difference in empathetic concern had to do with how parents disciplined their children. Children, they found, were more empathetic when the discipline included calling strong attention to the distress their misbehavior caused someone else: "Look how sad you've made her feel," instead of "That was naughty." They found, too, that children's empathy is also shaped by seeing how others react when someone else is distressed; by imitating what they see, children develop a repertoire of empathetic response, especially in helping other people who are distressed.

The Well-Attuned Child

Sarah was 25 when she gave birth to twin boys, Mark and Fred. Mark, she felt, was more like herself; Fred was more like his father. That perception may have the seed of an important but subtle difference in how she treated each boy. When the boys were just three months old, Sarah would often try to catch Fred's eye, and when he would avert his gaze, she would try to catch his eye again. Fred would respond, turning away more emphatically. Once she would look away, Fred would look back at her, and the cycle of pursuit and aversion would begin again, often leaving Fred in tears. But with Mark, Sarah virtually never tried to impose eye contact as she did with Fred. Instead, Mark could break it off whenever he wanted, and she would not pursue.

A small act, but telling. A year later, Fred was notably more fearful and dependent than Mark; one way he showed his fearfulness was in breaking off eye contact with other people as he had done with his mother at three months, turning his face down and away. Mark, on the other hand, looked people straight in the eye; when he wanted to break off contact, he'd turn his head slightly upward and to the side, with a winning smile.

The twins and their mother were observed minutely when they took part in research by Daniel Stern, a psychiatrist then at Cornell Medical School. Stern is fascinated by the small, repeated exchanges that take place between parent and child; he believes that the most basic lessons of emotional life are laid down in these intimate moments. Of all such moments, the most critical are those that let the child know her emotions are met with empathy, accepted, and reciprocated, in a process Stern calls "attunement." The twins' mother was attuned with Mark, but out of emotional sync with Fred. Stern contends that the countless repeated moments of attunement or misattunement between parent and child shape the emotional expectations adults bring to their close relationships, perhaps far more than the more dramatic events of childhood.

Attunement occurs tacitly, as part of the rhythm of relationship. Stern has studied it with incredible precision through videotaping hours of mothers with their infants. He finds that through attunement mothers let their infants know they have a sense of what the children are feeling. A baby squeals with delight, for example, and the mother affirms that delight by giving him a gentle shake, cooing, or matching the pitch of her voice to the baby's squeal. Or the baby shakes his rattle, and she gives him a quick shimmy in response. In such an interaction, the affirming message is in the mother more or less matching the baby's level of excitement. Such small attunements give an infant the reassuring feeling of being emotionally connected, a message that Stern finds mothers send about once a minute when they interact with their babies.

Attunement is very different from simple imitation. "If you just imitate a baby," Stern told me, "that only shows you know what he did, not how he felt. To let him know you sense how he feels, you have to play back his inner feelings in another way. Then the baby knows he is understood."

The Costs of Misattunement

Stern holds that from repeated attunements infants begin to develop a sense that other people can and will share in their feelings. This sense seems to emerge at around eight months, when they begin to realize they are separate from others, and continues to be shaped by intimate relationships throughout life. When parents are misattuned to a child, it is deeply upsetting. In one experiment, Stern had mothers deliberately over- or underrespond to their infants, rather than matching them in an attuned way; the infants responded with immediate dismay and distress.

Prolonged absence of attunement between parent and child takes a tremendous emotional toll on the child. When a parent consistently fails to show any empathy with a particular range of emotion in the child—joys or tears, needing to cuddle—the child begins to avoid expressing, and perhaps even feeling, those same emotions. In this way, presumably, entire ranges of emotion can begin to be obliterated from the repertoire for intimate relations, especially if through childhood those feelings continue to be covertly or overtly discouraged.

By the same token, children can come to favor an unfortunate range of emotion, depending on what moods are reciprocated. Even infants "catch" moods. Three-month-old babies of depressed mothers, for example, mirrored their mothers' moods while playing with them, displaying more feelings of anger and sadness and much less spontaneous curiosity and interest compared to infants whose mothers were not depressed.

One mother in Stern's study consistently underreacted to her baby's level of activity; eventually her baby learned to be passive. "An infant treated that way learns, 'When I get excited, I can't get my mother to be equally excited, so I may as well not try at all,'" Stern contends. But there is hope in "reparative" relationships: "Relationships throughout life—with friends or relatives, for example, or in psychotherapy—continually reshape your working model of relationships. An imbalance at one point can be corrected later; it's an ongoing, lifelong process."

Indeed, several theories of psychoanalysis see the therapeutic relationship as providing just such an emotional corrective, a reparative experience of attunement. *Mirroring* is the term used by some psychoanalytic thinkers for the therapist's reflecting back to the client an understanding of his inner state, just as an attuned mother does with her infant. The emotional synchrony is unstated and outside conscious awareness, although a patient may bask in the sense of being deeply acknowledged and understood.

The lifetime emotional costs of lack of attunement in childhood can be great, and not just for the child. A study of criminals who committed the cruelest and more violent crimes found that the one characteristic of their early lives that set them apart from other criminals was that they had been shuttled from foster home to foster home—life histories that suggest emotional neglect and little opportunity for attunement.

Such neglect can lead in adulthood to psychopathy, the incapacity to feel empathy or compassion of any sort or the least twinge of conscience. Robert Hare, a University of British Columbia psychologist, believes the callousness of criminal psychopaths is based in part on a physiological pattern he discovered: psychopaths about to receive an electric shock show no sign of the fear response that is normal in people about to experience pain. Because the prospect of pain does not trigger a surge of anxiety, Hare contends that psychopaths lack any concern about future punishment for what they do. And because they themselves do not feel fear, they have no empathy—or compassion—for the fear and pain of their victims.

Empathy is typically, and tragically, lacking in those who commit the most mean-spirited of crimes. The blotting out of empathy as these people inflict suffering on their victims is part of an emotional cycle that precipitates their cruel acts. This absence of empathy for their victims is one of the main focuses of new treatments being devised for violent offenders. In one of the most promising treatment programs, the offenders read heart-wrenching accounts of crimes like their own, told from the victims' perspectives. They also watch videotapes of victims tearfully telling what it was like to be molested. The offenders then write about their own offenses from the victim's point of view, imagining what the victim felt.

They read this account to a therapy group and try to answer questions about the assault from the victim's perspective.

Finally, the offender goes through a simulated reenactment of the crime, this time playing the role of the victim. The empathy they gain from this perspective-taking is an impetus for them to assume responsibility for their own crimes and try to reform themselves. From empathy arises compassion, even in the most hardened heart.

The Neurology of Empathy

As is so often the case in neurology, quirky and bizarre case reports were among the early clues to the brain basis of empathy. A 1975 report, for instance, reviewed several cases in which patients with lesions in the right area of the frontal lobes had a curious deficit: they were unable to understand the emotional message in people's tone of voice, although they were perfectly able to understand their words. A sarcastic "Thanks," a grateful "Thanks," and an angry "Thanks" all had the same neutral meaning for them.

By contrast, a 1979 report spoke of patients with injuries in other parts of the right hemisphere who had a very different gap in their emotional perception. These patients were unable to express their own emotions through their tone of voice or by gesture. They knew what they felt, but simply could not convey it. All these cortical regions, the various authors noted, had strong connections to the limbic system, the brain's emotional center.

These studies were reviewed as background to a seminal paper by Leslie Brothers, a psychiatrist at the University of California–Los Angeles, on the biology of empathy. Reviewing both neurological findings and comparative studies with animals, Brothers points to the amygdala—a structure in the limbic system that stores emotional memories—and its connections to the visual cortex as part of the key brain circuitry underlying empathy.

Much of the relevant neurological research is from work with animals, especially primates. That primates display empathy—or "emotional communication," as Brothers prefers to say—is clear not just from anecdotal accounts, but also from studies such as the following.

Rhesus monkeys were trained first to fear a certain tone sound by hearing it while they received a mild electric shock. Then they learned to avoid the electric shock by pushing a lever whenever they heard a certain tone sound. Next, pairs of these monkeys were put in separate cages, their only communication through a closed-circuit TV that allowed them to see pictures of the face of the other monkey. The first monkey, but not the second, then heard the dreaded tone sound, which brought a look of fear to its face. At that moment, the second monkey, seeing fear on the face of the first, pushed the lever that prevented the shock—an act of empathy, if not of altruism.

Having established that primates do, indeed, read emotions from the faces of their peers, researchers used long, fine-tipped electrodes gently inserted into the brains of monkeys. These electrodes allowed the recording of activity in a single neuron. Electrodes tapping neurons in the visual cortex and in the amygdala showed that when one monkey saw the face of another, that information led to neuron firing first in the visual cortex, then in the amygdala. This pathway is a standard route for information that is emotionally arousing.

But what is surprising about results from such studies is that they have also identified neurons in the visual cortex that seem to fire only in response to specific facial expressions or gestures, such as a threatening opening of the mouth, a fearful grimace, or a docile crouch. These neurons are distinct from others in the same region that recognize familiar faces. This would seem to mean that the brain is designed from the beginning to respond to specific emotional expressions—that is, empathy is a given of biology.

A similar physiological basis to empathy in human beings is suggested in research by Robert Levenson, a University of California–Berkeley psychologist who has studied married couples trying to guess what their partners are feeling during a heated discussion. His method is simple: The couple is videotaped and their physiological responses measured while talking over some troubling issue in their marriage—how to discipline the kids, spending habits, and the like. Each partner reviews the tape and narrates what he or she was feeling from moment to moment. Then the partner reviews the tape a second time, now trying to read the other's feelings.

The most empathetic accuracy occurred in those husbands and wives whose own physiology tracked that of the spouses they were watching. That is, when their partners had an elevated sweat response, so did they; when their partners had a drop in heart rate, their hearts slowed. In short, their bodies mimicked the subtle, moment-to-moment physical reactions of their spouses. If the viewers' physiological patterns simply repeated their own during the original interaction, they were very poor at surmising what their partners were feeling. Only when their bodies were in sync was there empathy.

This suggests that when the emotional brain is driving the body with a strong reaction—the heat of anger, say—there can be little or no empathy. Empathy requires enough calm and receptivity that the subtle signals of feeling from another person can be received and mimicked by one's own emotional brain. In other words, when we are less caught up in our own worries and ruminations, less trapped by the small concerns of the everyday self, we are more receptive to the needs and feelings of others. And from that receptiveness flows the impulse that undergirds a personal sense of universal responsibility.

Empathy and Ethics: The Roots of Altruism

One of the most famous lines in English poetry is an expression of the principle of universal responsibility: ". . . never send to ask for whom the bell tolls; it tolls for thee." John Donne's sentiment speaks to the heart of the link between empathy and caring: another's pain is one's own. To feel with another is to care; in this sense the opposite of *empathy* is *antipathy*. The empathetic attitude is engaged again and again in moral judgments, for moral dilemmas involve potential victims: Should you lie to keep from hurting a friend's feelings? Keep a promise to visit a sick friend or accept a last-minute invitation to a dinner party instead? When should a life-support system be kept going for someone who would otherwise die?

These moral questions are posed by the empathy researcher Martin Hoffman, who argues that the roots of morality are to be found in empathy, since it is empathizing with the potential victims—someone in pain, danger, or deprivation—and so sharing their distress, that moves people to act to help them. Beyond this immediate link between empathy and altruism in personal encounters, Hoffman proposes that the same capacity for empathetic affect, for putting oneself in another's place, leads people to follow certain moral principles.

Hoffman sees a natural progression in empathy from infancy onward. As we have seen, at one year of age, a child feels in distress herself when she sees another fall and starts to cry. Her rapport is so strong and immediate that she puts her thumb in her mouth and buries her head in her mother's lap, as if she herself is hurt. After the first year, when infants become more aware that they are distinct from others, they actively try to soothe another crying infant—offering them their teddy bears, for example.

As early as two years of age, children begin to realize that someone else's feelings differ from their own, and so they become more sensitive to cues revealing what another actually feels. At this point they might, for example, recognize that another child's pride might mean the best way to help them deal with their tears is not to call undue attention to them.

By late childhood, the most advanced level of empathy emerges, as children are able to understand distress beyond the immediate situation and see that someone's condition or station in life may be a source of chronic distress. At this point they can feel for the plight of an entire group, like the poor, the oppressed, and the outcast. That understanding, in adolescence, can buttress moral convictions centered on wanting to alleviate misfortune and injustice.

Empathy underlies many facets of moral judgment and action. One is "empathetic anger," which John Stuart Mill described as "the natural feeling of retaliation . . . rendered by intellect and sympathy applicable to . . . those hurts, which wound us through" wounding others. Another instance in which empathy leads to moral action is when a bystander is moved to intervene on behalf of a victim. The research shows that the more empathy bystanders feel for victims, the more likely they will intervene.

There is some evidence that the level of empathy people feel shades their moral judgments as well. For example, studies in Germany and the U.S. found that the more empathetic people are, the more they favor the moral principle that resources should be allocated according to need; the less empathetic, the more they favored the principle that people should be rewarded according to the effort they expend, regardless of need. Empathy, then, is the natural root of the altruistic impulse to take responsibility for those in need.

A Final Word

The Dalai Lama represents Tibet, the one great culture centered on a wisdom tradition to survive from classical times into the modern-day world. But the perilousness of our times is symbolized by the fact that even that future survives intact only in exile. Tibet represents a time capsule of sorts for the modern world, a message from an age when life was centered on the spirit, when the inner sciences—the art of being—were developed to the highest levels. At a time when the world is adrift and in crisis, we need more than ever to bring this wisdom to bear on our collective challenges.

Science and technology have brought immense control over nature, but power without wisdom is dangerous. We need to balance our modern capabilities with an ancient wisdom. His Holiness often speaks of the interconnectedness of all beings and the universal responsibility that this brings. In a sense, that means we are all in this together. He has said, also, that just because these times are so dire, it is a great honor to be alive now, at this moment, on this planet. It is we who bear the responsibility, who face the challenge, who must take care of the planet—not just for ourselves, but for the future of our children.

13

Universal Responsibility: A Christian Consideration

by Raimon Panikkar

His Holiness the Dalai Lama has asked us to meditate on the principle of universal responsibility. In fact, practically all saints of every tradition have preached and lived this principle. A saint, runs a Chinese saying, is a person who has the soul of the whole people. For the Indic tradition, such a person is a *mahatma;* and according to the Western classics, *magnanimitas* is the feature of saintliness. A "great soul" feels responsible for a wider field than a "narrow-minded" individual.

The extremely important call of the Dalai Lama to explore the notion of "universal responsibility" does not consist in asking us to work on one concept so as to get some further clarity on a particular subject. The call of His Holiness extends existentially the field of our responsibility by inviting us to become aware of its universal area. Most studies of this notion tell us that we are not responsible for things we are not aware of. We are only responsible if we are aware that we have to respond to a certain situation and are free in our response. This is why the notion is generally restricted to ethics.

The call of the Dalai Lama widens our horizon and reminds us of the otherwise traditional doctrine that our awareness is not limited to what we see with our eyes; comprehend with our reason; or, worse, "see" by means of satellites and mass-media information. Our awareness, and thus our responsibility, extends also to what opens up to our third eye, our faith, our deepest intuition. By doing this, he expands our responsibility into areas that until now were outside the concerns of modern man. Many people can go on with business as usual because they do not see beyond their private and individual field.

"Responsibility only enters in insofar as one can be called in question by another, and insofar as one can answer this summons," says theologian Waldemar Molinski in Rahner's *Sacramentum Mundi*. The Dalai Lama calls us into question. We have to add, of course, that he is not alone in this call. This is the call of practically all religions, which modern individualism has often overheard. Yet since the First World War, human, and especially Western, consciousness has been extended from its individualistic bulwark to the entire human history.

Now the spiritual head of one branch of the Buddhist tradition, in tune with the cosmology of ancient Buddhism, is not satisfied with just human history, and enlarges the field of human responsibility to all sentient beings. As a modern man, following our increasing ecological consciousness (that I prefer to call *ecosophical*), he suggests we should include in our responsibility the entire ecosystem of our planet and soon of our solar system. The shrinking of our human responsibility is the fruit of modern individualism, which limits man's concerns to himself and his immediate surroundings.

To be sure, these voices of concern—to which the powers that be and the routine of the mind are still reluctant to hear—come today with increasing consensus from all the intellectual and spiritual corners of the world. Humanity as such is responsible for its own destiny. Human history is confronting us with the dilemma of a radical anthropological, and thus civilizational, change *(metanoia)* or a collective suicide. If some survive, they will not be the humanly "fittest" but the most unscrupulous—who will destroy each other soon afterward. What we call human consciousness may "transmigrate" onto another nonhistorical realm. Hope may not be lost, but humanity collapses.

What follows is a Christian consideration on one single aspect of this formidable problem. It is a Christian commentary, however, which keeps in mind readers of other traditions. I could as well have written a Hindu or a Buddhist reflection on the topic, and it would be worth the effort to undertake a comparative study. We should be cautious, however, not to center every reflection on the single concept of responsibility, ignoring the many homeomorphic equivalents in other cultures. The Buddhist notion of *Pratitya-samutpada* (codependent origination, universal concatenation, or radical relativity), for instance, will stress more the awareness of a common belonging than the ability to respond. We need a pluri-perspectival approach to the problems of the world. This is a requisite for a healthy pluralism.

I choose the Christian tradition because His Holiness moves quite often among people of Christian extraction who have almost forgotten the archetypes of their religion—obliviousness to which modern Christianity has heavily contributed. For this reason I shall describe what I think belongs to the genuine Christian tradition, although expressed in an understandable way for our contemporaries to whom the old parlance may offer some difficulties—which in no way is it my intention to hide.

A consideration means the effort at bringing all the stars *(sidera)* together into one intelligible constellation. I could cite teachings—from the Gospels to Teilhard de Chardin (to quote just one name), passing through the Greek, the Oriental, and the Latin Fathers of the Church, the Middle Ages, Renaissance, and modern Christian thinkers—to substantiate the Christian notion of universal responsibility. But I will not use any telescope to gaze at those giant stars and shall use just my naked eye to present this consideration.

The very notion of universal responsibility entails fundamentally three aspects at least: human freedom, the universal connection of all things, and the capacity of things or events to respond to the human being.

1. Anthropological freedom. We would not be responsible if we were robots or puppets in the hands of a higher instance of whatever type, be it a God, a society, or a machine. I am responsible if I have in me the capacity to respond to the summons of what makes me precisely responsible. Human freedom is an essential ingredient of responsibility.

2. Universal solidarity. We are not responsible for what lies absolutely outside our field of action, or rather outside the effluvia of our being. Responsibility implies certain solidarity, the *karma, sarvam sarvatmakam, Buddha-kaya,* or the *pratityasamutpada* of other traditions.

3. Dialogical cosmology. We are not responsible, either, if the "other" for which we are allegedly responsible is a merely automatic or fixed thing, under the law of necessity impervious to human interference. If in one way or another I cannot influence that "other," I cannot have any responsibility. My response has to affect that for which I am supposed to be responsible. In a Newtonian universe, for instance, we are not responsible for an eclipse. In an astrological cosmology, our co-responsibility with the course of the eclipse is altogether another matter. Responsibility is meaningless in an utterly mechanical universe.

I shall limit myself exclusively to the second point—as much as I would like to scratch at least the third problem, since it touches a burning issue of our times: the modern scientific cosmology.

Most religious traditions have underscored the unity of the world, be it considered a creation or otherwise. Many traditions, including the Christian, have stressed in a special way the unity of humanity, without disputing the oneness of creation. Another pitiful restriction has also occasionally occurred. Some religions have *de facto* limited "humanity" to the people of their own tradition. The outsiders have been, if not totally forgotten, certainly neglected in the doctrinal elaborations of this unity of the human race.

The history of Christianity has from the very beginning been torn apart between an *inherited* idea of chosen people and an *inherent* idea of universality. The Jewish idea of chosenness does not claim universality. The Greek idea of universality does not pretend any privilege. This tension is not yet quite resolved in the present time. But after two millennia of history I detect that the prevalent trend today is to qualify chosenness and to reinterpret universality. "Catholicity," for instance, is not understood as a rather modern geographical universalism nor as being a holder of an exclusive truth, but as something closer to the universality of a mirror that reflects the whole without pretending to be the sole image of the whole. This was, incidentally, the primitive understanding of the word *catholic* up to times past St. Augustine's.

"Am I my brother's keeper?" asked the first normal human being in the Bible (Adam and Eve certainly were not ordinary people). "Yes, you are!" was the unambiguous answer. In order to escape this universal responsibility, the human race has ever attempted to reduce the extension of "brother." Responsibility was restricted to our "neighbors." "But who is my neighbor?" the Rabbi from Nazareth was asked; and he boldly replied that it was the foreigner, the stranger, the pagan . . . the *goi, kafir,* or *mleccha.* Our responsibility includes all people. Jesus summed up "salvation" as having had an active responsibility for the welfare of the downtrodden and identifying oneself with the naked, hungry, and suffering.

Let us reintroduce the problem from another more elementary perspective.

Why on earth should I be responsible for a murder committed in a distant island by an unknown fellow for reasons totally incomprehensible to me? Language is treacherous, for I should not have said "fellow," since the very word denotes a certain partnership, which is precisely what is at stake in the example. Is that distant person my fellow? Or do we have fellowship only with our family, clan, caste, nation, religion, or culture?

The only rational answer is to say that willingly or unwillingly, knowingly or not, we belong together and are not isolated individuals, unconnected monads, independent beings.

In a word, universal responsibility implies a certain type of universal *solidarity*. Individuals can only be linked by external ties, like a common interest. The moral responsibility that flows from a common goal is limited to the means used in the acquisition of that goal. It is a legal notion.

Philosopher F. H. Bradley wrote: "For practical purposes we need make no distinction between responsibility . . . and liability to punishment." This is the usual way of understanding responsibility in a predominantly economic worldview. I cannot be accountable for what lies outside my accounts. If there is no ontological unity of the human race, there is no universal responsibility. There is only accountability for the accounts into which we have put our investments.

This individualism is what leads modern citizens to express strongly: "If power lies exclusively with the people and I am the people, and I have not voted the Constitution [of a country, for example], why am I obliged to obey that law as sacrosanct?" Individuals feel united only if there is a common purpose (nationalism and communalism of all sorts) or if there is a threat from the law, the police, or the army. No wonder our planet has 40 million in the armed forces. They "enforce" law and order because there is no sense of responsibility.

Legal responsibility implies a prior contract, at least implicitly. Ethical responsibility demands an at least tacitly acknowledged moral code. We have responsibility toward others (legal) and toward ourselves (ethical). None of this alone can be the basis for universal responsibility. Here is the place and role of religion in general. It relinks humanity with something above the *merely* "human" by the active acknowledgment of a vertical dimension. Here is the place and role of God in the Christian tradition. Our response to this one God oversteps the boundaries of a mere responsibility toward society or toward my own self. God is not a discriminator of persons, says Christian scripture. The other in front of God—*in conspectus Domini,* repeated the Scholastics—has the same rights as I have.

We should not understand the *universal responsibility* to mean a single universal moral code. The *mores* of people are very different, and so are their ways of thinking. Each worldview offers the possibility of deriving from it a sense of universal responsibility, but each culture may have different visions and interpret and justify this responsibility in diverse forms. To be sure, our contemporary situation calls for the working out toward a political consensus for dealing with the problems of human conviviality, but no culture should impose its views on another.

We urgently need a political dialogical dialogue for our world, but this is different from assuming, for instance, that we should proclaim a global ethic, ignoring the function of the Divine so central in many traditions, just because it seems irrelevant in today's politics. The needed pragmatic rule of political behavior is something different from a global ethic; and, furthermore, different from our problem.

In sum, there is only universal responsibility if there is a universal human link of an ontological nature—well aware that this is a very specialized language. Our example is the Christian dogma of the mystical Body—to which I now turn.

The Hebrew Bible since its first lines stresses the unity of creation. The entire universe is the creation of one God, and the whole world sings the glory of its creator. The world is a unity.

The Christian scriptures, while fully accepting this oneness, emphasize the unity of the human race. The "recapitulation" of all things is done by one Man who becomes the Head of this Cosmic Body. Christ is a cosmic Christ, but he is foremost the head of humankind, besides being also the head of the whole cosmos, called a *makranthropos* (not dissimilar to the Vedic *purusa*) by the Greek Fathers. The "heresy" of the Ebionites was not to deny that Jesus was the son of Mary, but to deny that "Christ was before Mary" (to defend "Christum ante Mariam non fuisse," in the words of St. Jerome).

The confusion between Jesus and Christ has had dire consequences in Christian history. "Jesus is the Christ" is the Christian *mahavakya*, the Christian confession. Yet the Mystical Body of the Christian tradition is not just Jesus, the son of Mary, but the Mystical Body of Christ. This Christ—"light which illumines all Men," "splendor and image of the Godhead," "upholding all things by his word," "superior to all angels," "alpha and omega," "only begotten and firstborn of all creatures," who was "before Abraham," "in whom all things find their support," and so on—this Christ, "mystery hidden since the beginning in God," is discovered by Christians in and through Jesus of Nazareth.

Human solidarity in the Christian tradition has two pillars and one ground. The two pillars are the first Adam, created in the image and likeness of God; and the second Adam, Jesus the Christ, incarnated in time and history in order to reestablish the image and likeness of the Divine in Man. The ground is the eschatological expectation of a "new heaven and a new earth" at the *apokatastasis panton* or time of the "universal restoration" that St. Augustine sums up, saying, "And there will be one Christ loving himself" *(et erit unus Christus amans seipsum)* [*Epistula ad Parthos,* 10 (PL 35, 2055)].

The very word *Adam* means simply "Man," the Man, and not just an individual. All have been under "original sin" because of the universal human solidarity between the first Adam and the rest of mortals (otherwise why should we share the responsibility of Eve?). All have been restored to the undistorted Divine image because of the human solidarity between the second Adam and all the rest of humanity—theological distinctions and philosophical problems notwithstanding.

This is the explicit teaching of the Apostle Paul, confirmed by most of the so-called ecumenical councils. And all will be integrated into the *regressus,* or the return of all things to their origin from which they have emerged *(egressus),* so that at the end "God will be all in all things." This is the reason why St. Thomas, in the footsteps of Augustine's idea of evil as lack of Being *(privatio),* dares to affirm that sinners are not *(peccatores in quantum peccatores non sunt).* The Christian solidarity is universal and complete.

It is obvious that both the language and the ideas are all couched within a particular cultural context against the background of the worldview of the time. Just as Adam is a common name particularized in the story of creation, Christ is also a common name applied to the son of Mary. The action of the first Adam takes place at the birth of every person, and the action of the second Adam is witnessed in the rebirth of every human being. Both are historical and transhistorical events, even if a particular Christian theology has afterward interpreted the rebirth in a very particular manner—although never so exclusive as to deny many forms of that initiation into eternal life, which Christians call baptism.

Similarly, traditional Christianity has believed in the final oneness of both human history and the cosmos—so as to understand the entire reality as a radical Trinity: Father, Christ, and Holy Spirit. This Christ encompasses the whole history of the universe, the complete temporality of reality integrated in the divine Mystery. *"In rebus tantis trina coniunctio mundi"* sings the Christian liturgy, in a slightly different but applicable way. This radical Trinity is the truly *mysterium conjunctionis,* the "threefold conjunction" of the real.

In this manner the Christian believes in the total solidarity of the human race—extended also to the entire universe, as so many scriptural passages affirm and as it has been elaborated by the later tradition. It is the entire creation that "groans and waits for the total transformation of the cosmos" toward the "new heaven and the new earth." Little meaning it would have to believe in one creator if there were not one Creation. This is religion: we are all "linked" in the same adventure. It has been, in fact, a certain notion of universal responsibility that has triggered in all its ambivalence the missionary urge of the Christian churches. They felt, rightly and/or wrongly, responsible for the whole world.

We may now "bring all the stars together" by citing exclusively one single luminous planet of the Christian solar system. Our choice should be significant for the modern West inasmuch as we choose not an Oriental, a Greek, or a modern witness, but a Man who has decisively influenced (be it a blessing or not) the self-understanding of the most powerful branches of Christianity: St. Augustine, the 5th-century African bishop.

His leading idea follows in the wake of St. Paul and, of course, the Gospels:

> Extend your love over the entire earth if you want to love Christ, since the members of Christ are to be found every where in the world. If you love only one part you are divided, if you are divided you are not in the Body, if you are not in the Body, you are not under the Head [*Epistula ad Parthos*, 10 (PL 35, 2060)].

Or again:

> All Men are one Man in Christ, and the unity of Christians constitutes but one Man [*Psalm*, 127 (PL 37, 1686)].

And more:

> If he is the Head, and we are the members, then together he and we are the whole Man [*Johanem*, 21 (PL 35, 1568)].

There are dozens of such sentences. For Augustine, we can understand Christ in three ways *(tribes modis intelligitur, et nominator):* (1) as God equal to the Father, (2) as Man *(assumpta carne),* and (3) as the "whole Christ in the fullness of humanity" *(totus Christus in plenitudine ecclesiae)* [*Sermo,* 341, I].

For brevity's sake, we shall not proceed further, nor quote from the entire Christian tradition regarding this central tenet of the Mystical Body. We may refer here to the outstanding multivolume work *The Whole Christ,* written by Emile Mersch just before World War II.

I shall close with a few more general considerations.

Many authors discussing the problem of responsibility stress the moral responsibility of the person concerning our human actions. We are responsible for our actions, we are told, and according to them we shall be "judged." One of the best descriptions is that of Maurice Blondel, stating that "la responsabilité est la solidarité de la personne avec ses actes." It is interesting to know that already a century ago Blondel spoke of solidarity and not of congruence between our being and our actions. Responsibility is not the logical consequence of our ideas (as Kierkegaard would be inclined to defend), but the very manifestation of our being. Our responsibility is not the conclusion of a syllogism or the application of a rule, but the free response of our Being to the very challenge that existence confronts us with. A stone has not the responsibility to fall or a fire to burn without entering now in the degree of freedom of the so-called inanimate things.

In one word, we are not just responsible for our actions but also for our thoughts (as the famous incident of Ananias and Sapphira in the Acts of the Apostles shows: "You have not lied to men but to God"). The responsibility is not only toward ourselves, but toward the indwelling Divine Spirit in us. This is why Jesus also said that we shall be held responsible for every idle word coming out of our mouths, which is to say, for every word that does not effect what it says.

To continue the example cited earlier, I cannot know why that distant person in that distant island did what she did. I cannot know the results of my actions, and with the best of intentions I cannot foresee the good or bad effects of my words. The seat of our responsibility lies not in the good or bad example we set, not in the good or bad effect we have on others, but in our very being. The seat is inside us; it is ourselves. Responsibility is not mere prudence, and much less the fruit of an objective calculus foreseeing the effects of our words or actions. It is not cunning, nor a strategy for prestige, good name, and better results.

Responsibility is an ontological virtue because our Being is dialogical, and we are neither a solipsistic monad nor a dialectical individual. Our responsibility is based on the response we give to ourselves, to our being, because our being is constitutively related to all other beings. And this relatedness is a human relation—that is, dialogical, sharing our *logos* with all beings *(homo loquens)*. What links us with other beings, the traditional Christian answer will be, is not that we know about that distant person, but that we are all equally linked with the Ground of our Being, or God. God is the warrant of our universal solidarity. If I am not as I have to be, if I betray myself, if I do not live up to the divine calling that constitutes me, the entire universe suffers from my infidelity, and that "distant person" will commit that hideous act because, although in a minimal way, I have contributed to it.

It would be an undue extrapolation if we were to interpret what was just said in a mechanistic way and say, for instance, that my responsibility toward that "distant fellow" is simply one six-billionth part of the share. The greater my "soul," the bigger my responsibility. The being of a saint hallows an entire society. "To whom less has been given, less will be demanded." Every being is unique, and we cannot judge others. Interconnectedness is not a quantitative dimension, nor is relationship a mechanical one.

Paradoxically enough, this awareness of our universal responsibility bestows on us calmness and peace that saves us from the messianic syndrome of wanting to be the saviors of the world and falling into despair or indifference when we realize we cannot perform the task. It is not that we skip our duty or dilute our responsibility so thinly that it does not matter what we do. On the contrary, aware of our intrinsic responsibility in our very being, we do not frantically run to influence other people or "convert" them (to our ways, of course) by extrinsic means. Instead, it is the purity of heart that counts and the transparency of our lives. Not even the left hand should know the good acts that the right is doing.

Needless to say, ideas similar to the traditional Christian idea of God as the foundation for universal responsibility are present in other religions, with some variations. I mentioned the notion of *karma* and *Pratityasamutpada* as other homeomorphic equivalents for the foundation of universal responsibility.

It is an interesting feature of our times that there is an increasing shared awareness of human problems common to all rooted in our human experience in any doctrinal approach to reality.

Our contemporary awareness does not respond to deductive morality: There is a God; therefore I have to behave in a certain way. Lord Buddha said so; therefore I should do it. The Veda prescribes it; therefore I should behave in a particular manner. It is rather the other way around. We perceive the deterioration of the earth, the increasing exploitation of humans by other humans, human-made injustices, hunger, and so forth; and we then find both strength and remedies to address the issues, within our cultural context, later analyzing which methods or beliefs were the most effective.

The description of this modern myth needs but one important proviso. It would be a degradation of religion and demeaning to humans to see religion as a mere means and man as force in the universe. All religions warn us that man is not the absolute boss in heaven or on Earth; that our solidarity is not something we create, but that this *"solidum"* is something given; and that our responsibility is precisely this human capacity primarily not to ask, but to respond. Our responsibility entails the intuition that as beings we respond to a question we have not ultimately formulated. Universal responsibility means not universal lordship over reality, but a distinctly human power to respond freely to the mystery of reality, and, thus responding, steer also the very destiny of that reality. The Christian believes that he is not alone in this task.

14

GENTLE BRIDGES AND GOLDEN SEEDS: THE DALAI LAMA DIALOGUES WITH SCIENCE

by Swati Chopra

The writer attended the tenth Mind and Life conference at the official residence of His Holiness the Dalai Lama in McLeod Ganj near Dharamsala, India, in October of 2002.

I am on my way to Dharamsala to cover the tenth Mind and Life conference: a series of dialogues between eminent scientists and the Dalai Lama. It is a jolting overnight bus journey from Delhi. I am excited to be in the presence of the Dalai Lama and keen to witness the interaction between what appear to me to be the sciences of life and a science for living.

My thoughts are a jumble. My editor has agreed to this assignment because of the celebrity stir caused by Hollywood stars Richard Gere and Goldie Hawn walking the narrow streets of this hill town. But that is not my motivation. As a journalist, I have my, well, okay . . . "triple gems"—openness, awareness, and sharing. And in the darkened night, I think of these as being the qualities that drive both science and Buddhism, too—being open beyond beliefs and mindful of facts and experience.

I recall my conversation with my editor.

"Science and Buddhism? The Dalai Lama and scientists?"

I told him what I knew. That Mind and Life conferences are part of an ongoing process of dialogue between modern science and Buddhism initiated by a scientist (Francisco Varela) and a businessman (Adam Engle) in 1987, with active support from His Holiness.

"Why?"

Because Buddhism is, among other things, an ancient science of the mind. It has uncovered notions of reality that quantum physics is now slowly but surely arriving at. Because it also has a sophisticated science of ethics that can give geneticists and bio-engineers a perspective to resolve their dilemmas with. Because for the sake of our planet and ourselves, we must understand more about the interconnectedness that Buddhism talks about. Because a vocabulary is emerging, through interactions such as Mind and Life X, for the two to talk meaningfully to each other.

And because, as the Dalai Lama says, "with the ever-growing impact of science on our lives, religion and spirituality have a greater role to play reminding us of our humanity. . . ."

How this has happened is interesting. Science grows from a spirit of discovery; and I know that Buddhism, and certainly the Dalai Lama, have always been interested in leading explorations into the area beyond the circumference of doctrinal beliefs. I am particularly reminded of a public meeting some years ago, where I had been struck by the open attitude, and humbleness, of His Holiness. When asked about reincarnation, he had said: "In Buddhism, we believe in being open. For example, I now have flown in an airplane and have seen that there is no Mount Meru and that the earth is not flat. So I have proof that these are not true, even though they are believed in our scriptures. So far I believe in reincarnation because I have not seen proof that it isn't so."

As the rickety bus inches toward mist-cloaked McLeod Ganj, a tender dawn breaks out over the Dhauladhar Himalayas. Mind and Life X promises to be an engagement in openness and learning.

A cold morning. I race madly through the streets and bazaars of McLeod Ganj, Dharamsala, to reach it by "9 A.M. sharp," as the lama in charge had strictly warned me. Weaving through a crowd of little monks in training giggling at my haste, I arrive at the entrance to the "temple," the Dalai Lama's official residence. After a perfunctory security check, a tag bearing the legend MIND AND LIFE INSTITUTE, DHARAMSALA 2002 is placed around my neck with a smile. Multiple head silhouettes merge into a single, circular whole on the tag—an appropriate logo for the institute that has brought wonderful minds, scientific and Tibetan, at one table for the past 15 years.

A gong sounds. 9 A.M. All participants must gather.

Up the steep, double-helix-like winding graveled path to the Dalai Lama's residence, people walk in groups of twos and threes. I hear snatches of conversations peppered with terms like "dharma of gene expression," "cognition and consciousness," "physical reality/ ultimate reality" that convey a sense of a hybrid sciento-Buddhist idiom that the dialogue has bred. My guardian-angel lama materializes by my side and promptly introduces me to several participating scientists and the French monk Matthieu Ricard, who breaks off an animated discussion to say hello. Others' reactions are less enthusiastic, somewhat bordering on the frosty.

The issue is, as I gather, one of secrecy, which was apparently promised to scientists from the first conference onward. The Mind and Life conferences were to be semiprivate meetings, away from the media spotlight and, I imagine, the rest of the scientific community that might not take too kindly to its members hobnobbing with religion. A journalist's presence, therefore, is somewhat unwelcome.

Later, I discover that the one-sided celebrity gossip reports in Indian newspapers have also angered the scientists, who see it as a trivializing of the conference. They would rather have nothing to do with any journalist at this point, least of all an Indian one. A request is made to His Holiness, who, in his great compassion, lets me stay.

The meetings are being held in a large room overlooking the snow-covered Dhauladhars. Sunlight streams in from wide windows and warms the gleaming wooden floors. *Thangkas* depicting Buddhas past, present, and future line the walls. The participating scientists—Nobel laureate Steven Chu, physicists Michel Bitbol and Arthur Zajonc, biologist Ursula Goodenough, geneticist Eric Lander, and chemist Pier Luigi Luisi—sit in a semicircle in the middle of the room, with the Dalai Lama's seat in the center. The "observers" sit to his right, the monks to his left. The Dalai Lama himself would sit in the shadow of a gold Buddha, seated in *samadhi*, eyes half-closed in deep contemplation.

A young monk wearing trendy dark glasses walks in and takes his seat among the scientists somewhat self-consciously. I recognize the 17th Gyalwa Karmapa, Ogyen Trinley Dorje. In fact, of all the Mind and Life conferences, this one has the largest contingent of monks in attendance, who, I am told, are being taught Western science in their monasteries upon the Dalai Lama's encouragement. Tsoknyi Rinpoche, a gentle lama who has come from Nepal, explains that His Holiness is of the view that if Buddhism is to survive into the future, it must continue to change and adapt. In the present context, this means studying science and dialoguing with it.

So, is this a sort of a survival tactic, a Heimlich maneuver to remain relevant by a community struggling under the pressures of exile?

A sudden hush descends upon the gathering. A silence, and then . . . a belly laugh! His Holiness walks in, shaking hands all around. He takes his seat, with translators Geshe Thupten Jinpa and B. Alan Wallace by his side. Under the ever-watchful gaze of the golden Buddha, the conference begins.

In approximately ten sessions, morning and afternoon, spread over five days, the Mind and Life conference discusses "the nature of matter, the nature of life." Mornings are reserved for presentations by scientists about their respective fields, while in the afternoons the Dalai Lama presents related topics in Buddhism. The starting point is physicist Erwin Schrödinger's question, asked in 1943: "Can that which takes place inside a living organism be accounted for by physics and chemistry?" In many ways, this has been the perennial quest of science, to understand the mysterious nature of life and its equally enigmatic equation with matter.

In their presentations, Luigi Luisi and Ursula Goodenough talk about the origin of life on Earth and subsequent biological evolution. From very simple molecules increasingly complex phenomena emerge. Molecules become cells that form organisms, which have consciousness. So, a quality emerges that the original elements didn't have—consciousness. How does it arise? What is its nature?

His Holiness listens to the presentations with a great aliveness, and his occasional questions seem to arise from a place of knowing. As Matthieu Ricard, a veteran of several Mind and Life conferences, tells me over a doughnut during the midmorning coffee break: "I have noticed in this and previous meetings that the best brains in the world of science come here not really knowing what to expect. They are almost always pleasantly surprised to see the depth of Buddhist philosophical thought and how vast and complex it is. So a meaningful dialogue is built quickly, more than many of them expected in the first place. And His Holiness is always very eager to know and learn. The scientists discover that they can talk to him not as a beginner but even about the deepest issues, of ethics, of the natural world."

Quickly comprehending the essence of what is being said, I find that the Dalai Lama is able to look at it both from the scientist's point of view as well as that of his tradition and form the gentle bridges that enable one to reach out to the other. As the dialogue develops, there are several occasions to remember that one is in the presence of a fiercely modern mind that never quite lets go of its Buddhist perspective, often coming to rest in the middle ground between the two.

A delicate balance is in play. In the Dalai Lama's person, the Geluk lineage holder seems to exist in tandem with the adventurer who looks with wonderment at every new thing and thought. As he has often said: "I would have been an engineer if I had not been a monk!"

The group breaks up for the meals and coffee breaks that punctuate the conference day, but the discussions find a way of continuing. During car rides, at the guesthouse, while walking through the bustling lanes of McLeod Ganj at dusk, Mind and Life X constantly evolves through informal exchanges. Many scientists request private audiences after the day's proceedings end at five o'clock every evening to discuss issues further with the Dalai Lama.

Daniel Goleman, author and psychologist, who is attending his sixth successive Mind and Life conference, tells me that these tête-à-têtes often help break the ice. "Most scientists who come are not Buddhist practitioners, nor is it a requirement at all," he says, as the setting sun leaves its ochre imprint on the Dhauladhars. We are sitting in the veranda of the guesthouse where the scientists and observers are staying. "Some are quite skeptical, understandably so," he continues. "There are those who have not been as willing as we would like them to be to engage in dialogue. Some might think that they have to come here and teach the Dalai Lama their point of view, whereas actually this is a collaboration of different perspectives."

On the conference grapevine, however, I hear a marvelous story of a powerful, spiritual transformation. During a private audience with His Holiness during Mind and Life 2000, psychologist Paul Ekman suddenly felt himself full of heat. He said later that something happened in that moment that transformed him emotionally. Before that, he would have episodes of angry outbursts at least once a week. These completely stopped after the meeting. The tremendous insights he achieved during his conversation with His Holiness moved him enough to rewrite a considerable part of a book on emotions that he had been working on for 30 years.

How open can we really be? And how much a dialogue depends on this alone, I think as I trudge uphill in the swiftly gathering darkness.

The discussions in the conference turn to consciousness, as they often do in most Mind and Life dialogues. The Buddhist position on consciousness and its evolution is that . . . there is no evolution. In fact, there is no evolution not only for physical matter, but also for consciousness, which is seen as part of an endless continuum. His Holiness explains:

> Science talks of a big bang, formation of matter, appearance of life, and so on. But is this the full story? Is it all we have? In Buddhism, there is no concept of a beginning. It is impossible to accept that nothing becoming something. So the Buddhist perspective is of beginninglessness, of infinite big bangs, and not only of matter but of consciousness. "No beginning" might be difficult to imagine, but it is more logical, if you really think about it.

As this is hotly debated, I suddenly wonder how difficult it is for Buddhism and science to really converse at the same level, since they have in common neither paradigms nor basic assumptions. There are times in the conference when the dialogue seems to be going nowhere. When this happens, both the Dalai Lama and the scientists maintain their viewpoints, without one putting down the other. In that sense, there is no competitiveness, perhaps because of the privacy of the meetings that frees the scientists from their constituencies, and perhaps because there is an unspoken agreement not to hurt, to be gentle with one another. The Dalai Lama plays facilitator in those awkward moments, his laughter easing things along.

In times when tradition would dictate otherwise, the Dalai Lama has the rare quality to listen and be open to contrary views, modifying his own when sufficiently convinced. His is a dynamic mind that refuses to be dogmatic about anything, least of all his own tradition: very much in the spirit of the Buddha Shakyamuni, who instructed his followers never to accept anything, not even his own teachings, without adequate questioning and reasoning—only those that stood the test were to be applied, the others discarded, not unlike the research method of the contemporary scientist.

The bridges become visible again, spanning the turbulence of debate, riveted together by the search for truth, for reality, that is as much the Buddhist's as it is the scientist's.

The breakfast buzz before the morning session revolves around Steven Chu. "He is of Chinese origin," I am told, the remark laden with obvious political undertones. The Dalai Lama mentions this fact, but in passing, not as a political statement but to emphasize the need for greater participation of Asian scientists in Mind and Life conferences. That Dr. Chu is a Nobel laureate is also significant, and his presence is seen as being responsible for ratcheting up the conference's acceptability as a serious dialogue within the scientific community.

Dr. Chu presents the physicist's view of matter and life. He starts with outlining the quantum theory: that atoms are made up of electrons, protons, and neutrons, of which the last two can further be broken down into quarks. "Electrons and quarks are the most elementary particles," he says. "According to our current understanding of them, they have no size and are described as 'fields.'" He goes on to describe how the very act of observing the elementary particles changes their behavior.

The Dalai Lama is able to see subatomic particles and their behavior as an illustration of the Buddhist perception of reality. Says he:

> According to Madhyamika philosophy, there are two lev-
> els of reality—conventional and ultimate. At the ultimate level,
> nothing exists— it is *shunyata* (emptiness)— while at the conven-
> tional level what we perceive through our senses exists. But here,
> too, things cannot stand the test of deconstructive analysis and
> are proven not to exist intrinsically. Clinging to things obstructs
> the individual's ability to relate to the world openly, just as ob-
> serving the quarks changes their behavior. So Buddhism decon-
> structs the solidity of things we grasp at. In the end, everything
> we undergo has to do with human experience. And this is why
> ethics have to be part of research.

Ethics and science are further examined with Eric Lander's presentation about modern genetics and the choices it faced in the light of the Human Genome Project. The human control of genetic material, literally the matter of life, is forcing the making of certain choices. What should be the framework within which these are made? For instance, after unraveling the genome it is known that a particular disease—say, Alzheimer's—is caused by one particular gene. Would it, then, be all right to replace it? And if it was known that an embryo had genetic abnormalities, would it be okay to abort it?

Motivation is the key, says the Dalai Lama, aligning the karma of choosing with intentionality. A variety of factors must come into play, such as extent of suffering involved, motivation, the short- and long-term effects, and so on. Not once does he talk in absolutes and say something like, "I am a Buddhist, so all violence is bad," but insists on examining every question on an individual basis. "It is the motivation at the core of every choice that makes it ethical or unethical," he says. This gives scientists a point to ponder, since, as Arthur Zajonc points out, their research is often supported by companies whose "motives might not be pure but mixed."

Altruistic motivation must stem from compassion, the Dalai Lama's touchstone for any choice-making that needs to be done. No discussion in which he participates can be complete without a mention of compassion, the active loving-kindness for all sentient beings that arises from the Buddhist understanding of interdependence of life. This is a natural corollary to the theory of codependent origination, according to which everything exists because of everything else. There is no independent existence—we are all part of the gigantic web of life. Apart from its obvious implications for ecology and environmental-awareness movements, here, in the dialogue with science, compassion becomes the tool with which to make good choices. It recurs during Ursula Goodenough's presentation about intelligence and awareness.

"Is there a biological evolutionary basis for compassion? Where does it come from?" His Holiness asks her.

"Well, part of it is a question of survival. We are social beings because of that. There are examples in nature of empathy. For instance, when two chimps are fighting, an older chimp takes them by their hands and effects a reconciliation."

"Working together for survival is not really compassion," says His Holiness. "Honeybees don't know the Dharma, yet they work together beautifully. But these supposed examples among animals can only be of limited altruism, as they arise from necessity of some kind. Only human beings can develop infinite altruism because of their highly developed intelligence."

One is reminded of the bodhisattva's vow to defer nirvana, enlightenment, until he can help all sentient beings into it, and its centrality to the Dalai Lama's Mahayana Buddhism. Looking back at previous Mind and Life conferences, I find His Holiness often turning the conversation toward compassion and its place in human life—the practical never sacrificed for the theoretical and the abstract. For instance, in Mind and Life III, the Dalai Lama argued in favor of universal ethics based as much on compassion as on rationalism and individualism, overturning objections by participants who sought to link compassion with religion or deemed it an "unreliable" human trait. "If we look at history over all the millions of years that human beings have existed, I think there has been more construction than destruction. Ordinarily, when something destructive happens, we are shocked, because by nature we are compassionate," he said.

However, His Holiness is mindful enough of both the harsh reality of worldly suffering, as well as the possibility of transcending it, to point out that compassion is not necessarily a stand-alone, nor is it a sugarcoated medicine that will magically cure the world's ills. It needs to be coupled with wisdom and right action. Giving the simple example of making the choice between alleviating a person's hunger by feeding him once or finding him a livelihood, His Holiness says: "If you applied wisdom, you would think further: *How can I alter circumstances so that this person doesn't suffer in future?* Unless people make an effort to improve themselves, nothing can be done. It takes wisdom, not just sympathy, for people to move forward."

I coax my mind back to the interesting, if somewhat dense, presentations related to physical sciences that constitute most of Mind and Life X. I cannot help but feel that the dialogue is somewhat richer, more relevant to the behavioral sciences, where you deal with the human condition, and to ethics. This might be because there is a closer relation and much more commonality between the two. In fields of psychology and the neurosciences, for instance, Buddhist techniques are directly applicable, and so the dialogue is rendered more relevant.

It is the last day. Everyone gathers for the final session. There is much satisfaction about the levels of synergy that were achieved during the conference. Luigi Luisi says good-humoredly: "Earlier there was occasional flirting, but now it is a real marriage [between science and Buddhism]." But it is spoken too soon.

During his closing comments, Alan Wallace illustrates the need for provability of emergent phenomena by citing the example of reincarnation. "Of all religions, the Buddhist view is the only one that can be tested, since it involves a coming back into the world, unlike the Christian or Islamic views where the soul goes away into a hell or heaven, never to come back."

"Not so fast!" immediately interjects Eric Lander. *Reincarnation* seems to be the magic word that opens the doors of dissent in the conference. Barbed wires appear where there were bridges, and the room stands sharply divided. All scientists voice their denial strongly, while Wallace and Ricard try to argue the case for reincarnation, pleading for a lowering of "cultural resistance" to it.

"I remember a neuroscientist who once told me that he would believe in reincarnation if a yogi would direct his consciousness to a particular place and leave a letter giving the details of where he will reappear," says Alan. "And I told him that this has already happened 17 times, in the lineage of the Karmapas of Tibet, who leave detailed instructions about where and when they will be reborn!"

All this while, as the debate rages on, the Dalai Lama sits watchfully, listening quietly. He neither assents nor dissents. It reminds me of the Buddha's response of silence to the hairsplitting among scholars of his day over the issue of the existence or otherwise of God. Not wishing to get involved in any debate that was purely in the realm of conjecture and not directly connected with the practicalities of the human condition, the Buddha would simply become silent. As does His Holiness now.

Later, when the acrimony has settled and everybody is friends once again, he turns to the scientists and says: "I am an old man. If you promise there is no reincarnation, then I can relax. Else I will have to start the customary preparations for my next birth!" A belly laugh and a gentle bridge once again. No judgment, only quiet awareness.

As the day draws to a close, everyone lines up to receive the customary white silk *khatas* (scarves) as blessings from the Dalai Lama.

The bus curves on the serpentine hill roads, taking me farther and farther away from the pine-scented mountain air of Dharamsala. The editor comes into focus again, and I think that I did get the scoop, only rather than being about the Hollywood glamour, it is about synergy of the ancient and the modern, about gentle bridges and golden seeds, about frank dialogue and open minds. I marvel at the sustained effort that has kept the dialogue going for the past 15 years. And this despite the odds, the prejudices against all religion and spirituality that modern science harbors. I remember Daniel Goleman saying: "When we started 15 years ago, it was a rare scientist who would be open to a dialogue with the Dalai Lama, or anyone from any religion. It seemed not the thing a scientist should do. The level of scientists involved in the dialogue has gone up over the years. The scientific community has also started taking the dialogue much more seriously."

Gaps, fissures exist; but so do the golden seeds of shared wisdom, carefully sown and nurtured by His Holiness over the years. And the dialogue continues, with sincerity and commitment, mindfulness and sharing, over bridges past and present. . . .

15

THE DALAI LAMA AS A POLITICAL STRATEGIST

by Senthil Ram

"[A] young man who is much more intelligent and is better informed regarding world affairs than his advisors . . . [and who] is deeply conscious of the need for social and other reforms in Tibet."
— **Loy Henderson**, U.S. ambassador to India, about the young Dalai Lama in 1951

From Lhasa to Dharamsala, throughout the troubled times following the Chinese occupation of Tibet in 1950, the Dalai Lama's politics reflect the Buddhist notion of realistic understanding—in other words, pragmatism. Hence, in this essay I analyze the political philosophy of the Dalai Lama, who is revered by millions of Tibetans as "bodhisattva of compassion." While still he is at the height of his authority as the political and temporal leader of Tibetans, the appointment of Kalon Tripa—the Tibetan equivalent to prime minister—at least theoretically placed him on the backseat of the democratic vehicle of the Tibetan government in exile that is maneuvering toward a politically free Tibet.

Therefore, at this juncture, taking stock of the Dalai Lama's political contribution is crucial in order to comprehend the essence of Tibetan polity apart from visualizing its future course. Given the problematic in separating religion and politics, this essay proceeds with a modest objective to highlight the Dalai Lama's political role without undermining the influence of Tibetan Buddhism.

Background to the Tibetan Question

The 20th century has been a turning point in the Tibetan conflict, widely known as the "Tibetan question," that is rooted in unfathomable depths of centuries-old historical specifics, as claimed and constructed by both the main parties: the People's Republic of China (hereafter PRC) and the Tibetan government in exile (hereafter TGE). The British invasion and conquest of Tibet under Younghusband in 1903 and 1904 marked the beginning of the end of isolation of the kingdom of Tibet. The Qing dynasty in China, which had a representative in Tibet and treated Tibet as "politically subordinate," perceived this as an act of imperial aggression to its hegemony and attempted to increase its control over Tibet.

The sudden overthrow of the Qing in 1911 resulted in the proclamation of independence by the 13th Dalai Lama. During 1911 to 1951, Tibet functioned as a de facto independent nation and conducted all its local and international relations without interference from China or any other country. However, the Chinese claims on Tibet as part of its territory, the recognition of Chinese sovereignty over Tibet by the United States and United Kingdom, and the simultaneous refusal of these countries to recognize Tibetan independence had resulted in the invasion and occupation of Tibet by the Chinese Communists in October 1950.

Whether the Chinese intention was to liberate then occupy or occupy then liberate, Mao's "peaceful" strategy routed the poorly equipped Tibetan army of approximately 10,000 troops and forced the Tibetans to negotiate and relinquish their political sovereignty for the first time in Tibetan history. In return, the 17-point agreement promised to preserve the political and religious status of the Dalai Lama and not to introduce political and economic reforms until the Tibetans sought them. But the Chinese religious and economic reforms in eastern Tibet, and the consequent protests, slowly spread to central Tibet and created fear and mistrust among the Tibetans. As a result, both the Chinese and the 14th Dalai Lama could not honor the agreement.

Finally, after a major revolt in Lhasa, the Dalai Lama fled Tibet in March 1959, followed by an exodus of nearly 80,000 Tibetans, to India. There His Holiness established the TGE, denounced the 17-point agreement, and claimed Tibet's right to self-determination and independence. The PRC gave up the agreement as well and established a people's government in Tibet. Here lies the root of the disagreement over the issue of Tibet's political status vis-à-vis China. Over the years the conflict has become complex by encompassing various issues, including cultural survival, identity, governance, human rights, the environment, and development.

From exile, the Dalai Lama pursued various landmark reforms, on the one hand to democratize the Tibetan polity, and on the other to nonviolently handle the conflict with China. Although his democratization initiatives are constrained by practical considerations like "economic insecurity, traditional normative decorum, and lack of education," it is principally accepted as a method of polity due to his impartiality in dealing with various sects and regions and also the loyalty and affection of Tibetan people. Without costing any struggle or human life, the Tibetan democracy that originated from the ideas of the leader and came down to the masses is fittingly called the Dalai Lama's democracy or "one man's democracy." Importantly, his single democratic vision united the three diverse Tibetan regions of Ü-tsang, Kham, and Amdo and successfully prevented the conflict from reaching an overt level over the last more than 50 years.

Although nonviolence as a political tool of Tibetan policy sounds very natural given the nonviolence potential of Tibetans and the Buddhist tradition and culture, it should not be overemphasized. First, it is important not to overlook the violent potential of the Tibetan people. Like any other culture, Tibetans, too—although less prominently after Buddhism became the state religion in the 13th century—held on to weapons, waged wars, and maimed people for land and wealth. There were a lot of violent exceptions to the "noncoercive regime" of Tibet, particularly against foreign incursions, including the British invasion of 1904.

Tibetans bravely fought the advancing Chinese People's Liberation Army in 1950. Often monks, too, joined in the battles against the Chinese to regain territories and also fought with others belonging to different sects. The 1959 Lhasa uprising witnessed many monks carrying guns with the Khampas. Later, the Khampas used guerrilla tactics of "hit and run," with the clandestine support of the CIA, on and off until 1974.

Second, the political transformations to democracy in Buddhist countries did not take place in a nonviolent manner. For instance, in Thailand, Burma, and Sri Lanka, Buddhism was (and is) used to justify the violence of the nationalistic political activists. Therefore, at the political level, the Tibetan nonviolence is more chosen than inherent. What I want to stress is the deliberate choice of nonviolence becoming a political means with roots in Tibetan Buddhism during adversities, and the chief role of the Dalai Lama in contributing to a philosophical base called *middle path* with pragmatic political elements. Particularly from the 1980s, the middle-path policy of the Dalai Lama has formed the backbone of TGE's policies and became the driving force of the Tibetan nonviolent movement aimed to stop the Chinese population-transfer policy that threatened the ethnic composition in Tibet.

The Middle-Path Policy of the Dalai Lama

The middle path is not an end or a goal of the Tibetan movement. It is not a peace proposal, either. According to Thubten Samphel, *middle path* as conceived by the Dalai Lama is a method of conducting the struggle for freedom and justice for Tibetans. Thus, it does not represent or reflect the overall belief system of the Tibetans. Rather, it is a nonviolent technique advocated by the Dalai Lama, which can be crudely compared to the Gandhian *Satyagraha*.

The essence of the middle path is avoiding extremes. On the one side there is the necessity of not submitting to Communist Chinese policies that are against the survival of Tibetan culture and religion. The other side is the extreme measure of achieving a free Tibet at the cost of a vicious cycle of violence that might work against Tibetan culture and religion. Thus, taking a middle path is a moderate position that could guarantee the common minimum interests of all concerned parties. For Tibetans, it is the protection and preservation of Tibetan culture and religion; for the Chinese, it is the security and territorial integrity of the motherland; and for the neighbors and third parties, peace at their borders and peaceful international relations.

In essence, *middle path* becomes a pragmatic tool of policy to peacefully handle the conflict with China to achieve Tibetans' goal. The goal of the Tibetan struggle, according to the Dalai Lama, is to achieve a spiritual, religious, and cultural freedom conducive to Tibetans' performing their "universal responsibility" of preserving, maintaining, and disseminating the sublime cultural traditions of the unique inner sciences for the sake of the whole world in an autonomous political arrangement within the PRC.

Although the Tibetan conflict is defined by various researchers as "intractable nationalistic conflict," "ethno-nationalistic conflict," "nonviolent conflict," and an issue of "identity and autonomy," for the Dalai Lama it doesn't have any political motivation. The problem between Tibet and China, in his words, "is not the difference in ideology, social system, or issues resulting from clashes between tradition and modernity. Neither is it an issue of human rights violations, nor about a struggle based on ethnic claims. The root of the Tibetan issue lies in Tibet's long, separate history, its distinct and ancient culture, and its unique identity." Under his leadership, the Tibetan movement has a spiritual motivation to protect the religious tradition of Tibet that is rooted in compassion and nonviolence and facilitate the performance by Tibetans of their broader responsibilities to humanity.

Although sometimes on political platforms the Tibetans have highlighted the issue as a political problem, the current prime minister of the TGE reiterated the Dalai Lama's words:

The people of Tibet have inherited for centuries a responsibility to preserve, promote and disseminate a unique culture and spiritual traditions for the benefit of all sentient beings. To enable people of Tibet to fulfill these duties, we require a conducive social, political, economic and environmental situation. Human intelligence cannot awaken to its fullest extent in an atmosphere of oppression and terror. An uprooted cultural heritage cannot be properly preserved and promoted through replantation elsewhere. Therefore, political freedom is a means for Tibetans to fulfill their bounden duties.

Although for the Dalai Lama religious and political freedoms are inseparable and one can't exist without another, in the Tibetan nonviolent movement the religious freedom becomes central and the political freedom subsidiary. He firmly believed that an adequate political freedom would be the solution for the present Tibetan predicament. Therefore, the Dalai Lama proposed for autonomy arrangement within the PRC as a solution. He said:

> I do not seek independence for Tibet. I hope that negotiations can begin and that they will provide for genuine autonomy for the Tibetan people and the preservation and promotion of their cultural, religious and linguistic integrity, as well as their socioeconomic development. I sincerely believe that my "Middle Way Approach" will contribute to stability and unity of the People's Republic of China and secure the right for the Tibetan people to live in freedom, peace and dignity. (10 March 1999 statement)

The Dalai Lama has been advocating the political demand of a genuine autonomy informally from 1979, when Deng Xiaoping invited the Tibetans to discuss anything but independence, and formally from the 1989 Strasbourg Proposals, as a realistic proposition to settle the issue through negotiations. The Dalai Lama's "greater autonomy" proposal has been appreciated as reasonable by various parties to the conflict. Further, his proposal falls within the conflict-management processes recommended by conflict-resolution experts. Particularly when it comes to protracted social conflicts similar to Tibet that are about protecting unique cultural identity and seeking suitable form of governance, Edward Azar has suggested different forms of political structures within existing national setups. Ted Gurr and Deepa Khosla went one step further in suggesting autonomy as a realistic solution to the Tibet issue.

The most important constituent of a nonviolent movement is the precise and agreed-upon goals. Setting goals is not an easy task, as history has shown—from the Gandhian movement, which was caught between moderates and extremists in deciding its own route, to the recent democratic opposition in Serbia, which could not reach a decision in conducting the 2000 elections against Milošević until a few months before the date. Decision making over the goals often divided the house during difficult times. Similarly, in the Tibetan case, the nonestablishment line of thinking is in favor of a politically independent democratic Tibet. Their central argument is that even by giving up independence for nearly two decades, the TGE has failed miserably to convince the unwilling Chinese to work for a negotiation. Therefore, groups like Tibet Youth Congress (TYC) are against giving up Tibetan sovereignty and demand complete independence for the whole of ethnic Tibet encompassing the three traditional provinces of Ü-Tsang, Kham, and Amdo.

The root of this divisive stand lies more in the process of the decision making than the positions. Nonetheless, the TGE's stance, which is open for negotiation on the demand of autonomy, sounds—at least theoretically—practical, as it satisfies the basic needs of both Tibetans and Chinese without separation. For Tibetans, it guarantees the basic human rights, and rights to protect their unique cultural traditions. For the Chinese, it respects the territorial integrity and contributes to a stable and strong motherland. Thus, by addressing the national concerns of Tibetans and Chinese, this goal seems politically achievable.

Essentials of *Middle Path*

For Gandhian Satyagraha the basic precepts are: *truth, non-violence (ahimsa),* and *self-suffering.* For the Dalai Lama, the basic precepts of middle path are nonviolence and dialogue:

> . . . to live with less conflicts and bloodshed and in order to achieve this, it is important to follow nonviolence and to have dialogue . . . if our struggle through nonviolence with a compassionate feeling succeeds we will be creating a new way to solve problems and conflicts and thereby serve the interests of the entire humanity.

As is evident from his words, His Holiness believes that nonviolence and dialogue can be the only bases for peaceful conflict resolution. Over the years, both have occupied a central place in his middle-path policy. Dialogue, without a doubt, points to negotiations with the Chinese. Therefore, he conceived peace initiatives like the Five Point Peace Plan and Strasbourg Proposals to be the flexible ground for negotiations with the Chinese. Although the Dalai Lama did not explicitly say what he meant by nonviolence in the context of middle path, it essentially points to nonviolent action.

Dialogue is a central component of Tibetan Buddhism and, in turn, middle path. In the context of politics, he strongly advocated dialogue as a practical approach to solve the Tibet issue. He emphasized dialogue at two levels: (1) between the TGE and the PRC, and (2) between Tibetans and the Chinese people. He said:

> After a half a century of "liberation" the Tibetan issue is still very much alive and remains yet to be resolved. Obviously this situation is of no benefit to anyone, either to Tibet or to China. To continue along this path does nothing to alleviate the suffering of the Tibetan people, nor does it bring stability and unity to China or help in enhancing China's international image and standing. The only sensible and responsible way to address this problem is dialogue. There is no realistic alternative to it. (10 March 1999 statement)

Often he stressed the importance of dialogue in his speeches and statements. According to him, the distrust between Chinese and Tibetans could be overcome "only through face-to-face meetings and sincere dialogues." For his part, he said:

> I remain committed to the process of dialogue as the means to resolve the Tibetan problem. I do not seek independence for Tibet. I hope that negotiations can begin and that they will provide for genuine autonomy for the Tibetan people and the preservation and promotion of their cultural, religious and linguistic integrity, as well as their socioeconomic development.

In his March 10, 1996, statement, His Holiness also encouraged dialogue between Tibetans and Chinese so as to promote "a better understanding of our mutual concerns and interests." Thus, the Dalai Lama firmly believed that a lasting solution to the Tibet issue could be found through people-people contact between Tibetans and Chinese.

The Dalai Lama, the chief architect of Tibetan nonviolent politics, is a staunch follower of Mahatma Gandhi. His Holiness's endorsement of the Universal Declaration of Nonviolence, which states that "all forms of violence, especially war, are totally unacceptable as a means to settle disputes between and among nations, groups and persons" made him radical among other religious and political leaders. He strongly believed that nonviolent resistance is for the strong willed and the principled who refuse to rely on the warped illogic of stopping the enemy's bad violence with one's good violence.

The Dalai Lama said that it is shortsighted to believe that a lasting solution can be found through the use of force. He always expressed his firm conviction in following a nonviolent path. According to him, force and confrontation can only bring temporary gains. Therefore, the Dalai Lama encouraged nonviolent resistance inside Tibet.

Although he acknowledged that "Tibetan people expressing their deep sorrow through nonviolence is the correct way," he did not put in plain words the dynamics or the workings of Tibetan nonviolent resistance. This has made the holistic understanding of the ongoing Tibetan nonviolent movement hard to grasp, unlike Gandhian or Kingian movements. Therefore, here I am focusing on the lesser-known pragmatic elements of Tibetan nonviolence than the well-known Buddhist and Gandhian influences.

First, for the Dalai Lama, nonviolence is the most effective and appropriate method to resolve conflicts. He firmly believes in nonviolence as a political technique. He pointed out that "recent events such as the end of dictatorial regimes of Marcos in the Philippines and Pinochet in Chile, as well as the changes in Moscow and other countries, show quite clearly that the upheavals in the heart of the population were . . . the result of nonviolent action."

Further, he understood the importance of nonviolence for a friendly neighborhood. Since China and Tibet are always neighbors —past, present, and future—he argued that they must have a peaceful and harmonious relationship. Therefore, it is essential that the problems dividing them be resolved in a nonviolent way. Using violence in such situations leaves people with a lot of contempt and enmity for generations and thereby results in further violence. He gives the examples of protracted conflicts like Israel and Palestine and Bosnia, where violence was used to curtail violence.

Second, nonviolence is used in politics due to the understanding that the means of the struggle should not contradict its social goals or ends. Violence cannot be used to create a political system based on self-government and grassroots participation and bring about peace. Only through nonviolent methods can one attain nonviolent results. It is also important to note the connections between nonviolence and democracy as established by the Dalai Lama. Another crucial element of the pragmatic nonviolent approach is recognition that both parties have needs that must be resolved. Therefore, Tibetans have the dedication to pursue problem-solving negotiations as exemplified by peace initiatives like Five Point Peace Plan to achieve a solution equally beneficial to both Tibetans and Chinese.

Third, in the Tibetan situation, violence is not considered a realistic option against the Chinese and is seen as counterproductive to the Tibetans' objective. Even though nongovernmental organizations like the TYC advocate "violent means of struggle," the Dalai Lama strongly believes that nonviolence is the most effective method to deal with the Chinese under the present circumstances. The Dalai Lama also feels that a violent struggle against the militarily powerful China is an impossible task. He said, ". . . I ask the hotheads, let them visualize this: If we follow violent methods, a few hundred guns will not be effective. At least we need several thousand, at least a few thousand . . . around 100,000. Now from where will we get these weapons? Is there some country willing to supply us with them?"

In another place, the Dalai Lama reiterated that no one would give weapons to Tibetans, and even if a country were to provide weaponry, transferring it to Tibet would not be easy. "If half a million Tibetans took up arms against China, it would be suicidal." He believed that an armed uprising would be the best excuse for China to obliterate the Tibetans. Further, the dwindling Tibetan population definitely discourages the violent option and promotes nonviolence, as the latter could save a lot of lives.

Last, the Tibetan nonviolent position mobilized support from many corners, including the Chinese people. The Dalai Lama said, ". . . because of our nonviolent attitude, Chinese people both within China and abroad have already expressed sympathy and concern for our cause and as a result are openly demonstrating their support for Tibet's struggle for independence." He firmly believes that through nonviolence they can arrive at a solution that is mutually beneficial to the Chinese and Tibetans.

According to the Dalai Lama, the tremendous international support Tibetans enjoy, now more than ever, is due to the nonviolent character of the movement. The Dalai Lama often acknowledged the media's sympathy to the nonviolent movement and its importance to Tibet's cause. He believed that media interest in Tibet has attracted "people the world over . . . [to] the Tibetan cause." Therefore, the Dalai Lama attached "great importance to this interest . . . [and] the fact that our cause will gain recognition in this way will, I believe, inspire the Chinese government to show greater restraint in its dealings with the Tibetan people, and to take their needs into account."

Therefore, the Tibetan nonviolent struggle has indispensable pragmatic elements where nonviolence is realistically used as only one of several possible methods with which to respond to the conflict situation with China for a mutually beneficial settlement.

Strategy of the Tibetan Nonviolent Struggle

When the Dalai Lama visited India during 1956, he met many Gandhians and discussed the Tibetan situation. They advised that he return to Tibet and carry on the freedom struggle. The Dalai Lama said, "I did exactly that. But there were no results. So, finally in 1959, when there were no alternatives, I went into exile."

From exile, His Holiness tried to solve the issue through negotiation by initiating direct contacts with Beijing. The lack of progress in direct initiatives and the serious threat to Tibetan culture in the form of Chinese population-transfer policies compelled him to take the Tibetan nonviolent movement to a different level: internationalizing the Tibet issue, with the hope that it will pressure China to come down for a negotiation with Tibetans, without wavering from his chosen path of nonviolence and dialogue.

In his second Tibet Support Group conference address, in Germany in June 1996, the Dalai Lama clearly explained that the deadlock in the Chinese-Tibetan negotiations had compelled him to internationalize the Tibet issue. He said: "Because of this lack of response from the Chinese side, I was compelled to publicly announce my Five Point Peace Plan for Tibet. This was the result of lack of response from the Chinese side and thus there was no other alternative except to seek support from the international community."

Here the Dalai Lama emphasized the lack of response from the Chinese side for negotiation and lack of alternatives to deal with China as important reasons for internationalizing the Tibet issue. Since his immediate objective was a dialogue with the PRC to preserve Tibetan culture from the massive Chinese population-transfer policies, the Dalai Lama firmly believed that international moral, political, and economic pressure is the only feasible option the Tibetans are left with to find a timely solution. Therefore, he often publicly solicited "immediate international pressure [to] be exerted upon the Chinese government, with an aim to beginning significant negotiations as soon as possible."

Thus, having nonviolent action and dialogue as central components, the middle-path policy attempted to mobilize international pressure so as to compel the PRC to come down for a negotiated political settlement over Tibet. Pressure was exerted on China by making Tibet an issue in the international governments through introducing the agenda of various parliaments and passing resolutions and bills in favor of Tibet. This legislative effort—that is, taking Tibet into governmental forums, particularly legislative branches, to effect changes in government policies worldwide—has become the core strategy of internationalization.

This strategy has evolved from 1987 by encompassing four dimensions: (1) nonviolent resistance inside Tibet, (2) dialogue with the PRC, (3) constructive programs in exile to protect Tibetan culture and religion, and (4) internationalization and media mobilization of the Tibet issue.

While nonviolence resistance inside Tibet on the one hand conveyed Tibetan people's genuine grievances to the PRC and the outside world, the dialogue through peace initiatives has formed the basis for negotiation with Beijing. The Constructive Program of the TGE aimed to protect and promote Tibetan religion and culture and actualize a democratic free Tibet in exile. Last, the internationalization of the Tibet issue mobilizes international public, political, and media support to put pressure on China for a peaceful resolution through negotiations.

While scholars belonging to the realist or positivist school condemn the internationalization strategy, the second group of scholars, who are in line with political idealism and pluralism, appreciate the internationalization of the Tibet issue. Although both groups agree that Tibet is a strategic concern for China and the Tibetans' cultural survival is in peril, they offer quite different solutions. The realists recommended active third-party governmental (particularly U.S.) involvement in the reconciliation and the return of the Dalai Lama to protect the lives of Tibetans, without making any structural changes on Tibetan political position vis-à-vis China. Barring the international economic and social boycotts as recommendations to pressure China for negotiations, the idealists propose an active Tibetan nonviolent engagement with China to save the Tibetan people and culture from destruction.

However, both groups, in their obvious quest to handle the conflict in a way that can meet both parties' needs, have missed the crucial element of resolving asymmetrical conflicts—that is, balancing the power relationship between the TGE and PRC for a long-term, sustainable peace. Their ideas highlight the efficacy of nonviolent action and third-party involvement as crucial factors to alter the power balance and impact a peaceful change in the Chinese-Tibetan sociopolitical relationship. Theoretically, these two activities contribute a great deal in managing any asymmetrical conflict: nonviolent actions will raise the conflict to overt levels, and third-party support can help balance the power relationship of parties. Fittingly, these two elements form the core of the Dalai Lama's middle-path policy. Therefore, *middle path* is more than a religious or moral principle. It is political and practical as well.

Although this four-dimensional strategy has not brought the PRC to the negotiating table, when considering the political success of garnering international support and solidarity and the costs involved, it can be said that this nonviolent political strategy has achieved more than some of the contemporary violent conflicts in Asia. Particularly, it is successful so far in forestalling the conflict's taking a violent turn in the "roof of the world," as Tibet is known. Undoubtedly, violence in Tibet will kick-start a spiral of violence exacting immense human and material costs to all the parties, when considering the enduring resistance in Tibet and other ethnic-minority nationalities within the PRC. Violence in Tibet in the globalized context will also affect the present status quo of the conflict and provoke intervention at the regional level, particularly from India, where nearly 80,000 Tibetan refugees live; and at the international level, mainly from United States, where the Tibetan lobby is very active.

Nonetheless, the asymmetrical conflict situation, which is knotted in the unbalanced social and political relationship between the powerful PRC and the powerless TGE, poses tremendous challenges to conflict resolution. Since the structure helps the dominant and powerful win and the minority or the powerless lose, the conflict can be resolved only by changing the structure through raising the conflict to manifest level. Nonviolent actions through polarization are the only effective method to do so and effect a peaceful transformation. Although the Tibetan nonviolent actions are so far unsuccessful in removing the existing latent violence in Tibet and have kept the conflict at the latent level—with minor exceptions like the protests of 1959, 1987, and 1989—it is the only key to increase the conflict to manifest level, bring in structural changes, prevent future violence in Tibet, and transform the Tibetan conflict toward a peaceful settlement.

Conclusion

The purpose of this essay is not to challenge or deconstruct the Dalai Lama, who shares the Gandhian view on the inseparable nature of religion and politics. Rather, it is a humble attempt to highlight the realistic aspects of his politics that are driven by the Buddhist spiritual values. This critical analysis of the Dalai Lama's middle-path policy is of importance to the ongoing nonviolent movement and evolving democratic politics.

On the other hand, the Tibetan case offers a new nonviolent way of conflict handling that can be tailored to meet similar or different situations against dictatorship or authoritarian governments to provide an effective alternative to violent means. Thus, following the traditions set by peace philosophers like Tolstoy, Gandhi, and King, the Dalai Lama, too, has challenged Machiavellian notions of violence and advocated and worked for improving the peaceful conditions of the world.

Although he is utopian in his desire to break conventions for idealized politics, he is also pragmatic, since he actualized his vision in "this world" by peacefully handling the conflict with China and democratizing the Tibetan polity. His policies show his penchant for optimism—he drew inspiration from hopes rather than traumas and developed alternatives rather than assumptions. His Holiness's handling of the Tibetan issue and revolutionizing of Tibetan politics clearly reflects his motivation to improve the system as a whole where Tibetans, the Chinese, and their neighbors benefit together. Hence, his political philosophy, particularly middle-path policy—rooted in Buddhism, Gandhian *Satyagraha,* and realistic understanding of international politics—becomes sound material for peace research.

16

His Holiness the 14th Dalai Lama: A Monarch or a Socialist

by Ela Gandhi

Since his exile at the tender age of 24, His Holiness has been trying to negotiate a peaceful settlement with China. He continues to struggle for his country and his people on the Gandhian path of nonviolent resistance, bearing all suffering while continuing to love and pray for his adversaries, that someday they may see light. India, a leading member of the nonaligned movement, gave asylum to His Holiness. But in addition, the country also gave a place for the thousands of Tibetan exiles who have now built a Tibetan village in exile at Dharamsala.

The Western bloc has in many ways supported the struggle for freedom of the Tibetan people. How much of the support is for the Tibetan cause and how much of it is against the last post of the Communist world is a moot point. His Holiness is as yet breaking ground in getting the support of the developing world. The introduction of the debate on the Tibet issue has been outvoted at the United Nations.

This lack of support from the emerging nations of the world raises the issue of the dilemma that has been created by the historical roots of systems of monarchical governance, which have been overthrown through popular revolutions in many parts of the world. Did Tibet also have a monarchical rule by a person who is believed to be the reincarnation of the Buddha?

The idea of reincarnation of the Buddha is not acceptable to modern scientists, to populist culture, to nonbelievers, and to those who do not subscribe to reincarnation. Such people would, therefore, feel that this is just another cult—another exploitative regime—and would have no sympathy with the people.

By no means are the opponents of the Dalai Lama a homogeneous group. By the same token, by no means are those who support the struggle of the Tibetans a homogeneous group. The supporters of the Tibetan cause range from Chinese scholars to ordinary Chinese workers, from people belonging to the leftist movements in various countries to those belonging to the ultra-Right. Within these diverse groups lie various motivations for supporting this struggle, as also for not doing so.

While there are vast numbers of people who are highly concerned about the blatant human rights abuses and feel deeply the repression suffered by the people of Tibet, there are, too, those who are driven by their own motives. These could range from preserving capitalism to preserving some narrow self-interest, to a much wider interest in maintaining a hold over a strategic position. The whole globalization and antiglobalization movements have revealed to us one truth: that such self-interests have very strong links, and although driven by a small group, they often wield power in many ways.

We live in a modern world, a world that has become a neighborhood, yet a world divided in terms of diversities of many kinds: religious differences, ideological differences, wealth and poverty, black and white and a million shades in between, rural and urban, modern and traditional . . . the list can go on. But instead of enriching the world with the vast mosaic of this diversity, man is killing man, nations are killing nations, and in the midst of all this there are millions who desire peace. They are desperately seeking peace. His Holiness is among the leaders who are trying desperately to alter the course humankind has set for itself. Will he succeed?

Tracing the history of China, one sees the overthrow of the oppressive monastic feudal-type social order in China, replaced by a socialist movement. The merits and demerits of this movement are not the subject of this essay, and so suffice it to say that a popular movement deposed the wealthy barons of China.

The story is that the peasants in China rose up under the guidance of successive socialist leaders and eventually deposed the Chinese empire under the leadership of Mao Tse-tung. The empire was replaced by the People's Republic. A new social order was established. The story goes on to maintain that for the first time the poverty-stricken and oppressed peasants were able to live with self-respect. On the whole, therefore, the story is that the stark poverty that confronted millions of Chinese had come to an end.

Yet history records that time and again those who faced repression of the most terrible kind have little compunction in repressing other people. How this happens is difficult to fathom. But there are millions of examples throughout the ages of people who continue to repress, and forget their own oppression at the hands of others. So the Chinese did not hesitate to conquer Tibet. Ostensibly, they were bringing a better life for the Tibetan people, who, they argue, were living under a feudal system. They were bringing a new socialist, Communist order to replace the feudal system that the people of Tibet were living under. In reality, they wanted occupation of Tibet. His Holiness recognizes this but has never condemned the Chinese. Therein lies his magnanimity and humility.

When one begins to read the many books written on him, the story of his life, and the story of his people, a picture emerges of a visionary, a compassionate spirit, and a totally liberated soul. He said in his book *Essential Teachings,* for instance, "Look around us at this world that we call 'civilized' and that for more than 2,000 years has searched to obtain happiness and avoid suffering by false means: trickery, corruption, hate, abuse of power, and exploitation of others."

His Holiness is a simple smiling monk who is not affected by the inhumanity of the Chinese aggression. One sees the deep pain and hurt when he talks about the destruction of his beloved land, the deaths of almost a million of his people, and the continued imprisonment and torture of hundreds of Tibetans. His concern, nevertheless, is not based on narrow self-interest or just the interests of his people, but for him the world and the universe are issues of concern.

The pollution of the pure mountain water; the degradation of the environment through the clearing of indigenous forests; the flattening of mountains by dynamiting; and the killing, torture, and incarceration—all these have an effect not only on him and his people, he constantly reminds us, but also on the world's ecosystem. Although his ever-smiling face and jovial nature may hide the pain and deep hurt of this continued destruction, there are times when one can see the deep-set lines of his face crying out for help, crying out to the world to heed the warnings of nature.

For some, he is but a monk; to others, he is a head of a feudal society; and for many, he is a unique personality who could indeed be a reincarnation of the Buddha, although he himself dismisses this possibility. In this chapter I want to dispel the myth of him as a feudal lord. He has said in *Essential Teachings,* "If in India, Africa, and other countries misery and famine rule, it is not because natural resources are lacking, nor that the means of bringing about lasting well-being are flawed. It is because each person has looked only for his own profit without fear of oppressing others for selfish goals. . . ."

His Holiness, with the kind of power he wields, chose to use his power to begin a process of reform of his order. In 1963, he shed his power in favor of democracy. One person, one vote was introduced. A democratic parliament was elected in exile. The Tibetan people at his instigation drafted a constitution that reflects democratic principles. He declared that once Tibet is free, an interim government would be set up with the specific purpose of establishing a constitutional assembly to draft a new constitution. He has further declared that after accomplishing this task, he will retire and live as an ordinary monk, transferring all his power to the newly elected government.

His five-point plan is as follows:

1. Transformation of the whole of Tibet into a zone of peace

2. Abandonment of China's population-transfer policy, which threatens the very existence of the Tibetan people

3. Respect for the Tibetan people's fundamental human rights and democratic freedoms

4. Restoration of Tibet's natural environment and the abandonment of China's use of Tibet for the production of nuclear weapons and dumping of nuclear waste

5. Commencement of earnest negotiations on the future status of Tibet and of relations between the Tibetan and Chinese people

He has recently added the stoppage of the oil-and-mineral-wealth excavations.

This plan reflects the reasonable nature of his offer to bring an end to this long and brutal aggression against his people. He is in fact extending a hand of friendship to the Chinese, whom he refers to as his brothers and sisters. He recognizes that they share a common religion, have a common history, and are neighbors dependent on each other. Many Chinese deeply admire and feel great reverence toward His Holiness. Despite the repression suffered by his people, he believes that the two nations can live in peace as neighbors.

In his writings, His Holiness advocates compassion, sharing simplicity, living close to the earth, conserving the environment, and leading a wholesome life. While retaining his traditional beliefs, he has a deep understanding of the modern age. Like Mahatma Gandhi, His Holiness advocates adhering to good traditional values and discarding those customs and traditions that are oppressive and inhibit development.

In his book *The Art of Happiness,* His Holiness says of human beings:

Generally speaking, you can have two different types of individuals. On the one hand, you can have a wealthy, successful person, surrounded by relatives and so on. If that person's source of dignity and sense of worth is only material, then so long as his fortune remains, maybe that person can sustain a sense of security. But the moment the fortune wanes, the person will suffer because there is no other refuge. On the other hand, you can have another person enjoying similar economic status and financial success, but at the same time, that person is warm and affectionate and has a feeling of compassion. Because that person has another source of worth, another source that gives him or her a sense of dignity, another anchor, there is less chance of that person's becoming depressed if his or her fortune happens to disappear. Through this type of reasoning you can see the very practical value of human warmth and affection in developing an inner sense of worth.

His Holiness clearly sees modern materialism as a source of destruction. He has said that real happiness comes from within, from satisfaction and reconciliation with yourself, and not by acquiring material objects. Clearly he expounds socialist and not feudal ideals, and it must be remembered that despite belonging to a traditional society, His Holiness has spoken about the rights of women, something that the Tibetan constitution upholds.

Moves are being made to involve women at all levels of society and to accord them equal status. Tibetan women play a prominent role in international women's organizations and locally within Tibetan society. They are also taking leadership positions in the liberation movement, and many have been imprisoned for their participation in the struggle.

Yet in trying to come to terms with why the Chinese have occupied Tibet, why some people support the struggle of the Tibetans and others do not, and what is that which draws people to His Holiness even as people were drawn to Mahatma Gandhi, one needs to develop a deeper understanding of Buddhism.

His Holiness is an excellent scholar of Buddhist philosophy, and in his works he explains in simple terms the very essence of the philosophy. It is when we begin to understand this philosophy that we get a glimpse into a mind that is so sharp and yet full of compassion, that is so concerned about the future and yet content in the present, that is so active and yet still. Such a being can never fit the cloak of a monarch. His ideas are socialist in nature, and his life and work will live on to inspire generations to come.

17

THE DALAI LAMA
AND INDIA

by Dalip Mehta

For the past 50 years, India has had the great good fortune of the Dalai Lama's presence on its soil. The nation has long enjoyed renown as a land where great spiritual leaders flourished, a land where persecuted people found refuge and eventually made their home, adding one more piece to the rich mosaic that is India's pluralistic, multicultural society. The arrival of the Dalai Lama in March 1959, followed by thousands of his people, provided welcome proof that these cherished traditions were still alive.

The Dalai Lama came to India at the young age of 24. In his own country he was revered as a god-king, but little known outside it. During his long years of exile in India, he has grown into one of the world's most beloved and respected leaders. Equally remarkably, he has succeeded in keeping alive the aspirations and hopes of the Tibetan people and in preserving Tibet's unique culture. He has achieved the delicate task of adhering to his principles and at the same time not jeopardizing the interests of his adopted homeland. And he has ensured that the Tibetan diaspora—not just in India, but elsewhere in the world—has developed and progressed in the modern world, even while remaining rooted in their traditions. In his quest for "freedom in exile" in India, the Dalai Lama has perhaps achieved far more than he would have if destiny had not forced him to flee Tibet.

China's invasion and occupation of Tibet in 1950, and its brutal suppression of the Tibetan national uprising in Lhasa in 1959, finally persuaded the Dalai Lama to seek political asylum in India. In the turbulent years that followed, the Chinese systematically destroyed Tibet's culture and civilization in the hopes that it would become just another indistinguishable region of the People's Republic, losing its distinct and separate identity.

Differing views exist on the legal status of Tibet, but it has been convincingly argued—by the Dalai Lama, among others—that throughout its history Tibet has remained an independent country and that it was never a part of any other, although like many, it had been subjected to invasions and had in turn occupied territories that belonged to other countries. It, therefore, came as a bitter disappointment to the Tibetans when in 1954 India signed an agreement with the People's Republic that recognized Tibet as a part of China. In so doing, India, in a sense, changed the political and historical identity of Tibet. By describing Tibet as the "Tibet region of China" in an official agreement, Chinese sovereignty over Tibet was given legitimacy.

Nevertheless, the Dalai Lama's request for asylum was immediately granted by Prime Minister Jawaharlal Nehru's government, which received him with honor when he arrived in India at the end of March 1959, and it is in India that he has continued to live ever since, inspiring his people both inside and outside Tibet, and keeping their spirit of freedom alive. Nehru's decision was indeed a courageous one, for he fully realized that the already difficult relations with China would be further complicated at a time when he believed that friendship between India and China was essential for peace in Asia. While granting asylum to the Dalai Lama was not the sole reason for the souring relations between the two countries, it has continued to be a source of friction over the years and something for which the Chinese have never forgiven India.

The Dalai Lama left his homeland with the greatest reluctance and amid much debate among his advisors, for it was not an easy decision to leave behind his six million compatriots, who regarded him as their god and king—and in their difficult times, their savior and only hope. However, it was the Dalai Lama's belief that he could do more for his people and country from the freedom that he would enjoy in India than under the suffocating constraints placed on him by the Chinese in Lhasa that finally persuaded him to leave his country.

At the age of 24, the Dalai Lama found himself far removed from the cloistered, medieval world he left behind in Tibet and thrust into the hurly-burly of the complex relations between nations at the highest levels, where the players were towering personalities like Nehru, Mao Tse-tung, Chou En-lai, among others. In this world, the inexperienced Dalai Lama sought to achieve his twin goals of independence for Tibet and the preservation and continuance of his country's religious and cultural traditions. He realized early in his political career that violence and force could never defeat the might of the Chinese. He learned from Mahatma Gandhi, whom he greatly admired, that nonviolence is the only way to conduct politics, and far from being a passive response, it was one of great moral courage and far more effective than the use of force.

Soon after arriving in India, the Dalai Lama established his government in exile, and although never formally recognized by the Indian government, it has throughout been allowed to function unimpeded. As the Dalai Lama himself has said, often the Indian government vehemently opposed his point of view but never did anything to prevent him from holding it, much less from expressing it. There was no interference from Delhi over how he and the Tibetans conducted their lives. As Nehru told him, India was a free country, so he had "complete freedom to follow his own conscience." Today the Dalai Lama's government, known as the Central Tibetan Administration, functions for all purposes as a body that guides the destiny of the more than 100,000 Tibetan diaspora scattered in a dozen countries.

Over the years the Dalai Lama has interacted with every prime minister of independent India. Relations with some have been close; with others, formal though correct. Yet without exception they have all held him in high regard. The Dalai Lama recalls with special warmth his association with such Indian political figures as Rajagopalachari, Rajendra Prasad, Jaya Prakash Narayan, Acharya Kripalani, among others. He regarded Lal Bahadur Shastri as an outstanding leader who had left a powerful impression on him. His relations with Nehru, often complicated by differing political compulsions, sometimes led to frustration and disappointment, but did not detract from his admiration of a man of great humanity, liberalism, and magnanimity. He also enjoyed a close personal rapport with Indira Gandhi, who often confided in him, even regarding matters of state.

In all his dealings with the Indian leadership, the Dalai Lama has always kept India's sensitivities and national interests in mind, even while pursuing his own objectives, and has unfailingly expressed his immense appreciation for the warmth and hospitality he has received from the Indian people and government. It was in his early interactions with Nehru that the Dalai Lama had his first experience of the harsh world of realpolitik, where moral and ethical considerations often had to bend to the more pragmatic imperatives such as national security.

While he greatly appreciated Nehru's humanism and his genuine concern for the welfare of the Tibetan people, the Dalai Lama realized that for Nehru, relations with China had higher priority. Yet the Dalai Lama has never forgotten that it was Nehru who took the crucial and in a sense lifesaving decision to grant him asylum in India, fully sensitive to its consequences, and to accommodate the more than 80,000 Tibetan refugees who crossed over into India.

Over the years the Dalai Lama has made various overtures to the Chinese leadership in the hopes of securing his country's legitimate interests within parameters he thought realistic and acceptable to the Chinese. For example, in his address to the U.S. Congress in September 1987, he outlined his Five Point Peace Plan, which he continues to believe could be the basis for a permanent solution to the Tibetan question. It calls for making Tibet a zone of peace and nonviolence, the abandonment of population transfers that are changing the demographic character of Tibet, respect for the Tibetan people's fundamental human rights and democratic freedoms, the protection of Tibet's environment, putting a stop to using Tibet for all nuclear activities, and, finally, the commencement of earnest negotiations on the future status of Tibet and the relations between the Tibetan and Chinese peoples. All reasonable suggestions, but to which the Chinese have reacted by accusing the Dalai Lama of attempting to split the country.

Chinese intransigence led to a complete breakdown of contacts for a decade, until the visit of the Dalai Lama's envoys to Beijing in September 2002. From the Tibetan point of view, the visit served to explain to the Chinese leadership what has since come to be known as the Dalai Lama's Middle Way Approach, which in essence calls for Tibetan self-rule within the People's Republic of China. The Dalai Lama has drawn a distinction between freedom and independence, for with his characteristic pragmatism, he realizes that complete independence is no longer feasible.

According to the Middle Way Approach, China would control Tibet's foreign and defense policies; while internal administration, culture, religious affairs, and the economy would be left to the Tibetans. In other words, the Dalai Lama no longer calls for the independence and separation of Tibet from China, but his Middle Way Approach does provide for genuine autonomy for the entire Tibetan region and its six million people, to enable them to preserve their distinctive culture, religion, and way of life.

In his annual March 10 statement in 2003, the Dalai Lama spoke of the necessity for dialogue as the "only sensible, intelligent and human way to resolve differences" and to put behind "decades of bitterness, distrust and resentment and to form a new relationship based on equality, friendship and mutual benefit." As he pointed out, "looking around the world we cannot fail to notice how unattended conflicts with ethnic roots can erupt in ways that make them extremely difficult to solve."

He hopes that China's new leadership will take a more humane and accommodating view of Tibet's aspirations as embodied in the Middle Way Approach. China, however, remains inscrutable. There are those who believe that China is merely biding its time and willing to wait until the present Dalai Lama passes away so that they can then install a successor of their choice who will do their bidding.

The Dalai Lama has been extraordinarily successful in arousing the conscience of the world to the plight of his people and country. The Tibetan question is very much on the world's agenda, although governments still balk at outright support. Nongovernmental organizations espousing Tibet's cause have mushroomed, such as the International Campaign for Tibet, which seeks to influence various governments' policies to support the "legitimate aspirations of the Tibetan people."

The Dalai Lama's quiet, sustained effort, without polemics or provocation, has won the Tibetans friends and supporters around the world. His indefatigable energy has taken him to countries across the globe, patiently explaining, seeking understanding and support for his cause, without the slightest trace of rancor or recrimination. His peaceful and nonviolent approach in trying to resolve even this most intractable problem won him the Nobel Peace Prize in 1989, which also symbolized international recognition for all the profound spiritual values he stands for. The Nobel Committee said, "The Dalai Lama has developed his philosophy of peace from a great reverence for all things living and upon the concept of universal responsibility embracing all mankind as well as nature."

The Dalai Lama has often said that his ideas about "universal responsibility" have evolved from ancient Indian traditions, and that as he is a Buddhist monk, his entire training has its roots in the culture of India. For him India is in many ways his spiritual home. As he points out, Buddhism went to Tibet from India, along with many other important cultural influences. He has even gone to the extent of saying that in his opinion India had a better claim to Tibet than China, "whose influence at best was only slight." The Dalai Lama has likened the relationship between India and Tibet to that between a teacher and a pupil.

Fundamental to the Dalai Lama's political philosophy is the belief that love, compassion, and forgiveness can lead to peaceful change, and that a nonviolent revolution, which may seem unrealistic to some, is indeed possible. He is aware that many Tibetans feel that the time has come to resort to more militant ways to deal with the Chinese. The Dalai Lama has, however, been steadfast in his belief in *ahimsa,* and has said that if the movement for freedom turns violent, he would abdicate.

Exile in India has provided the Dalai Lama with the opportunity to overhaul and modernize various archaic Tibetan practices and institutions, in a manner both pragmatic and farsighted. The rigors of protocol surrounding his person have been reduced and simplified, making him more accessible to his people. The age-old theocracy has been transformed into a functioning democracy with, most remarkably, the Dalai Lama voluntarily abdicating his temporal powers to institutions that now determine the destiny of the Tibetan people, to the extent that the elected assembly, by a two-thirds majority vote, can remove the Dalai Lama from office.

This indeed was revolutionary and unprecedented at the time of its enactment in the early '60s. The Dalai Lama has since stated that when Tibet eventually regains its freedom, he would have no political or administrative role in the government, as without such responsibilities, he would be better placed to serve his people as an elder statesman, who when called upon would advise and assist. It is his firm belief that if Tibet is to survive in the modern world it must reflect the collective will of its people rather than just that of an individual.

Today the Tibetan government in exile functions from Dharamsala and has all the necessary departments to run its affairs. The executive is headed by a council of ministers, elected by and responsible to the assembly. An independent judiciary exists. The constitution, known as the Charter of the Tibetans in Exile, adopted in 1991, adheres closely to the Universal Declaration of Human Rights and provides all Tibetans equality before the law and the enjoyment of rights and freedoms without discrimination on the basis of sex, religion, race, language, or social origin.

Throughout his many years in exile, an abiding concern of the Dalai Lama has been the welfare and rehabilitation of the refugees from Tibet. Apart from the obvious humanitarian aspect, the Dalai Lama has all along believed that the only way to preserve Tibet's culture, religion, and way of life is by building strong and vibrant communities abroad. With the support and assistance of the Indian government, the refugees have been resettled in several centers around the country, where they have been able to reorganize their lives and preserve and continue their traditions.

Today Tibetan civilization remains alive in India, having been largely destroyed on its own soil. The initiatives taken by Pandit Nehru and followed by successive governments in Delhi have produced a multitude of schemes for the rehabilitation of the refugees. In a typical manifestation of his enlightened and liberal approach, Nehru had said that in order to preserve Tibetan culture, it would be necessary to have separate schools for the refugees, and for this purpose he created the independent Society for Tibetan Education within the Indian Ministry of Education. Nehru also advised that while Tibetan children should have a thorough knowledge of their own history and culture, it was vital that they should be fully familiar with the ways of the modern world, and for this it was essential to know English and to use it as the medium of instruction, as it is the international language of the future. This advice, well taken, has helped the scattered Tibetan community make its presence felt internationally, far out of proportion to its small size.

Agriculture, carpet weaving, the manufacture of garments, the food-and-restaurant business, and the service sector have been the mainstays of the 85,000-strong Tibetan community in India. Another 20,000 or so Tibetans live in other countries around the world. Today there exist over 80 schools, with close to 30,000 students, in India and Nepal, 54 settlements and welfare offices, and a dozen missions in various countries; apart from cultural institutes, libraries, archives, publishing houses, and charitable trusts. Religious establishments include more than 200 monasteries and nunneries, with around 20,000 residents, representing all the sects of Tibetan Buddhism. Tibet's rich and unique arts and crafts, as well as its medical and philosophical traditions, are alive and flourishing.

Last but not the least is the Foundation for Universal Responsibility, established by the Dalai Lama from the money he received with the Nobel Prize. According to its charter, it seeks to benefit people everywhere, regardless of nationality, race, or creed; to cultivate the common ground between different faiths; and to assist nonviolent methods, foster communication between science and religion, and secure human rights and democratic freedoms. The Foundation recognizes the interdependence not only of nations and communities but of all living things, and in fact represents the Dalai Lama's moral and political thinking in action.

Among the programs the Foundation currently supports are those of Women in Security, Conflict Management and Peace (WISCOMP)—which has done courageous work among the victims of militant violence in Kashmir and has awarded scholarships to enhance the professional efficacy of Asian women in international relations—and projects for environmental regeneration. Other programs run by the Foundation enable students to spend time in Tibetan monasteries and religious leaders to visit the places of worship of one another's faiths.

The Dalai Lama believes that people all over the world are basically the same; they seek happiness and the avoidance of suffering. Suffering is caused by ignorance, selfishness, and greed. True happiness comes from a sense of peace and contentment—which, in turn, is achieved through compassion, empathy, and love; and by the elimination of anger, hatred, and greed. The problems that the world faces today are all human-made: violent conflicts, poverty, hunger, and the destruction of the environment, among many others. They can all be resolved by human effort, understanding, and the development of a universal brotherhood. The Dalai Lama has spoken out time and again against religious intolerance, which inevitably sows mistrust and divides communities.

The Dalai Lama embodies the very qualities that he preaches: love, compassion, and goodness; forgiveness and charity; and universal responsibility. His teachings are simple and lucid; devoid of jargon and metaphysical tangles; and communicated with directness, charm, and an unfailing sense of humor. His joie de vivre and sense of fun, as well as his easy manner of delivery, immediately establish a close personal rapport with all those who come to hear him speak or are fortunate enough to meet him.

He is completely free of pomposity and is a person of true humility. I recall an occasion when the Dalai Lama called on Indian president Venkataraman on the eve of a trip abroad to seek his advice on how he should respond to various issues that could be raised. "Who am I, a mere mortal," replied the president, "to advise a god incarnate on earth!" The Dalai Lama's response, after a moment of complete surprise, was to break into a loud, infectious laughter.

When once asked how he wished to be remembered for posterity, the Dalai Lama replied: "Just as a human being; perhaps as a human being who often smiles." That remark sums up the essence of the Dalai Lama's personality: deep wisdom, deep love and compassion, deep humility.

18

THE DALAI LAMA AND THE TIBETAN MONASTIC ACADEMIA

by Thupten Jinpa

Once in the early '60s, His Holiness the Dalai Lama paid a brief visit to the Tibetan refugee community in Dalhousie, formerly a summer retreat for the officers of the British imperial Raj, located in the hills of what is today the state of Himachal Pradesh in northern India. Part of the community was a small group of monks from Sera, Drepung, and Ganden—the three great monastic universities of Tibet, known for their tradition of logic and philosophical scholarship. A few hours after his arrival, so the story goes, His Holiness convened a session of debate.

As all the scholars gathered inside the hall, the Dalai Lama sat down comfortably, prepared for a long session of intellectual feast. He selected two monks at random and asked one to sit down to defend and the other, who was standing, to open a debate. Unfortunately, the two selected turned out not to be the best of the scholars in the group. Nevertheless, they began their debate. Quite soon it became obvious that they were at their wit's end. As the exchanges between the debaters progressed, the two monks' eastern Tibetan dialect became heavier and heavier, and soon no one could understand what was being said. Needless to say, the

Dalai Lama politely asked them to stop and called for two other monks to take their place.

This is a well-known anecdote among the scholars of the Tibetan monastic colleges, now reestablished in India. The story, although amusing, tells us the depth of the Dalai Lama's passion for Tibet's thousand-year-old intellectual tradition of logic and philosophical debates. It also serves as a warning to the students in the monastic colleges, for the story reminds us that anyone could easily be in a situation similar to that of those two monks when His Holiness visits the monastic universities.

I first had the privilege to participate in a debate in the presence of His Holiness in 1980. This was during one of his visits to Drepung and Ganden monastic universities in Karnataka, south India. I was then a young student at the Shartse College of Ganden. Apart from my own nervousness, what I remember most about this event is the single-pointedness—I could say almost a meditation-like absorption—of His Holiness's attention to the exchanges. Since then, I have had the privilege of experiencing this deeply inspiring sight on many occasions.

What follows in this brief essay is a glimpse into one aspect of the Dalai Lama's intellectual life, of which, despite its critical importance, very little is known outside Tibetan circles. I am referring to the role and influence of the Tibetan monastic academia on the life and thought of the Dalai Lama. Thanks to his two successful autobiographies,[1] and more recently, Hollywood's two films *Kundun* and *Seven Years in Tibet,* many people outside the Tibetan community have a sense that monks and scholars played an important role in the Dalai Lama's upbringing. But few are aware of the exact nature of this role, for how can they be expected to know the scope and nature of the unique education the Dalai Lama received in his youth?

My approach here is more impressionistic than systematic, weaving personal observations with anecdotes I heard as a young student at Ganden. I shall make no attempt to present any comprehensive account of the Dalai Lama's intellectual life, a task better left in the hands of professional biographers and historians. Furthermore, there are other important aspects of the Dalai Lama's intellectual life—such as the development of his social and political thought, his extensive engagement with modern science, his interaction with theologians, and so on—which must remain outside the scope of this essay.

Today, there are so many important matters competing for the Dalai Lama's time and attention. Needless to say, the plight of the Tibetan nation and its six million people must weigh heavily on his shoulders. On any given day, when he is in residence in Dharamsala, India, one can see a stream of new Tibetan refugees coming to visit him with obviously distressing news about his people back home. Within India, the Dalai Lama and his government in exile not only coordinate the campaign for the freedom of the Tibetan people, but they also oversee the welfare of the thousands of Tibetan refugees scattered all over the world today. The cause of Tibet is undoubtedly the Dalai Lama's primary responsibility; and he seems to have a deep, historical sense of this duty.

In addition, the Dalai Lama has taken upon himself the responsibility of promoting closer understanding between the world's major faith traditions.[2] As part of this effort, he has, besides participating in countless numbers of interfaith services, initiated several high-profile joint pilgrimages to the holy sites of the different traditions, such as Jerusalem and Lourdes.

There is, however, a third area of concern that also makes a strong demand on the Dalai Lama's time. This is what he calls the "promotion of basic human values." At the core of this mission lies the belief that fundamental ethical values such as love, compassion, and tolerance are indispensable for basic human happiness and must therefore be accepted as universally binding moral principles.

As a human being living in an increasingly complex and ever more interconnected world, the Dalai Lama sees this mission as an important personal responsibility.[3] Since he won the Nobel Peace Prize in 1989, the demands on his time with matters relating to this third mission have increased exponentially. Today, His Holiness is increasingly seen by millions as a powerful symbol of peace, justice, compassion, and environmental awareness.

All of these three "missions" of the Dalai Lama take him away, and often far, from his exiled Tibetan community.

Despite demands on his time—and more important, despite his emergence as a tremendously respected international figure—the Dalai Lama has continued to retain his traditionally close ties with the Tibetan scholastic monasteries. He visits them regularly, lectures on important classical texts, keeps close contact with senior scholars, and follows the progress of the young emerging scholars. The Dalai Lama's relation to the Tibetan monastic academia in general and the three Geluk[4] scholastic monasteries—Sera, Drepung, and Ganden—in particular is intriguing. One could say that the large monastic universities, especially the well-known trio, form a special constituency for the Dalai Lama. On the one hand, he is a former student whose formal accreditation of education is conferred by the authorities of these institutions.

Thanks to the archival instincts of some individuals, modern television audiences all over the world can still witness the formal ceremony of the Dalai Lama's final examination in Lhasa in the presence of several thousand monks. Prior to this event, he had visited each of the three monastic universities to sit for separate debate examinations.

On the other hand, the Dalai Lama is not on the rolls of any of these colleges. Moreover, the appointment of the abbots of the individual colleges of the three monastic universities, although based on candidates selected by the members of the monasteries, is still finalized by the Dalai Lama.

Historically speaking, up until the time of the Great Fifth, formally the Dalai Lamas were one, although very high, reincarnated lama of the Loseling college of Drepung monastic university. In fact, the name of the Dalai Lama's government in Tibet, *Ganden Phodrang,* previously belonged to the Dalai Lama institution at Drepung. Since the Great Fifth's assumption of temporal power in the mid-17th century, the Dalai Lama's institution became the Tibetan government.[5] Nevertheless, the Dalai Lamas have continued to be educated in strict accordance with the curriculum of the Geluk scholastic monasteries, and their tutors have been graduates of these universities.

For example, of the two main tutors of the Dalai Lama, Kyabje Ling Rinpoche was a scholar of formidable reputation from Drepung, while Kyabje Trijang Rinpoche was one of Ganden's most renowned personalities of the 20th century. In addition, the present Dalai Lama had several scholastic assistants *(tshen shap)*, such as the Mongolian scholar Ngodup Tsoknyi and the late Serkong Tsenshap Rinpoche, all of whom were graduates of the Geluk monasteries.

The core of the Tibetan monastic academic curriculum entails a highly systematic training in logic and epistemology, philosophical investigation into the nature of reality, a detailed investigation into the nature and varieties of religious experience, psychological and phenomenological inquiry into the nature of the mind and its modalities, and, of course, a detailed study of ethics. Together, these five fields of knowledge are known as the study of the Five Great Treatises *(shung chen ka pö nga)*:

— Of these, study of the **first** discipline, logic and epistemology, is based primarily on the works of the Indian thinkers Dignaga (c. 400–485 C.E.)[6] and Dharmakirti (c. 650 C.E.) and their subsequent Indian and Tibetan commentators.

— The study of the **second** discipline, which is perhaps best characterized in contemporary language as metaphysics and ontology, is based principally on the works of the highly influential Indian philosopher Nagarjuna (c. 150–250 C.E.) and his main interpreters, such as Buddhapalita (c. 470–540 C.E.) and Chandrakirti (c. 650 C.E.).

— On the **third** field of study, the writings of Indian masters such as Maitreyanatha (c. 270–350 C.E.), Asanga (c. 310–390 C.E.), and Haribhadra (c. 8th century C.E.) form the core texts.

— For the study of psychology and phenomenology, the **fourth** field, the principal works that constitute the basis for inquiry are those by Asanga and his brother Vasubhandu (c. 320–400 C.E.).

— Finally, for the **fifth** field of study, ethics, the central texts that are utilized are those that pertain primarily to the detailed analysis of the precepts of monastic discipline.

The mastery of these five fields of study is required if the candidate is to qualify for the title of Geshe Lharam, which is the Tibetan equivalent to a doctorate in divinity. Incidentally, this is the formal higher-education degree the present Dalai Lama holds.

The principal medium of the Tibetan monastic academic training is debate—a highly systematic, Socratic style of disputation that operates through drawing out a series of consequences, often unacceptable to the defender, based on the premises of the opponent's stated theses. This system of debate employs extensively principles of identity, contradiction, and the law of the excluded middle, which lie at the heart of the logics of deduction and induction.

Tibetan historians credit Chapa Chökyi Senge (1109–1169) with the development of this sophisticated system of inquiry. Chapa is believed to have authored several short texts that were collectively entitled "Collected Topics" *(Dü dön),* which presented in an ingenious instructional manner a critical treatment of many logical and epistemological themes from Dharmakirti's seminal work "A Thorough Exposition of Valid Cognition" *(Pramanavarttika).*[7] Chapa's brilliance lies in illustrating the logical principles in a series of structured debates using the example of common, everyday objects.

Today an entire genre of literature exists within Tibetan monastic academic studies that carries the label "Collected Topics." These texts are written in such a way that they can be used effectively, which is the case today, as manuals for training young students in the art of debate and making them familiar with the operation of the key logical principles.

It is this kind of rigorous intellectual training that the Dalai Lama had received in his student years. The Tibetan education theorists speak of three aspects of intelligence that must be cultivated and developed:

1. "Clear intelligence," which refers to an ability to perceive questions with an unconfused mind.

2. "Sharp intelligence," which refers to the ability to swiftly grasp an issue without much difficulty.

3. "Penetrating intelligence," which refers to the ability to view a problem with greater depth and comprehensiveness.

Debate is believed to help enhance the individual in all these three aspects of intelligence, which are critical for the development of a learned mind. It is said that those who excel in the first type of intelligence are often highly gifted in their power of articulation, while those who excel in the second become seasoned debaters, capable of dismantling the solidity of the opponent's positions. Finally, those who excel in the third type of intelligence are said to become great defenders, capable of adopting a panoramic perspective on any chosen subject under inquiry. Those who have heard the Dalai Lama would recall all these three aspects of intelligence at play.

If there is one thing the Dalai Lama feels he lost in his youth, it is perhaps not having had the freedom that an average monk normally enjoys as a student in the monastic colleges. He occasionally idealizes what is called the life of a *drapa drakyang,* which is best translated as the life of an ordinary monk, simple and unattached. In fact, he once told me when I was a student at Ganden that I was fortunate to have, unlike him, this unique opportunity to be a student as a simple, ordinary monk. I must admit I was a bit surprised at the time.

Perhaps, from the point of view of contemporary education, one of the most admirable features of Tibet's scholastic debate training is that it underlines the critical importance of openness. The debating courtyards in the scholastic monasteries are among the best places for the teaching of humility. On any given day, students and seasoned scholars are constantly exposed to the humbling experience of having to modify their standpoints, some of which they may have held for a long time with a high degree of confidence. In fact, when this occurs, the individual is said to gain greater maturity as he or she obtains what is called a "burst of growth in understanding" *(lo kye)*. When this happens, there is often a palpable sense of collective acknowledgment on the part of everyone participating in the discussion.

This burst of growth in understanding arises in the context of one's exchanges with debating colleagues. It is, therefore, often said that one's debating colleagues are as much teachers as one's professors. It is this kind of academic training that conditions the individual to have the preparedness to modify his or her position in the light of new insights. Such debate training also teaches students not to take themselves too seriously. Anyone who has witnessed a live performance of this monastic art of critical inquiry would recall the laughter and liveliness of the atmosphere that unmistakably accompanies the exchanges between the various parties in the debate. There is also something very scientific about this method of critical inquiry.

The Dalai Lama's classical academic training appears to have left a lasting impact both on his personality and his thinking. Despite his extensive exposure to modernity and contemporary Western thought, his appreciation of the scholastic tradition of Tibet remains as strong as ever. In fact, his worldview remains deeply rooted in the ancient teachings of the Buddha and the philosophical tradition that developed on their basis for a period of more than two millennia in India and Tibet. Belief in ethical-religious ideas—such as karma, the possibility of rebirth, the natural potential for perfection that is thought to exist in human beings, and so on—form the bedrock of the Buddhist worldview, and these still retain their cogency and vitality for the Dalai Lama.

On the philosophical level, it is Nagarjuna's antiessentialist metaphysics and his rejection of any reified notions of substantial reality that inform the Dalai Lama's understanding of the nature of reality. As he often points out, almost in the fashion of a motto, according to the Dalai Lama, everything is a "dependent origination" and exists within a nexus of "interrelationships," with no independently existing, discrete entities "relating" to each other.

It is this basic philosophy of the world's interconnectedness that underlies the Dalai Lama's perspectives on the natural world.

One of the most memorable experiences of my monastic years was catching a glimpse of the Dalai Lama's heavily annotated personal copy of Nagarjuna's philosophical classic "Fundamentals of the Middle Way" (*Mulamadhyamakarika*).[8] I was traveling with His Holiness as his interpreter, and we were waiting in the airport lounge in Mumbai (formerly called Bombay) for our Indian Airlines flight, which was just announced as being delayed by several hours. As soon as the official protocol business of being received by the airport authorities was completed, the Dalai Lama opened his small shoulder bag and took out his copy of Nagarjuna's book and launched into a deep study. To see His Holiness approach this text almost as a student was a truly humbling yet most inspiring experience, particularly since I was then "lecturing" on this text at Ganden monastery.

Among Tibetan thinkers, undoubtedly Tibet's great reformer and philosopher Tsong Khapa (1357–1419) appeared to exert the greatest influence on the Dalai Lama's philosophical views. There are some unmistakable strands of Tsong Khapa's thought that constantly resonate in the Dalai Lama's more philosophical writings. For example, His Holiness often invokes an important methodological principle, first developed fully as a crucial principle by Tsong Khapa, which underlines the need to distinguish between what is negated through a particular method of inquiry and what has not been observed through such a method. In other words, he reminds us not to conflate the two processes of "not finding something" and "finding its nonexistence."

So, just as for Tsong Khapa, for the Dalai Lama, too, not seeing something is not equal to seeing its nonexistence. This is a crucial methodological principle the Dalai Lama brings to bear when he engages in dialogues with contemporary thought, especially modern science. Furthermore, in his unshakable belief in the liberating potentials of critical thinking, which he calls "analytic meditation," one can also see the unmistakable influence of Tsong Khapa's writings.[9]

Similarly, the Dalai Lama's understanding of the human psyche—the nature of emotions, the relation between reason and emotion, the connection between certain emotions and behavior, how to deal with the destructive tendencies of certain emotions, and so on—derives from the long history of Buddhist psychological and phenomenological thinking, rather than contemporary Western thought. This latter includes, among others, the influential psychoanalytic theories of Sigmund Freud and, of course, many aspects of cognitive-scientific disciplines.

This is not to suggest that there exist no convergences between the two intellectual traditions. For example, parallel to the psychoanalytic notion of the unconscious, in Buddhist psychology there is a notion of what are called "propensities" for specific emotions.[10] Unlike the emotions themselves, these propensities are thought to be not actual, manifest, felt states of cognition. Rather, they exist more as "subconscious" forces.

In dealing with the cognitive aspects of the human psyche, the Dalai Lama's understanding of the nature of perception and experience, the cognitive processes involved in generating inference, the definitions of knowledge, and so on are based, again, on the writings of Buddhist philosophers and not on the works of contemporary cognitive science. I remember once, at a dialogue with some cognitive scientists, the Dalai Lama, after listening to a scientific understanding of how a moment of perception occurs, immediately attempted to translate this into the language of Tibetan epistemology.

At the heart of this Tibetan system is a sevenfold typology of cognitions: (1) perception, (2) inference, (3) correct assumption, (4) inattentive perception, (5) subsequent cognition, (6) doubt, and (7) false cognition. The nature, causation, and the interrelation of these seven classes of cognitions constitute a major focus of Tibetan epistemological thinking to this day.

The point I am trying to make is this: The Dalai Lama's intellectual and ethical worldview remains firmly rooted in the classical Tibetan heritage. His advocacy of compassion as a universal spiritual principle, his belief in the basic goodness of human nature, his persistent belief in the power of nonviolence as a means of resolving human conflicts, his passionate advocacy of altruism as an effective means of achieving individual happiness . . . all have their roots in the teachings of the Buddha.

Here again, two classical Indian thinkers stand out in terms of their influence on the Dalai Lama. They are Nagarjuna and Shantideva, the author of the well-known 7th-century Buddhist classic "Guide to the Bodhisattva's Way of Life" *(Bodhicharyavatara)*.[11] Those who are familiar with the Dalai Lama's writings will note the frequency with which he cites Shantideva in his lectures. In fact, the Dalai Lama has repeatedly stated that his greatest source of inspiration is the following verse from Shantideva:

> For as long as space remains,
> For as long as sentient beings remain,
> Until then, may I too remain
> And dispel the miseries of beings[12]

One area where the Dalai Lama's views are firmly grounded in modern science rather than his own inherited classical Buddhist thought is cosmology. Here, the Dalai Lama appears to have abandoned the entire cosmological system derived from the highly influential Buddhist classic entitled "Treasury of Knowledge" *(Abhidharmakoshakarika)*, written by Vasubhandu in the 4th century. Like many cosmological theories current in ancient Indian thought, in Vasubhandu's cosmology, known as the "Abhidharma cosmology," the sun and the moon revolve around the earth, and the latter is thought to be supported by forces of the four elements, which are stacked upon each other in an ascending order.

Judging by his comments on classical Abhidharma cosmology, it seems that the Dalai Lama was never convinced of the cogency of the system. There is also the simple coincidence that before the young Dalai Lama was exposed to the intricacies of the classical Abhidharma cosmology, which traditionally happens much later on in one's academic scholarship, he was already introduced to some powerful symbols of modern cosmology, such as the globe atlas and photographs of the volcanic craters on the surface of the moon. He was also aware of the scientific, as opposed to the classical Buddhist, explanations of the occurrence of solar and lunar eclipses and so on.

Once His Holiness lamented that he did not understand why many of the senior Tibetan scholars in the monastic colleges are so reluctant to let go of the ancient cosmological theories. In his mind, most of this cosmology had been falsified by the weight of empirical evidence gathered by modern scientists. And given that the scholastic monks trained in the system of philosophical debates are conditioned to modify their views in the light of new insights, His Holiness felt that it was only emotional attachment to old theories that came in the way of their accepting the new cosmology.

I sensed a rare note of impatience in him. I was then a graduate at Ganden, one of the three scholastic universities, and felt that I should at least try to present the case for these senior Tibetan scholars.

Politely, I reminded His Holiness that regardless of its lack of modern scientific foundation, the Abhidharma system "works," so far as the proponents of the system are concerned. For example, based on this system, almanacs are produced, highly accurate predictions of solar and lunar eclipses are made, the changing lengths of daylight are predicted, and accurate calculation of stellar positions are developed as well. In other words, the Abhidharma system makes predictions of events that are observable and highly relevant to the everyday life of the people. It would be unrealistic, I opined, for the monks to abandon this model until it's explained to them how each of these facts are supported, too, in the alternative, new cosmology—which, in addition, has solid empirical foundation. Ever since, I have noticed that His Holiness has been much more appreciative of the perspectives of his senior colleagues on cosmology.

It is this kind of complex background that brings the Dalai Lama often back into the folds of the classical Tibetan monastic academic monasteries. Not only is he present to observe the progress of the emerging scholars, he is there also to stimulate his own intellectual development. This becomes all the more necessary as he ventures deeper and deeper into dialogues with scientists and thinkers from various contemporary disciplines.[13]

In this context, it may be worth noting the special relationship that the Dalai Lama has had for a long time with a unique Tibetan scholar. I am referring here to the late Shakor Gen Nyima-la from Drepung Loseling monastic college, who was one of the 20th century's greatest interpreters of Nagarjuna's and Tsong Khapa's philosophical writings. Once, in a conversation, His Holiness told me that he felt that in Gen Nyima-la he had found someone who had not only penetrated the depths of Nagarjuna's insights, but who was also able to bring them to life. He then lamented the fact that hardly any of Gen Nyima-la's lectures were ever recorded! I have myself had the privilege to attend one series of lectures this great scholar gave on an influential work of Tsong Khapa at Drepung.

It must be truly refreshing for the Dalai Lama to intellectually engage with a senior scholar such as Gen Nyima-la who was able to relate to His Holiness as a genuine colleague. Unlike most Tibetan scholars in the exile community in India and Nepal, Gen Nyima-la was not overwhelmed by the Dalai Lama's presence. This is partly because, like the Dalai Lama's two late tutors, Gen Nyima-la has seen his intellectual development from when he was a young student.

It is also conceivable that the Dalai Lama finds the atmosphere of the monastic academia a rather sobering counterpoint to the many other areas of his very public life. It is one sphere where he is not expected to be the "great" authority. Furthermore, exchanging diverse and often opposing views is a part of the intellectual culture of the monastic academia. Every now and then, the Dalai Lama gives a series of formal lectures on an important philosophical treatise at one of the three monastic universities. These lectures, on average, last for two to three weeks. During these occasions, formal debate sessions are held in the evenings, where the top scholars of the monastic academia debate on the issues addressed in the text the Dalai Lama is lecturing on, while he listens with total absorption. Needless to say, these are truly stimulating events.

It is perhaps too early to judge what will be the lasting intellectual legacy of the Dalai Lama insofar as the Tibetan monastic academia is concerned. Unlike many of his predecessors, the present Dalai Lama has so far not chosen to pen any major scholarly treatises in Tibetan. Yet, among all Tibetans who have had a truly classical education, he has engaged most with the various scholarly disciplines of contemporary Western thought, especially science. No doubt historians would take particular note of this fact and come to realize that in many ways the Dalai Lama's life mirrors the wider picture of classical Tibetan culture's encounter with modernity.

Endnotes

1. The Dalai Lama, *My Land and My People* (New York: McGraw-Hill, 1962) and *Freedom in Exile* (New York: HarperCollins, 1991).

2. For an informative account of this aspect of the Dalai Lama's stated mission, see the Dalai Lama, et al., *The Good Heart: The Dalai Lama Explores the Heart of Christianity* (London: Rider Books, 1996).

3. The Dalai Lama has devoted an entire book to the promotion of what he calls secular ethics, entitled *Ethics for the New Millennium* (New York: Riverhead Books, 1999).

4. The latest of the four main schools of Tibetan Buddhism (the other three being *Nyingma, Sakya,* and *Kagyü*), founded by Tibet's great reformer and philosopher Tsong Khapa (1357–1419).

5. For a concise history of Tibet and, in particular, the emergence of the Dalai Lama's rule, see Lee Feigon, *Demystifying Tibet: Unlocking the Secrets of the Land of Snows* (Chicago: Ivan R. Dee, 1996).

6. All my dates of the classical Indian thinkers are from Hajme Nakamura, *Indian Buddhism: A Survey with Bibliographical Notes* (New Delhi: Motilal Banarsidass, 1987).

7. Dharmakirti's thought is today a major area of focus in contemporary academic scholarship on Sanskrit and Buddhist studies. To date, four international conferences on Dharmakirti have taken place, attended by scholars from the continents of Europe, Asia, and North America.

8. For an accessible translation and study of this important Buddhist philosophical classic, see Jay Garfield, *The Fundamental Wisdom of the Middle Way* (New York: Oxford University Press, 1995).

9. Various aspects of Tsong Khapa's thought have received extensive attention in contemporary scholarship. See, for example, Robert Thurman, *Tsong Khapa's Speech of Gold in the Essence of True Eloquence* (Princeton, NJ: Princeton University Press, 1984); and Thupten Jinpa, *Self, Reality and Reason in Tibetan Philosophy: Tsongkhapa's Quest for the Middle Way* (London: RoutledgeCurzon, 2002).

10. For a concise study of the key parallels between Buddhist psychology and contemporary psychoanalytic thought, see Mark Epstein, *Thoughts Without a Thinker* (New York: Basic Books, 1995).

11. For a lucid translation of this influential Buddhist classic, see Santideva, *The Bodhicaryavatara* (Oxford World's Classics) (New York: Oxford University Press, 1996), translated by Kate Crosby and Andrew Skilton.

12. This translation is mine. For Oxford World's Classics version, see Santideva, op.cit., p. 143.

13. The Dalai Lama has had close friendships with several influential contemporary thinkers—in particular, the late British philosopher of science Sir Karl Popper, the late physicists David Bohm and Carl Von Weizsäcker, and the late Chilean neurobiologist Francisco Varela. Especially since 1987, the Dalai Lama has been engaged in ongoing conversations with scientists and philosophers on the interface between Buddhist thought and contemporary science, entitled Mind and Life conferences, which take place once every two years at his residence in India. The proceedings of some of these meetings have been published under the following titles: *Gentle Bridges* (Boston: Shambhala, 1992); *Sleeping, Dreaming, and Dying* (Boston: Wisdom, 1997); *Healing Emotions* (Boston: Shambhala, 1997); and *Consciousness at the Crossroads* (Ithaca, NY: Snow Lion, 1999).

19

AN UNCONVENTIONAL
TIBETAN PERSPECTIVE

by Bhuchung Tsering

What does His Holiness the Dalai Lama mean to young Tibetans? On the face of it, this question may seem to be an unnecessary one. Don't all Tibetans have the same approach toward His Holiness?

Yes and no. There is the traditional Tibetan perspective of His Holiness, which is also shared by followers of Tibetan Buddhism along the Himalayas, including in Mongolia, the Russian Federation, Nepal, Bhutan, Arunachal Pradesh, Himachal Pradesh, Sikkim, Ladakh, and so on. This perspective is that of His Holiness as the manifestation of Chenrezig (Avalokiteshvara), the bodhisattva of compassion, and the *Kyabgon Rinpoche,* the precious source of refuge. He is someone who has the capacity to be fully enlightened, but has chosen to come back to this human world for the sake of sentient beings.

In essence, he is god in a human form, and thus beyond the reach of ordinary mortals in Tibet. He is virtually regarded as the Buddha of our age, with many Tibetan Buddhists referring to him as *Sangye* (the Enlightened One), one of the many Tibetan terms for the Buddha.

Prior to 1959, an average Tibetan could only hope to meet some-one who may have been fortunate enough to get a glimpse of His Holiness from a distance. At best this glimpse may have been at a religious teaching or when the Dalai Lama undertook his irregular travels in Tibet. It would be rare to meet someone who had an audi-ence with His Holiness.

The structure of Tibetan society in independent Tibet was such that there was very limited access to His Holiness or to the senior officials of the Tibetan government. Elaborate protocol was the rule of the game. Therefore, ordinary Tibetans did not have the opportunity to interact with His Holiness at close quarters. To them, he was their *Gyalwa Rinpoche,* the Victorious One, who was the focus of their daily prayers. Nobody even dreamed of any close encounters with him.

But in the post-1959 period, following the flight of His Holiness into exile forced by Chinese incursion into Tibet, the institution of the Dalai Lama underwent a dramatic transformation, much to the delight of the young 14th incarnation. Aided by circumstances, the institution became less protocol-heavy, more accessible to the public, and more practical. Over a period of time, this led to a close interaction between His Holiness and the Tibetan people, a historical development of sorts.

The most obvious indication of this metamorphosis is the increase in the number of Tibetans with the first name Tenzin. Almost every other Tibetan who is born in exile and under the age of 20 may have this first name. As Tibetans know, Tenzin is the name that His Holiness gives when Tibetans resort to the convention of approach-ing a lama for providing a name to their child. Prior to 1959 only a privileged few Tibetan children may have had the opportunity to get their names from His Holiness.

Life in exile has also led to His Holiness's interaction with the outside world, mainly by way of his visits throughout the world, pro-viding Tibetans with a new side of the Dalai Lama. This has become clear to young Tibetans, particularly those who have the good fortune to be growing up in a free society. While most still hold strong to their Buddhist faith, and thus subscribe to the traditional perspective of the Dalai Lama, they have also been able to see his human side and to appreciate it as such. His Holiness has become a role model for young Tibetans.

I belong to the generation of Tibetans who grew up in exile, a generation that had to be the spokesman for our people without having the direct experience of life in Tibet. This change in our situation, however, has given me a fresh insight into the Dalai Lama and has provided people like me with the opportunity unimaginable for my parents' generation.

Growing up in the Tibetan settlement in south India in the 1970s, or attending high school in Darjeeling or college in New Delhi in the beginning of the 1980s, I did not dream even for a minute that one day I would be in the same room as Kundun, the Presence, let alone be able to strike a conversation with him. But that day arrived in the late 1980s and is fresh in my memory even now.

I was accompanying an Indian photojournalist to the residence of His Holiness in Dharamsala as part of my work at the Department of Information and International Relations. Between photo sessions, His Holiness looked toward me, just a newcomer to the Tibetan civil service, and asked me from which part of Tibet I was. That one ordinary-sounding question altered the course of Tibetan social history, to me at least. Kundun had spoken to me, an ordinary Tibetan, and acknowledged my presence. Since then I have been privileged to interact with His Holiness on quite a few occasions in the course of my work.

My interaction with His Holiness is in a way symbolic of the transformation of the institution of the Dalai Lama that the 14th incarnation, Tenzin Gyatso, has brought about. The significance of the transformation can be comprehended only when one has looked at the history of modern Tibet, as well as that of the 14th Dalai Lama. To be objective, the course of modern Tibetan history dictated certain changes in the institution as well as in Tibetan society as a whole.

However, things might not have changed as rapidly as they did had the 14th Dalai Lama not complemented historical development with his own liberal outlook and foresight. My fascination (if I even dare use this term) with His Holiness is more to do with his social activism and less with his religious role. While his outreach to the international community—in the field of religion and spirituality, as well as in drawing attention to the plight of the Tibetan people—is acknowledged internationally, not many know much about his influence on the social thinking of the Tibetan people and his other followers.

The establishment of a system of universal modern education to young Tibetans, mainly with the assistance of the Indian government, in the wake of his flight to India in 1959 was the most important factor in changing the Tibetan society in exile. That one act by the Dalai Lama not only provided an even playing field for Tibetans at all levels of society in terms of educational opportunity, but the blend of modern and traditional education that was part of the curriculum resulted in a new generation of Tibetans, modern in outlook and also having knowledge of their cultural heritage.

His Holiness is a social reformer and an iconoclast. Relying on his moral authority and the well-founded justification of Buddhism as a rational religion, His Holiness has altered the theological perceptions of Tibetan Buddhists when these did not conform to scientific reality. This included asking monks to accept the earth as round instead of being flat, as is found in Buddhist scriptures; and removing the mystery behind the institution of the Dalai Lama, and thereby forcing the very many *Tulku* institutions to follow suit. He has encouraged doing away with irrelevant monastic rituals and political protocols. He has transformed Tibetan Buddhism from being ritualistic to a practice relevant to any individual interested in it.

His Holiness has been able to make effective use of his coveted position to change the social system not only of the Tibetans but also of communities that share the same cultural values as Tibetans. For example, although people living in the Tibetan cultural environment do not have a caste system, people following certain professions are still looked down upon.

There is a story of how a simple act by His Holiness changed the outlook of the Ladakhi community toward the musicians in their society. During one of his visits to Ladakh, His Holiness took the drumsticks of the person with the *dhama* (a drum traditionally used with another musical instrument, *suna*, for official functions) and beat the drum himself a couple of times. It is said that dhama players are traditionally looked down upon in Ladakhi society.

One issue that has personally affected me is His Holiness's contribution in changing the dietary habits of Tibetans. Tibetan Buddhists traditionally consume meat, and the reasoning goes that Tibet in the past did not have adequate nonmeat products. Since 1959, Tibetan society has changed greatly. Today, Tibetans, whether living in exile or inside Tibet, do have access to vegetarian food. However, meat continues to be an integral part of the Tibetan diet even now, much to the consternation and confusion of outside observers, who tend to equate Buddhism with vegetarianism.

Many people do not comprehend the significant role His Holiness has been playing in promoting vegetarianism. Through his personal example (he became totally vegetarian for some years, but then had to resume a nonvegetarian diet on the advice of his physicians) and consistent advocacy using his coveted position, His Holiness has started leading the meat-eating Tibetan society along the path of vegetarianism. He has encouraged food workshops promoting vegetarianism in the Tibetan community. A meat-eating society has overnight started taking gradual steps toward vegetarianism. This is a significant development. There are increasing numbers of Tibetans, like myself, who have become vegetarians, and our encouragement has come from His Holiness.

His Holiness is also a role model for a balanced approach to life. He can interact easily with royalty and heads of state as well as with a simple monk in a meditation cave. I overheard one Swiss tourist exclaiming *"Sehr einfach"*—"very simple"—when he found that he was traveling in the same tram car as His Holiness several years back. He can be very solemn in a ritual-filled Buddhist ceremony or be jovial among schoolchildren in a Tibetan settlement.

Generally, Tibetans believe in the ability of His Holiness to liberate them from the suffering of this material world. That is a spiritual and subjective belief that only people subscribing to Tibetan Buddhist principles may comprehend. But the new perspective of His Holiness as a role model is one that is shared by Tibetans and non-Tibetans alike.

20

A Journey Through Bylakuppe

by Anees Jung

I never did see Tibet when it was Tibet. Now that I would like to, it is no longer Tibet. The Potala Palace, that overwhelming symbol that is indelible in the imagination of every Tibetan, is today "a somber shipwreck beached on the shores of an alien city" in the words of Sonam Tenzin, a returning Tibetan native. Its mythical outlines loom ghostlike, empty of life, empty without the presence of the man who lived in it and lent it the magic of his being. I have no desire to go to Tibet and join the horde of men and women who buy tickets to visit the apartments where the Dalai Lama once lived. To see Potala Palace as a tourist seems a sacrilege. It would be as if one were visiting a monument abandoned and disgraced.

What seems grounded in Lhasa is the skeleton of the wrecked ship. What it contained has sailed on, invisibly, finding a mooring miles away, in a land without an imposing palace, without majestic hills, without the snows shimmering down. But the presence that once prevailed in Lhasa now reigns over Bylakuppe in a distant corner of south India where it never snows but rains. Bylakuppe by its very name means "a place of rains." In the presence of the Dalai Lama, even the rains, it seems, decide to step back.

Bigger than the rains is the happening of the Dalai Lama's yearly visit to Bylakuppe. I am fortunate to be among the thousands of Tibetans who have traveled distances for his *darshan* (beholding). They line the routes he travels, standing in single file—hundreds of men, women, and children, with heads bowed, fervently clutching white scarves of peace and bunches of wildflowers, offerings so finely wrapped in devotion. Their eyes are lit, their faces are wreathed in anticipation. They present a picture not of ebullience but of quiet animation. To see such quietude in a crowd is a rare sight.

Looking at the Tibetans always gives me a good feeling. I find in their faces a peace unfazed by the rigors of the hardships they have borne so heroically, so stoically. I have been a witness to crowds before, the kind that gather or are gathered to cheer political leaders. They are more in the nature of a spectacle, disorganized, frenzied, more curious than expectant. But to see a crowd of Tibetans standing hours in the rains is to witness a picture of serenity, of humility and patience born of an unyielding faith. It is a moving sight to see the old, the dying, and the disabled being brought out, lying on their beds, with tears in their eyes, clutching a flower or two in trembling hands, their last offerings. It is as if the Buddha has returned.

As indeed he has. But this Buddha, it seems, belongs to another time. He carries his mantle lightly, is less like a god, more like a friend. Pomp and grandeur reminiscent of the shades of the last emperor circle Sera-je monastery, a replica of what existed in Tibet. But the one who is seated on the throne-like chair is a humble monk, like those assembled around him. The air is charged with vapors of ritual, resonant with sounds that remind one of Gregorian chants. Mixed with mournful strains of the Tibetan clarinet, and cymbals crashing like thunder, they strike an eerie contrast with the quietude of the still red sea that the presence of the lamas evokes. Robed in maroon is the Dalai Lama, smiling, waving a hand, gazing indulgently at the long line of devotees who walk past him carrying offerings—from flowers to white scarves to bags of rice and maize, the fruits of their new earth. Watching their faces, I choke.

When he speaks to the crowd that has gathered through the night (some had brought their bedding and slept in the drizzle), he again seems to talk to each one. He even recognizes in the melee faces that he has met, smiles at them, waves now and then a hand of affirmation, watches with glee a child pursuing a yellow balloon. The face of the crowd is lit. Sitting on the throne-like chair while waiting for the microphones to begin working, he gazes into the eye of the crowd that is not restless. Nor is His Holiness. The wait is indefinite but does not seem long because of the serenity that prevails. The microphones refuse to work.

"Why not go and have your lunch, stretch your legs, and return?" suggests His Holiness with a laugh. "By the time you return, the microphones may start working." The crowd bursts into laughter, echoing his short laugh. There is not a trace of protest from a crowd that has waited a whole night to hear him.

Dutifully and in good humor, they are back again, sitting patiently between intermittent sun and rain. A sea of people, their faces darkened in the strong Karnataka sun, old men and women turning prayer wheels, counting beads, many of whom have probably braved the journey from Tibet. Across from them are children in a disciplined crowd dressed in crisp blue uniforms. And as happy as the children are the lamas dressed in maroon and saffron robes gathered in another mass. Hundreds of colorful umbrellas unfurl when the Dalai Lama gently advises that they protect their heads against the glare. They hang on to each word he utters.

When he talks, the tone is not of a man espousing a sermon but of a person who is reflecting and searching for answers himself. He constantly seems to question the changing realities of his time and seeks new answers and solutions. Buddha did it in his own time, leaving behind a path that the Dalai Lama now walks on. It has been for him, as for his people, a long, arduous road that together they have traveled, finding a freedom that is charged with sunshine and laughter.

Bigger than a place are a people who give that place a definition, fill it with the aura born of a collective racial memory and nostalgia. I never did see the mythical grandeur of Tibet, but I was fortunate to witness the miracle of how a people, so visibly doomed, can rebuild not only their lives but a place that is bound to their destiny and their very existence. That's what the Tibetans have done, turning Bylakuppe into the Tibet of their dreams and imagination.

When the first batch of them arrived in this desolate corner of Karnataka, so generously given to them by the state government, they bowed, as Tibetans so naturally do, in deep gratitude. It was an alien landscape, a wilderness where elephants lived and tigers roamed at night, animals they had never seen in their native Tibet. Some succumbed to the wild animals, but many did not. They learned how to challenge the great animals by gathering in groups and beating tins. Soon the elephants receded. As did the tigers. But not the snakes and the scorpions. Some of them died when bitten or stung; some became wary and cautious, slowly learning to fend them off. The men cleared the jungles; the women gathered the wood and burned them.

Soon there were clearings where fields could be plowed and planted with unfamiliar grains—maize, tobacco, cotton, and ginger. Around the fields rose homesteads, small houses with red tile roofs, the kind their Indian neighbors lived in. Like them, the Tibetans used to harness the bullocks. Gone was the familiar yak, that beast of their burden, whose meat gave them the strength and heat. In this distant land green with the perennial rains, they made vegetable gardens, got acquainted with their color and taste, and without realizing it, slowly became vegetarians. It suited the climate and way of life. It was less violent, as the Dalai Lama told them. Having once watched a chicken being killed and then turned into a meal for him, he gave up eating chicken; he advised Tibetans not to raise poultry and pigs but grow less violent foods.

Today the poultry farm in Bylakuppe is an old-age home. His Holiness makes it a point to visit the elderly each time he travels to Bylakuppe. He never fails to stop at the pond on the way to feed the fish that sweep up in shoals to eat out of his hand. He makes an unexpected stop on the road to lay a white scarf on the grave of a Chinese man who left Tibet to make his home here. These are gestures that speak broadly and loudly. They speak of his compassion for animate and inanimate beings, for the friends and so-called enemies.

I am reminded of a story that Sonam Tenzin quotes of how a lady from Lhasa dressed in the traditional striped apron and *chuba* traveling in a bus asked him if he had ever seen Kundan, referring to the Dalai Lama by the name he was called as a child. "You are fortunate," she told him. "We have no freedom at all. . . . It's as if we are lying on a bed of thorns—we never know when things might change for the worse."

This sad reality has escaped the thousands of Tibetans who have lost a home but gained another—a home that radiates in the presence of Kundun, who lives among them. Unlike the woman in Lhasa, they deem themselves fortunate to get a glimpse of him and be blessed by his presence. He remains not only a spiritual light but a leader in the true sense who has been shepherding their journey; watching over each stop of their growth, development, and progress; and giving them friendly advice, care, and concern not the way a leader does when he is elected, but as one who loves them as much as they revere and trust him. Their well-being is his victory.

21

IN PRAISE OF HIS HOLINESS THE 14TH DALAI LAMA

by Lama Thubten Zopa Rinpoche

His Holiness the Dalai Lama is the great treasure of infinite compassion embracing all sentient beings, the sole source of benefit and happiness, and the sole refuge. His Holiness is incomparably kinder to us—the fortunate disciples in many countries of this world who are able to see his holy body and hear his holy speech—than all the past, present, and future Buddhas.

The kind Guru Shakyamuni Buddha, out of his great compassion, descended to this world of Dzambu in the Arya land of India for the sole purpose of bringing benefit and happiness to migratory beings by leading us to liberation and full enlightenment.

It is said in the White Lotus Sutra:

> At one time when the Buddha was residing in Milk-Plant Park, he turned to face the north and smiled. Five rays of light issued from the curled hair between his eyebrows. When the bodhisattva Meaningful to Behold asked why, the Buddha replied, "O son of the Mahayana type, there is a land in the north known as the Land of Snow where the Buddhas of the three times have not yet put their holy feet. However, in the future, the holy Dharma will spread and flourish there like the rising sun and all

the living beings there will be liberated by Lord Avalokiteshvara, who once made the following prayer:

> *May I liberate all sentient beings in the Land of Snow, who are difficult to subdue. May I subdue them. May I lead the sentient beings in that outlying barbarous country [Tibet] on the path to liberation and full enlightenment. May even that barbarous country become a field that is subdued by me. May all the holy Dharma taught by all the Tathagatas be spread and flourish for a long time in that country. May the sentient beings there enjoy the holy Dharma by hearing the name of the Triple Gem, going for refuge and achieving the bodies of happy migratory beings.*

The bodhisattva Meaningful to Behold, to whom Guru Shakyamuni Buddha predicted the spread of Dharma in Tibet, saying, "In the future when my teaching has degenerated in India, the sentient beings in the Land of Snow in the north will be the objects to be subdued by you, the bodhisattva," and the Compassion Buddha who made all those prayers and achieved extensive benefits, illuminating with the light of Dharma . . . are none other than the present Dalai Lama.

Even ordinary people can realize that the incomparable qualities and the holy actions of His Holiness's body, speech, and mind benefiting other sentient beings signify the infinitely compassionate aspiration that he made in the past. Not only did His Holiness make prayers to extensively benefit Tibet by subduing the sentient beings there, but nowadays he shines the light of Dharma to eliminate the darkness of ignorance and bring the sunshine of peace and happiness even in the Western world.

It is proven that His Holiness is the present, living Compassionate-Eyed Looking Buddha, Avalokiteshvara, even from the lineage of the incarnation, which starts from Avalokiteshvara and during Buddha's time, the bodhisattva Meaningful to Behold, King Jigten Ngawang, and the Brahmin Khyeu Nan-che . . . then continues through Sangye Gyalwa; Nyatri Tsenpo; the first king of Tibet, Chogyal Trisong Duetsen; Chogyal Songtsen Gampo; Lama Atisha's translator, the great Dromtönpa, who is the 45th incarnation; the 1st Dalai Lama, Gendun Drubpa, who founded Tashi Lhunpo Monastery; Gendun Gyatso; Sonam Gyatso; Yonten Gyatso; the 5th Dalai Lama; Tsangyang Gyatso; Kelsang Gyatso; Jampal Gyatso; Lungtok Gyatso; Tsultrim Gyatso; Khedrup Gyatso; Trinley Gyatso; Thubten Gyatso; and the present Dalai Lama, Tenzin Gyatso, the 64th incarnation.

His Holiness Serkong Dorje Chang, who passed away in Tibet, had a dream in which a spontaneously arisen statue of Avalokiteshvara with five faces predicted that he would see the Compassion Buddha the following day. The next day he saw His Holiness.

One day the great scholar-yogi Tehor Kyoerpen Rinpoche—renowned in Sera, Ganden, and Drepung monasteries—told all his disciples that they were going to meet Dromtönpa, an incarnation of the Compassion Buddha. They then went to see His Holiness.

His Holiness is preserving the complete teaching of the Buddha, the three higher trainings of morality, meditation, and wisdom in the three basket teachings, which is the essence of the Hinayana teaching and the foundation of the causal Mahayana Paramitayana path and the resultant secret Vajrayana, which flourished in the past in Tibet and now flourishes even outside Tibet. Because of that, His Holiness is able to produce many hundreds of thousands of holy scholars and highly attained yogis, like stars in the sky.

Even nowadays in various parts of the world, so many people are able to receive teachings from highly qualified practitioners—teachers from the monasteries of Sera, Ganden, and Drepung and also from those of the other traditions. So many Westerners and others from many countries around the world are able to study with them in depth and learn everything they wish. By putting these teachings into practice, they are able to make their lives meaningful and find fulfillment. They have so much opportunity to enjoy peace and happiness and are able to direct their lives toward liberation and enlightenment, and this is increasing every year. This is solely due to His Holiness's kindness.

Without His Holiness, Buddhism would suffer, and it would be extremely difficult to continue the preservation of the entire Buddhadharma. Without the teaching of the Buddha, sentient beings suffer, because it is the only medicine to cure all diseases, delusions, negative karma, and their imprints. His Holiness is completely liberated from all the fears of samsara—the circling aggregates that cause suffering—and is highly skilled in liberating others from all suffering. Therefore, from the bottom of our hearts, we should always pray for His Holiness to have a stable life until samsara ends.

His Holiness's holy body, speech, and mind are the source of peace for all living beings. He is ultimate among those who are learned, ultimate among those who are pure in morality, and ultimate among those who are warmhearted. He is unstained by delusion and ego-seeking happiness for the self. He is unstained by even the subtlest obscurations.

For us sentient beings, both human and animal, just seeing or touching his holy body purifies our minds and makes our lives meaningful. It brings unforgettable peace and happiness and plants the seeds of liberation and enlightenment in our mental continuum. It gives incredible inspiration and the hope for a better life.

The ever-loving smile and compassionate face of His Holiness radiate warm rays of light that pacify all fears and anxieties, all the karma and delusions of sentient beings. No matter how much one looks at the holy body of the Compassion Buddha, one never feels satiated. There is no limit to the qualities of the stainless holy body and to the extensive benefits that sentient beings receive from it.

From one hour or even a few minutes of the gentle, soothing nectar of his holy speech, people can understand immediately the very essence of Buddhism and make their lives most beneficial and meaningful. His holy words—which come solely from ego-less, compassionate, loving thought—present everything in a very simple, clear, logical way and suit exactly the nature and mind of each person who hears them. Even if 100,000 people listen to His Holiness, every single one is uplifted with unbelievable joy and finds the answers to his questions. The problems in their lives are immediately solved.

In the very short time it takes to hear a few of his holy words, they receive a profound wisdom that illuminates the darkness of ignorance obscuring the clear nature of their minds. They develop the wisdom to know what is right and to be practiced, and what is wrong and to be abandoned. They are able to practice the Dharma and benefit others, as well as obtain the ultimate happiness of liberation from samsara, and full enlightenment.

Western countries are highly developed in the fields of science, technology, psychology, and so forth; yet they are unable to find answers for many of the complicated issues of life, especially relating to birth and death. Within Western countries, there are many unresolved doubts and wrong views concerning economic, legal, and social problems. Each of His Holiness's holy words is a sword that immediately cuts through these problems. He gives simple solutions—none of which are separate from Dharma—not only to problems related to religious practice but also to business, family relationships, and other aspects of our daily lives. Everything he advises is based on not harming others and on benefiting them. There is no contradiction between the spiritual and political because his advice comes not only from a pure motivation of compassion but from wisdom as well.

His Holiness's holy speech takes care of the earth and the living beings inhabiting it. If people were to put his holy speech into practice, it would protect even the environment from destruction. He gives so much love and compassion that each person's mind is transformed *into* that love and compassion. Each person who hears His Holiness speak and then practices according to his words transforms his mind into the qualities His Holiness speaks about, and brings peace and happiness to the world. Millions of people have heard his holy speech and been inspired with hope and courage in their lives. They become more sensitive to others, with the loving, compassionate thought of caring for others' rights and needs. At the very least they decide not to kill other beings.

Even if they cannot completely stop harming others, if one person in an audience stops causing harm to others—for example, by refraining from killing or getting angry—it brings peace to all other living beings. All this peace given to the world by one person refraining from causing harm came from hearing His Holiness speak. There is no question of the benefit when millions of people put his holy speech into practice. Therefore, it is easy to understand how His Holiness is the source of all the temporary and ultimate joy and peace for all sentient beings.

With a very few words, he gives us insight into the whole path to enlightenment, bringing us incredible light. The qualities of His Holiness's speech, as well as the benefits sentient beings receive from it, are limitless.

As to the attributes of the holy mind, His Holiness has infinite qualities—such as the ten powers, the four fearlessnesses, the 18 qualities of unmixed dharma, and so forth—which cannot be comprehended by even a tenth-level bodhisattva, let alone by an ordinary sentient being. Each pore of his holy body is able to perform the function of his holy mind and directly see all existence and benefit all sentient beings. His holy wisdom, which is immovable forever from emptiness, without concept simultaneously manifests and works for all sentient beings exactly in accordance with their karma.

A special quality of His Holiness that ordinary people can see is that he seeks to benefit even those who harm him. Even though some criticize His Holiness, unlike common people and even other religious leaders, he only blesses them in return. He feels even greater compassion for them and cherishes them most in his heart. He praises their qualities and prays only for their well-being, for their temporary and ultimate happiness up to enlightenment. This leaves no doubt that His Holiness is a bodhisattva, the Compassion Buddha.

When the Chinese Communists invaded Tibet, they caused unbelievable destruction of buildings, especially monasteries, and of the environment; and tortured and killed not only ordinary people but many high lamas and highly educated monks and nuns. Not only did they destroy buildings and holy objects in the monasteries, but they prevented monks and nuns teaching Buddhism, particularly the higher training of morality.

In such a situation, there is no doubt that an ordinary world leader would hold a grudge and regard the Chinese Communists as enemies. His Holiness, however, is not solely concerned about the freedom, peace, and happiness of the six million Tibetan people and the future of the most precious, profound culture in the world, which preserves the entire teaching of the Buddha. He also cherishes deeply the Chinese Communists. He is greatly concerned about their sufferings and always prays for their freedom, peace, and happiness. He feels a special concern and unbearable compassion for Mao Tse-tung. There is no question that this is His Holiness's attitude and action, and it proves even to an ordinary person that he is a bodhisattva, that in reality he is Avalokiteshvara, the Compassion Buddha.

If the Chinese Communists are unable to open their hearts to His Holiness and accept his holy wishes, it will be a great pity and a great loss of opportunity. If they *can* open their hearts, it will mean not only freedom, peace, and happiness for six million Tibetan people, but the opportunity to continue to preserve and strengthen the whole of Buddhism, as happened previously in Tibet, where so many highly attained beings experienced the path shown by Buddha and were enlightened. It will also mean that the rest of the world will be able to deepen their understanding of the cause of joy and suffering and have the opportunity to attain enlightenment, which is the ultimate source of peace and happiness for all.

In addition, millions of Chinese will receive unbelievable peace and happiness from His Holiness. If the key figures in the Chinese government used him to communicate with and help their people, there would be incredible benefits in terms of peace and happiness, which these nonreligious officials cannot offer because they lack his qualities. In the past, the emperors of Chinese dynasties invited prominent Tibetan lamas to China so they could learn from them. They received many teachings and initiations and studied the path to enlightenment in order to bring the greatest benefit to their lives.

All sentient beings receive loving-kindness and compassion from His Holiness without discrimination. He works to benefit all sentient beings, regardless of whether they have benefited him or not.

In particular, this present Dalai Lama has been able to benefit the West, where he has opened the hearts of millions. He shows an understanding of everything about the Western world and culture and is able to deal with issues by bringing them down to Earth with a humor that uplifts the spirit. Every time His Holiness comes to the West, he brings many thousands of people unforgettable joy, peace, and satisfaction. He brings great benefit to those who are religious by giving them essential, practical advice about how to make their lives most profitable and enjoyable. He also shows others who are not religious practical ways to make their lives meaningful.

Such extensive benefits were not offered in this way by previous Dalai Lamas. His Holiness has accomplished much more in the world than the independence of Tibet for six million people. Therefore, this aspect is extremely important for us sentient beings, who are in danger of nuclear war and of dying from new diseases, and who suffer so much from desire, violence, anger, and the gloom of ignorance.

Most precious is the Buddha's psychology, the Buddha's way of pacifying suffering and achieving happiness. There is no way that we can repay the kindness of His Holiness, who is preserving the doctrine, even if we offer the whole world filled with wish-fulfilling jewels for eons. Through hearing His Holiness's teachings, we make unbelievable strides in preparing our mental continuum for every happiness, including liberation and enlightenment. So we should practice his essential advice of loving-kindness and compassion, caring more for others and serving them. We should put into practice as much as possible all his holy teachings and fulfill his holy wishes, particularly his wish to free the Tibetans from the misery and fear they are now facing and help them have freedom like before.

With palms together, we should constantly pray for His Holiness to guide us continuously in all our lifetimes until we achieve enlightenment, and for our lives to be most beneficial for all sentient beings—just like His Holiness, the Compassion Buddha.

When we see His Holiness the Dalai Lama, what we are actually seeing is the holy body of the Compassion Buddha in human form. His Holiness the Dalai Lama is the actual living Compassion Buddha, so besides hearing his holy speech, even just seeing his holy body is great purification—it makes preparation in our minds for us to be liberated from the oceans of samsaric suffering and plants the seed of enlightenment.

Even a yogi who is not enlightened but has realizations of the graduated generation stage, which ripens the mind, and the completion stage, which liberates the mind, of the path of the highest yoga tantra, or *Maha-anuttara*, is unbelievably meaningful for us sentient beings. Merely to be able to see the holy body or be in the same place as such a yogi is meaningful. It is said in the *Heruka* root tantra, "Just by seeing, touching, hearing, and remembering [the yogi], one gets liberated from all negative karmas [sins]. There is no doubt that it happens exactly like that. And one gets born in the race of the Tathagata and will become a king endowed with Dharma." This is the benefit of someone who is practicing the Heruka.

The same Heruka root tantra text also says, "The hero or heroine, the supreme yogi, wherever he or she is abiding, blesses the whole place and the living beings in that area." Such a yogi extensively benefits not only the human beings but even the insects in that area, purifying their negative karmas and liberating them. Even when a practitioner of Heruka is passing over a bridge, the insects under it are purified and liberated.

Besides the actual yogi, an unenlightened being who has those realizations or even a practitioner of the Heruka deity becomes meaningful to behold for sentient beings. So there is no question of the benefit of seeing an actual enlightened being, what is historically known as Avalokiteshvara. We can understand from these valid quotations from the Heruka root tantra how much benefit we get by being near His Holiness.

This is just the benefit of being able to see or be near the holy body. Then with each hour that we hear the holy speech, it plants the seeds of liberation and enlightenment—so much preparation is made in our mental continuum to achieve liberation from samsara, as well as full enlightenment. His Holiness's holy speech is simplified and easy to understand, but it contains the depth and extensiveness of everything that is explained in Buddha's holy texts.

Each word is like an atomic bomb that destroys our inner enemy, the delusions, and defeats the strong selfish mind. His Holiness's words also destroy the creator of not only human problems but all samsaric sufferings—the mind unknowing the ultimate nature of the "I" and the ultimate nature of the mind, which creates death and rebirth, old age and sickness, dissatisfaction, emotional pain, and other sufferings.

As *amrita* nectar is the most enjoyable thing we can drink, His Holiness's speech is the supreme nectar for our minds. And even though at the moment we cannot see His Holiness's infinite qualities, we can see that he is filled with wisdom, offering the solutions to every difficulty in every aspect of life and showing all those people who think their lives have no meaning and no hope—not only in the East but in the West, also—how to make their lives most meaningful. We can also see that His Holiness is filled with loving-kindness, compassion, and respect for everyone, whether they praise or criticize him, whether they are rich or poor.

By being near His Holiness, especially by hearing his holy speech, and by seeing all his qualities, the hearts of many millions in the world have been filled with hope, joy, and peace. Of course, we *should* see His Holiness in the pure aspect of Buddha Avalokiteshvara, in the aspect of the Compassionate Buddha Avalokiteshvara's holy body, but as it is mentioned in the teachings, "Even if all the Buddhas actually descend in front of us, one does not have the fortune to see the holy body with the holy signs and exemplifications except the present appearance (the ordinary impure appearance projected by the ordinary impure mind) until one is free from karmic obscuration."

Since ordinary beings like ourselves only have the karma to see the Buddha in a human form, His Holiness has manifested in this inspiring human form exactly in accordance with our karma, giving us the opportunity to hear and see directly this aspect. This kindness of His Holiness is without limit or measure, like the infinite sky. By being able to see His Holiness and hear his holy speech, we can awaken or enlighten our minds—this is the best gift we can receive in this life.

By showing the Four Noble Truths, His Holiness introduces true suffering and where it comes from—its true causes. Because they are dependent arisings, existing in dependence upon cause and conditions, they can be ceased by other causes and conditions, so we can achieve the cessation of suffering. How is this possible? Because there is the true path, and by showing us the Four Noble Truths, His Holiness liberates sentient beings from the oceans of samsaric suffering and brings us to liberation. This is the most important education a teacher can give.

Many of us have no idea what the "I" is, what the mind is; we have no idea of ultimate truth and conventional truth. Our minds are totally dark. Even though everything—including the "I," the self—exists merely by being labeled by the mind and because of that is totally empty, we are constantly overwhelmed by a wrong belief in apparently true appearances projected by ignorance. All that we see as real, His Holiness sees as empty; he sees all phenomena as existing because they are labeled so by the mind. Not only that, but all the sense objects appear most pure to His Holiness.

We constantly suffer, overwhelmed by negative emotional thoughts—if not by anger, then by ignorance or desire—like a city covered by the ocean waves. But His Holiness's holy mind is totally free from obscuration, from disturbing emotional thoughts such as desire and so forth. His Holiness's holy mind does not have even the slightest stain or taint of this.

We are like oil spilled on paper. Whatever we do, even breathing in and out, we are totally overwhelmed by self-cherishing thought. But numberless eons ago His Holiness became free from the stain of self-cherishing thought, with no thought arising even for a second of seeking happiness for the self.

His Holiness has made even being the political leader of Tibet total Dharma, which means only benefiting others. In this world, the best politician, the one who gives no harm to any being but only benefits them, is Guru Shakyamuni Buddha and Avalokiteshvara—His Holiness. His Holiness is also purest in morality, or ethics, and is the Omniscient One whose compassion embraces numberless sentient beings, never giving them up even for one second.

In conclusion, until we remove the cause of suffering, which is within us—the wrong concepts, the delusions, and their imprints left on our mental continuum—those negative imprints will give rise to delusions, which motivate karma, then create the suffering of samsara. We need to develop wisdom, analyzing the spiritual path and then practice it.

There is no way to repay the kindness of each word of advice or teaching, even if we offered up the whole universe, filled with billions of dollars or jewels. Putting into practice whatever advice we are given is the best way to repay the kindness. And along with that, everyone should pray for the freedom of the Tibetan people to occur as quickly as possible, which is one of His Holiness's main holy wishes, and do what they can to help this cause. And, finally, we should constantly petition His Holiness to live until samsara ends and guide us all the time.

The Praise of the Dalai Lama: Musings

by Jeffrey Hopkins

When the Chinese Communist government in Beijing hears that the Dalai Lama has been invited to visit a country, it immediately objects to that country, which all too often then finds his visit to be inconvenient, or downscales it, or makes it "personal." What do they fear? The Dalai Lama has no army, no economic pressure, no political cards to play. He advocates nonviolence and compassion. What do they fear?

The Chinese Communist government in Beijing offered to negotiate anywhere at any time if the Dalai Lama would not bring up the topic of independence. He said he would do this, but the response has been to refuse to talk. What do they fear?

He has inspired the rebuilding of Tibetan cultural institutions outside of Tibet. He has asked the religious and political leaders of the world to look beyond narrow interests to the greater good. He has advocated attention to the basic need of society regardless of religion or politics—kindness. Is this what is feared?

His power comes from a life of ethics, the force of truth. In Tibetan, he speaks with a range, depth, inspiration, humor, and sincerity that inspire insight and motivate dedication to others' welfare. I have often wished that all the world could hear this marvel in his own tongue.

The Dalai Lama's longer name is *rJe btsun 'jam dpal ngag dbang blo bzang ye shes bstan 'dzin rgya mtsho srid gsum dbang bsgyur mtshungs pa med pa'I sde dpal bzang po,.*

In English, syllable-by-syllable, it means "leader, holiness, gentleness, renown, speech, dominion, mind, goodness, primordial, wisdom, teaching, hold, vastness, ocean, being, triad, controlling, unparalleled, glory, integrity."

> **Leader** *of the world recognized for true* **holiness,**
> **Gentleness** *personified in persuasive* **renown,**
> **Speech** *of compassion pervading the planet in its* **dominion,**
> **Mind** *of altruistic endeavor reaching all in its* **goodness,**
> **Primordial** *in the depth and range of profound* **wisdom,**
> **Teaching** *encompassing all phenomena in its* **hold,**
> **Vastness** *of love's deeds rippling throughout life's* **ocean,**
> **Being** *so merciful is played in suffering's* **triad,**
> **Controlling** *the unruly through kindness* **unparalleled,**
> **Glory** *in forms of endeavor sealed in total* **integrity,**
> *May the teacher of the world bearing compassion*
> *And wisdom indissoluble see all obstacles dissolve.*

Middling Exposition of the Stages of the Path

At lectures by the holy
Misconceptions are removed,
Previous realizations increase,
And the unrealized newly dawns to the mind.

At your lectures on the *Stages of the Path,*
Twenty-two new dawnings occurred for me.

Just as the past was quick,
So one should consider the future will be.

The purpose of meditating on impermanence
Is to realize that suffering quickly comes.

Like being deceived by a small present,
All compounded things are deceptive phenomena.

The body is an anode of afflictive emotions,
Assisting the generation of afflictive emotions.

That afflictive emotions are difficult to abandon
Is because they seem to act like protectors to oneself.

At birth one is alone
Without helpers and friends, a pathetic time.

If one remembered one's birth,
One would think, *May this not be needed!*

Contaminated pleasures
Are not at all unfabricated pleasures.

The function of ethical behavior
Is to stop coarse ill-deeds.

The doctrine is the actual object of refuge,
Realized by taking it to practice.

When going for refuge it is necessary
For true cessation to dawn well to the mind.

Nagarjuna and Asanga relied on the Perfection of Wisdom Sutras
As sources for the profound and vast.

All sentient beings filling space
Are equal in wanting happiness and not wanting suffering.

One should think that since others are so great in number
They are so much more important than oneself.

Because a consciousness knows something,
Although emptiness is difficult, it can be known.

The way things appear to exist inherently
Is that they appear to cover their bases of designation.

It is necessary to identify the root afflictive emotions
And secondary afflictive emotions that arise from ignorance.

Due to having a conception of one's own inherent existence,
One gets angry at a mouse that has eaten barley.

A sign of realizing just the nonexistence of a self-sufficient person,
Is that upon searching for the mental and physical aggregates
    they still are found.

One should meditate on the person, the qualificant,
And the reality of emptiness as mutually dependent.

Although a Buddha's exalted body is supreme
It is incontrovertibly empty of inherent existence.

A Buddha's good qualities
Are a source of insatiable perception.

Since in that way religious awarenesses
Arose dependent upon your speech,
I respectfully bow to Your Holiness.
What teacher other than you is there!

(Written in 1972 on the occasion of H.H. the Dalai Lama's discourse on Tsong Khapa)

Six Collections of Reasonings

At the discourse on the Six Collections of Reasonings and
    Avalokiteshvara initiation,
Hearing mind-transforming words helped from the depths.
As before, twenty-two sets of meanings arose.
For the sake of remembering them, I will set them down here.

In this one short human life
It is difficult to find speech causing understanding of the profound.

The inherent nature refuted in the *Fundamental Wisdom*
Is with all whatsoever phenomena.

The mode of appearance as if covering the spot of the basis of
    designation
Is to appear as if existing concretely where the monastic is sitting.

If the sense of pointability dawns stably,
One will think, *What is there more true than this!*

If something is other from its own side,
It must be other without reliance on another.

If one analyzes, the mode of being exists right there.
One does not at all need to search elsewhere.

Though it is easy to experience the sign that is not to find the
    thing,
It is difficult to realize the boundary of the self-instituting status
    refuted by it.

Just as upon seeking a human appearing in a dream, it is not
　　Foundation for Universal Responsibility
But its appearance is not contradictory, so it is with a human.

Through reasoning analyzing harmer and harmed
A consciousness conceiving their true existence is refuted but not
　　the conventions.

Though the current conception of inherent existence is strong,
Cultivation of the mind of selflessness will make it limitless.

The clear light pervading the entire circle of objects of knowledge
Transcends anything fabricated by mind.

If Buddhahood is not attained quickly,
Opportunities to help others will be wasted.

Since sentient beings are a Buddha's special objects of intent,
One should not view them as lower than oneself.

Since sentient beings are the field for accumulating merit,
One should perforce view them as higher than oneself.

One should make use of each short moment
For the sake of helping others.

Among the many good qualities of a Buddha,
It is most difficult to attain the qualities of speech helpful to
　　others.

In a palace whose "substance" is exalted wisdom
A moon of compassion dawns at the heart.

The emptiness of that dawns as a vajra.
If so, one surely becomes definite in the Great Vehicle lineage.

Through the "substances" of very subtle body, speech, and mind
One becomes fully purified in Buddhahood.

The difference between sutra and mantra is made by meditative
     stabilization.
The difference in speed is that in mantra the realization of
     emptiness is stronger.

The meaning of the non-duality of the three exalted bodies and
     of the profound and the manifest
Is symbolized by *om mani padme hum*.

Because such doctrine of the union of the profound and vast
Came to be heard in your presence,
It is difficult to express the benefit of encountering you.
I bow to Your Holiness from the depths.

(Written in 1972 on the occasion of H.H. the Dalai Lama's discourse on Nagarjuna)

THE DALAI LAMA AND HISTORY

by U. R. Anantha Murthy

It is only Truth that triumphs in history,
Believe the Dalai Lama's Tibetan Buddhists—
compassionate and mystical that they are.
Whatever triumphs will become Truth,
Believe the Chinese—
shrewd and cunning that they happen to be.

At Delhi, on some day,
The Dalai Lama noticed a black ant
on his saffron robe, even as he was speaking
with intense concentration and concern
about the plight of his unfortunate countrymen
trapped in the vicissitudes of modern history—
Gently smiling throughout.
The soft-spoken sanyasi stopped speaking,
held the ant gently and carefully by the tips of his fingers,
let it out to move around safely on the table,
proceeding to talk, smilingly.
The Dalai Lama thus waits—
even though it appears for the moment
that the Chinese have triumphed in history—

in the countless moments and the infinity of time,
for Truth to triumph.

(Translated from the Kannada by N. Manu Chakravarthy)

Contributors' Bio Notes

U. R. Anantha Murthy is a prominent Indian poet and writer of novels such as *Samskara* and *Bharatiputra* whose writing emphasizes his existential approach to life. He is an activist and academic; has been the president of the Sahitya Akademi, New Delhi; and is presently the Chairman of Film and Television Institute of India, Pune.

Swati Chopra is a Delhi-based journalist who writes on spirituality and religion. Her interview with His Holiness the 17th Karmapa has appeared in *Tricycle: The Buddhist Review,* and her writing has been featured in *Resurgence* magazine. She has written two books and has edited *The Best of Speaking Tree.* Swati is editor of the magazine *Life Positive Plus.*

Mary Craig is a former broadcast journalist and the author of 14 books, including a trilogy on Tibet. Its first book, *Kundun,* looks at the family of His Holiness. The other books in the trilogy are *Tears of Blood* and *Waiting for the Sun.* She lives in England.

Ela Gandhi is the granddaughter of Mahatma Gandhi and is a revered social worker and political activist based in South Africa. She is a member of the African National Congress and works closely with international organizations on peace issues, as well as with Tibet support groups.

Daniel Goleman is a psychologist and journalist who has authored several international bestsellers, including *Emotional Intelligence* and *Working with Emotional Intelligence*. He is the founder and CEO of Emotional Intelligence Services, allied with a global consulting firm. He recently authored *Destructive Emotions: How Can We Overcome Them? A Scientific Dialogue with the Dalai Lama*.

Isabel Hilton is a staff writer for the *New Yorker* magazine and a London-based writer and broadcaster. She is an expert in Chinese affairs. Her last book was *The Search for the Panchen Lama*, as a follow-up to her documentary film *Kingdom of the Lost Boy*, an account of the titular search.

Jeffrey Hopkins is Professor of Tibetan Buddhist Studies at the University of Virginia. Eight of his twenty-eight books have been collaborations with His Holiness, for whom he served as chief interpreter into English on lecture tours from 1979 to 1989.

Pico Iyer is a well-known journalist, author, and essayist who has written extensively on a range of issues, including Tibet, for the world's leading publications, from *Time* to the *International Herald Tribune*. Pico first visited His Holiness in Dharamsala in 1974. He is a contributing editor to *Tricycle: The Buddhist Review*.

Thupten Jinpa is a former monk based in Canada; is the principal English interpreter to the Dalai Lama; and has translated and edited more than ten books by His Holiness, including *The World of Tibetan Buddhism, The Good Heart: The Dalai Lama Explores the Heart of Christianity,* and the bestseller *Ethics for the New Millennium*.

Anees Jung is a Delhi-based writer and journalist who has authored many books, several of which have chronicled the concerns and predicaments of South Asian women. She was educated in Hyderabad, India, and the United States. Her books include *Unveiling India: A Woman's Journey; Beyond the Courtyard: A Sequel to Unveiling India;* and *Peace in Winter Gardens: Ordinary People, Extraordinary Lives.*

Dalip Mehta served in the Indian Foreign Service until 2002. During his career, he was closely involved in India's relations with its immediate neighbors. He served as ambassador in central Asia, based in Tashkent and Bhutan, and was dean of the Foreign Service Institute in New Delhi. He serves as a trustee of the New Delhi–based Foundation for Universal Responsibility of His Holiness the Dalai Lama.

Alexander Norman worked closely with His Holiness in the writing of his autobiography *Freedom in Exile* and *Ethics for the New Millennium*. He has also contributed numerous articles on Tibet to publications such as *Financial Times*.

Raimon Panikkar is a philosopher, theologian, and expert in interreligious dialogue. A professor emeritus in the Religious Studies Department of the University of California–Santa Barbara, he is also the president of the Spanish Association for the Science of Religions. He was raised in Spain by a Catholic mother and a Hindu father and was ordained a Roman Catholic priest in 1946.

Bharati Puri is a journalist and scholar who is currently a postdoctoral fellow working on a study, "Deconstructing Engaged Buddhist Ethics," with the New Delhi–based Centre for the Study of Developing Societies. She received her Ph.D. from Jawaharlal Nehru University in 2001.

Senthil Ram completed a Ph.D. in Central Asian Studies from Jawaharlal Nehru University, New Delhi. He is currently a visiting researcher in the Department of Peace and Development Research at the University of Gothenburg, Sweden, and is working on a monograph, *Nonviolent Approaches to Conflict Resolution: The Case of Tibet,* for the Centre for Peace Studies, University of Tromsø, Norway.

Nick Ribush is a medical doctor who first encountered Buddhism at Kopan Monastery in 1972 when he became a student of Lamas Yeshe and Zopa Rinpoche. He is the founder of the Tushita Mahayana Meditation Centres in New Delhi and Boston, as well as the Lama Yeshe Wisdom Archive in Boston.

Matthieu Ricard is a former scientist who chose to become a Tibetan Buddhist monk. He is His Holiness's interpreter in French, has translated numerous Buddhist texts, is a noted photographer, and is the co-author of *The Quantum and the Lotus* and *The Monk and the Philosopher.*

Lama Thubten Zopa Rinpoche, born in Nepal, was recognized as the reincarnation of the Lawudo Lama at the age of three. A disciple of Lama Yeshe, he currently serves as spiritual director of the Foundation for the Preservation of Mahayana Tradition, and has traveled the world with his teacher, establishing centers of Dharma.

Sulak Sivaraksa is a prominent and outspoken Thai intellectual. He is a teacher, scholar, publisher, and social activist; the founder of many organizations; and the author of more than a hundred books and monographs in both Thai and English.

Brother Wayne Teasdale was a "Benedictine monastic in the Sannyasa tradition." He was based in Chicago and served on the board of trustees of the Parliament of the World's Religions. He worked with His Holiness on the 1991 Universal Declaration on Nonviolence and the interdisciplinary symposium "Synthesis Dialogues." He died in 2004.

Robert A. F. Thurman is the director of Tibet House in New York City that he co-founded. He is a scholar, author, former Tibetan Buddhist monk, and friend of His Holiness. Currently, he is the Jey Tsong Kappa Professor of Indo-Tibetan Buddhist Studies at Columbia University.

Bhuchung Tsering came to India with his family from Tibet in 1960 and joined the Tibetan government in exile in Dharamsala in the 1980s. He worked as editor of the official journal of the Tibetan government, in addition to writing for several journals and newspapers. Currently, he is director of the Washington, D.C.–based International Campaign for Tibet.

ACKNOWLEDGMENTS

The Foundation for Universal Responsibility and I owe our deep gratitude to all the contributors to this book for their generous and spontaneous response to our request for these essays. It is a truly collective effort toward cultivating a deeper appreciation of the many facets of a great master and to provide contemporary commentaries on him for posterity.

My thanks to David Davidhar and first commissioning editor Krishan Chopra, who were truly indulgent and gently supportive in the early years of my struggles as an editor and author. Just when it seemed it was time to quit and explore other pastures, Ashok Chopra and Hay House have played a decisive and catalytic role in my continuing to work as an author. Ashok has been a friend and mentor, the kind of publisher authors can only dream about. This book in its current incarnation would not have been possible without him.

My gratitude to Tulika Srivastava, Nandita Surendran, and R. Lalitha for their continuing help in putting the manuscript together.

ABOUT THE EDITOR

Rajiv Mehrotra was educated at St. Stephen's College, Delhi, and the University of Oxford and Columbia University.

He manages (as the Honorary Secretary/Trustee) the Foundation for Universal Responsibility of His Holiness the Dalai Lama. He has been a student and disciple of the Dalai Lama for more than 25 years and traveled with him to Oslo when His Holiness received the Nobel Prize and announced the establishment of the Foundation with a part of the prize money.

Rajiv works as Managing Trustee, Executive Producer, and Commissioning Editor of the Public Service Broadcasting Trust, which has produced more than 300 documentary films, winning some 50 awards. He has won nine national awards for documentary films from the president of India and several international ones.

Rajiv has twice addressed plenary sessions at the World Economic Forum at Davos and was nominated a Global Leader for Tomorrow by them. He was also a judge of the Templeton Prize for Spirituality and has served on the governing council of the Sri Aurobindo Society and the Film and Television Institute of India.

Until recently, he was host to one of India's longest-running and most widely viewed talk shows on public television, *In*

Conversation, which has been through several incarnations over more than 20 years.

Rajiv has published a number of books, including *The Mind of the Guru; Understanding the Dalai Lama; The Essential Dalai Lama;* and *Thakur,* a biography of Sri Ramakrishna. In addition, he has edited *In My Own Words* by the Dalai Lama and *All You Ever Wanted to Know from His Holiness the Dalai Lama on Happiness, Life, Living, and Much More.* Awaiting publication is *The Spirit of The Muse.* He is currently working on a biography of His Holiness the Dalai Lama and a 25-part series for television on Swami Vivekananda.

We hope you enjoyed this Hay House book. If you'd like to receive a free catalog featuring additional Hay House books and products, or if you'd like information about the Hay Foundation, please contact:

Hay House, Inc.
P.O. Box 5100
Carlsbad, CA 92018-5100

(760) 431-7695 or (800) 654-5126
(760) 431-6948 (fax) or (800) 650-5115 (fax)
www.hayhouse.com® • www.hayfoundation.org

Published and distributed in Australia by:
Hay House Australia Pty. Ltd., 18/36 Ralph St., Alexandria NSW 2015
Phone: 612-9669-4299 • *Fax:* 612-9669-4144 • www.hayhouse.com.au

Published and distributed in the United Kingdom by:
Hay House UK, Ltd., 292B Kensal Rd., London W10 5BE • *Phone:*
44-20-8962-1230 • *Fax:* 44-20-8962-1239 • www.hayhouse.co.uk

Published and distributed in the Republic of South Africa by:
Hay House SA (Pty), Ltd., P.O. Box 990, Witkoppen 2068 • *Phone/Fax:*
27-11-467-8904 • orders@psdprom.co.za • www.hayhouse.co.za

Distributed in Canada by:
Raincoast, 9050 Shaughnessy St., Vancouver, B.C. V6P 6E5
Phone: (604) 323-7100 • *Fax:* (604) 323-2600 • www.raincoast.com

Tune in to **HayHouseRadio.com**® for the best in inspirational talk radio featuring top Hay House authors! And, sign up via the Hay House USA Website to receive the Hay House online newsletter and stay informed about what's going on with your favorite authors. You'll receive bimonthly announcements about Discounts and Offers, Special Events, Product Highlights, Free Excerpts, Giveaways, and more!
www.hayhouse.com®